Forgotten History
of the Western People

13 Nov 2014

To Alicia from Dad.

Psalm 90 v1-2

1) Lord, you have been our dwelling place in all generations.

2) Before the mountains were brought forth, or ever you had formed the earth and the world Even from everlasting to everlasting,

You are God.

Forgotten History of the Western People

From the Earliest Origins

Mike Gascoigne

Anno Mundi Books

ISBN 0-9543922-0-5

Published by:
Anno Mundi Books
PO Box 752
Camberley
GU17 0XJ
England

Table of Contents

Table of Contents

Preface

In the dim and distant murky past, when it was hardly possible to distinguish between gods and men, there emerged a thing called 'history'. The earliest histories, when mortals and immortals are supposed to have inhabited the earth together, are called 'classics'. There comes, eventually, a period when it is realised that we are all mortal, and the 'gods', whoever they were, are left far behind. This is the period of history proper, when it is no longer called 'classics'. The study of God (or the gods in the case of paganism) became known as 'religion' or 'theology'. History emerged as a separate discipline, about the activities of humans, although it may from time to time include a few acts of divine intervention (for example the storm that wrecked the Spanish Armada is widely believed to be an act of God).

In recent times, during the last 150 years or so, there has been an attempt to eliminate God altogether, from the study of both science and history, using something called 'evolution', with the result that our earliest histories are eliminated. There is a gap in our history, just at the point where history and classics merge together, and it remains in place to prevent us from grasping another kind of forbidden fruit, from the tree of knowledge of where we came from.

When I was at school, during the 1960's, which seems a long time ago, I used to argue with my teachers about evolution. Those of us who dropped biology were given a special course called "Evolution", but it wasn't really about evolution, it was about genetics. The teacher must have thought that if the presentation was good enough, we would all believe in evolution, because that's what it was called. We were taught about genes, chromosomes, DNA and cell divisions, and it was all very interesting, but I couldn't see how any of it was related to the past.

That's the problem with all of science. You can observe what is happening in the present with the greatest accuracy, but the past and the future are less certain. The use of science to investigate the distant past, over long timescales, is virtually impossible, because you have to assume that the observations and methods which apply to the present time have been valid for all time. The use of science to predict the distant future is equally difficult, for the same reasons.

The best use of science, for historical work, is to validate something that is already known, and fill in some of the details. For example, if a murder has been committed, you might use forensic science (fingerprints, blood samples etc.) to find out 'whodunit'. But the process doesn't work in reverse. It would be ridiculous if a detective found a fingerprint on a lamp post and decided "A murder must have happened here".

Science can do many things, but it cannot produce a detailed reconstruction of the past. The only way we can know about the past is to use the historical records left behind by our ancestors, and in this book I have argued that history does not favour evolution. Instead it favours our descent from one man and one woman, and a family of their descendants who survived universal annihilation by getting into a boat. These people had not evolved over millions of years, and the family who survived the flood was only the tenth generation of all who ever lived. I have argued the case, not from the Bible, but from other ancient sources, since anything outside of the Bible is much more likely to be believed.

Not only did I have problems with the evolution class at school, I also had problems with the history class. I didn't know why at the time, but I found it boring and irrelevant, so I dropped it at the age of 14. I studied sciences, eventually leading to a degree in chemical engineering. Now, with the benefit of hindsight, I can understand why history was boring. It was because it never had a beginning. It was like watching a film that was already half-way through. If you miss the beginning, you can't understand what it's about. I would rather see the first half of a film and miss the end, because once they have set up the characters and hatched the plot, you can use your imagination to work out what happens next.

In the history class we were told about the stone age, the bronze age and the iron age. We were told about ignorant savages who lived in caves and clothed themselves with animal skins. Then they started building huts out of mud and straw. At first they lived only by hunting, but then they learned about agriculture and became farmers. The earliest tools were made of stone, but then they learned how to make bronze out of a mixture of copper and tin, and finally they learned how to make iron. And that was the sum total of all that we learned about pre-Roman British history. The first person who appears on the scene with an actual name wasn't even British. He came from Rome and he was called Julius Caesar.

This is the point where the film usually starts, but in this book I have attempted to wind it back, to show the names and deeds of the Ancient Britons, some of whom are descended from the scattered remnants of the burning city of Troy. Others came from Egypt, with a princess called

Scota, and they inhabited Ireland and then Scotland. The film winds back further, to show the foundation of Troy, and further back to the Egyptian Osiris who can be identified with the Greek Zeus and the sons of the Biblical Ham. Two generations earlier we come to Noah, the Emperor of all the world. But that's not all. The story goes back even as far as Adam, where all history begins. And that's where science creates problems for history. It doesn't allow us to wind the film back that far. The beginning of the film has been censored.

In this book, I have attempted to bring history to life by starting from the beginning. During the pre-Darwinian period (which constitutes most of the history of the world), all history books were like that. They used to start with a few lines about creation, or at least they would give a brief account of the dispersion of the three sons of Noah after the flood, but they were not considered to be religious books. They were history books. This book is also not a religious book, it is a history book in the pre-Darwinian style.

Those who are familiar with the classics will understand that a wide variety of meanings can be attached to the Greek and Roman mythologies. The number of interpretations is dependent only on the fertility of our imagination, which is the reason why the mythologies exist in the first place. I have attempted to simplify the matter by taking the approach of Euhemerus, a Greek mythographer who believed that all the gods were deified humans, and all the myths were grossly embellished versions of real history. From his name we get the practice of *Euhemerism*, which means unravelling the myths to find the real history behind them.

In taking this approach, I doubt that I have made any discoveries that are absolutely new. It is more likely that I have encouraged a renewal of existing knowledge and brought it into the public domain. I do not claim anything with absolute certainty, regarding my interpretation of the ancient world, except that there is One True God who started it all off and has occasionally intervened in the affairs of men when our folly became too great. On matters of detail, I am prepared to give way to anyone who can come up with new material that proves me wrong. Any retractions or amendments to this work will be published in a new edition, or will be displayed on my website:

www.write-on.co.uk/history/index.htm

Ancient and Medieval Sources

Among the historical sources used in this book, there are works of great antiquity of which only fragments remain, and there are other works that are surrounded in controversy. The complete list of sources is given in the Bibliography, but it is necessary to comment on a few of them here.

For our knowledge of the early Babylonian history, beginning with the creation, we are indebted to Berosus (sometimes spelled Berossus), a Chaldean priest of Bel at Babylon who went to Asia Minor and then to the island of Cos near Rhodes, after the conquest of Alexander the Great. He was an astronomer, and he had an observatory and founded a school of astronomy on the island. He was also a historian, and he wrote three books in Greek during the early 3rd Century BC. The first was about the creation of the world, and the appearance of Oannes and the Annedoti, the fish-men who came out of the sea and taught people the arts and sciences. The second and third books describe the ten kings before the flood, then the flood itself, then the kings after the flood.[1]

Unfortunately, the books of Berosus are now lost, such are the ravages of time and circumstances. However, he was quoted by other historians such as Abydenus,[2] Apollodorus,[3] and Alexander Polyhistor,[4] and then re-quoted by Josephus,[5] Eusebius,[6] Syncellus[7] and others, so that fragments of his work have been preserved. These were collected together and published, during the 19th century, by Isaac Preston Cory in

---

[1] For a brief description of Berosus, see Hodges, E.R., *Cory's Ancient Fragments*, pp.43-45. See also *Encyclopaedia Britannica*.

[2] Abydenus was a disciple of Aristotle, the Greek philosopher and scientist of the 4th century BC.

[3] Apollodorus of Athens, 2nd century BC. He was a student of Aristarchus of Alexandria, but he left the city about 146 BC, perhaps for Pergamon, and then he went to Athens.

[4] Lucius Cornelius Alexander Polyhistor, 1st century BC, philosopher, geographer, and historian.

[5] Flavius Josephus, b. AD 37/38 - d. AD 100. Jewish priest and historian.

[6] Eusebius Pamphilus, b. 264 - d. about 338. Bishop of Caesarea, polemicist and historian.

[7] George the Syncellus, 8th century Byzantine historian.

his *Ancient Fragments*,[8] together with fragments from other ancient authors. An enlarged edition was later published by E. Richmond Hodges[9].

In addition to the work of Berosus, we also have fragments from a much more ancient Phoenician[10] author called Sanchoniathon, who lived before the Trojan wars of the early 12th century BC. His works are lost, also because of the ravages of time, but fragments have survived because they are quoted in polemic arguments between Eusebius and his anti-Christian opponent Porphyry.[11] These are also available in Cory's *Ancient Fragments*. Sanchoniathon gives an account of creation from a different viewpoint, yet compatible with Berosus. He describes the decadence that preceded the flood, although there is no surviving fragment of the flood itself. Then he describes Ouranos (Heaven) and Ge (Earth), who can be identified as Noah and his wife, and he tells some of the story of their descendants.

During the renaissance period in Italy, there appeared some additional histories, purported to be from Berosus and his Egyptian contemporary Manetho. They were published by a Benedictine Friar called Annius of Viterbo, but are widely regarded as fabricated. However, I have included these histories because of their influence on Tudor period literature and the need to recognise them where they occur. There is also the possibility that some of the work of Annius might have a basis of fact, although not the basis that he claimed. These histories give a genealogy from Noah to Dardanus, the founder of Troy, and at the same time give the Celtic (or Samothean) line of descent from Japheth.

The relatively later period of Celtic history in Britain, from the arrival of Brutus the Trojan to the Saxon invasion, is easier to substantiate, although it has come in for some criticism. This period is documented by Geoffrey of Monmouth, the 12th Century Welsh historian, in his *History*

---

[8] Cory, I.P., *The Ancient Fragments; containing what remains of the writings of Sanchoniatho, Berossus, Abydenus, Megasthenes, and Manetho*, 1828.
[9] Hodges, E.R., *Cory's Ancient Fragments*, 1876.
[10] The Phoenicians are the Caananites who were driven out of the land by the Israelites returning from Egypt. They went to Anatolia (Turkey) and then to Carthage (Tunisia) and were eventually wiped out by the Romans.
[11] Porphyry, c.234 - c.305. Anti-Christian opponent of Eusebius.

of the Kings of Britain.[12] Geoffrey says that he received a "very ancient book" from Walter, Archdeacon of Oxford, and he stands accused of falsely claiming to have translated it from Welsh into Latin. In reality, he merely used it as a source book to write his own history. Such has been the indignation about his claim, that some historians have doubted that his "very ancient book" ever existed. Yet it can be shown that a separate Latin translation was made, by Walter himself, and it was used by another historian called Geffrei Gaimar to write his *L'Estoire des Engleis*[13] in Anglo-Norman.

The controversy over Geoffrey of Monmouth is to some extent a distraction, because the history of the Britons is not dependent on him. A shorter version of the same history was written much earlier, by the 9th century Welsh historian Nennius,[14] who collected together what remained after the country had been decimated by the Saxons. He made no attempt to paraphrase things into his own words, and instead he began his *British History* by saying: *"I have therefore made a heap of all that I have found ... "*. Even earlier, we have Gildas[15] during the 6th century, who wrote his *Ruin of Britain*, lamenting that the demise of the Britons was a consequence of their decadent spiritual state. He was not writing historical narrative for the purpose of passing it on to posterity, but his work nevertheless contains some useful history.

In this book, I have quoted from these sources and many others. In some cases, where quotations are in medieval English, I have tidied them up to make them more intelligible to the modern reader.

---

[12] Thorpe, L., *Geoffrey of Monmouth: History of the Kings of Britain.*
[13] Bell, A., *Geffrei Gaimar: L'Estoire des Engleis.*
[14] Morris, J., *Nennius: British History and the Welsh Annals.*
[15] Winterbottom, M., *Gildas: The Ruin of Britain.*

Chapter 1 - Creation and the Flood

Now these things a certain Sanchoniathon has handed down to posterity … He supposes that the beginning of all things was a dark and condensed windy air, or a breeze of dark air, and a chaos turbid and black as Erebus;[16] and that these were unbounded, and for a long series of ages destitute of form. But when this wind became enamoured of its own first principles (the chaos), and an intimate union took place, that connection was called Pothos;[17] and it was the beginning of the creation of all things. And it (the Chaos) knew not its own production; but, from its embrace[18] with the wind, was generated Môt, which some called Ilus (mud); but others the putrefaction of a watery mixture. And from this sprung all the seed of the creation, and the generation of the universe. And there were certain animals, not having sensation, from which intelligent animals were produced; and they were called Zophasemim, *i.e. observers of heaven*, and they were formed similar to the shape of an egg. And Môt shone out with the sun, and the moon, and the less and the greater stars. …

… And when the air began to send forth light, by its fiery influence on the sea and earth, winds were produced, and clouds, and very great defluxions and outpourings of the heavenly waters. And after that these things were divided and separated from their proper place by the heat of the sun, and then all met again in the air, and dashed together, whence thunders and lightnings were formed; and at the crash of those thunders the above-named intelligent animals were awakened and frightened with the sound; and then male and female moved on the earth and in the sea. …

… Of the wind Kolpia[19] and of his wife, Baau, which is interpreted Night, were begotten two mortal men, Aeon and Protogonus[20] so called, and Aeon

---

[16] Erebus appears in Greek mythology, representing the darkness of the underworld.

[17] Pothos or Desire. This seems to be the same as Eros or Cupid, who in Greek Mythology is considered to be the prime cause of all things.

[18] This union was symbolised among the heathen, and particularly by the Phoenicians, by an egg enfolded by a serpent, which disjunctively represented the Chaos and the Aether, but when united it represented the hermaphroditic first principle of the universe, *i.e.* Cupid, or Pothos.

[19] This compares with the Hebrew Kol-pi-Yah, the voice of the mouth of Yah, or Jehovah. The early Phoenicians spoke a language almost identical to Hebrew.

[20] Orelli, an editor of the Ancient Fragments who is referenced by Hodges, says that Aeon is Eve and Protogonus (first-born) is Adam.

discovered food from trees. The Those begotten from these were called Genos and Genea[21], and inhabited Phoenicia, and when great droughts came (*upon the land*) they stretched forth their hands to heaven, towards the Sun, for this (he says), they supposed to be the only God, the Lord of Heaven, calling him BEELSAMIN, which name among the Phoenicians signifies Lord of Heaven, but among the Greeks *is equivalent* to Zeus, or Jupiter.

Eusebius, on Sanchoniathon.[22]

It could be argued that some of this supports evolution, and even Eusebius himself admits that the first paragraph, up to the formation of the Zophasemim, could be used to promote atheism. However, I doubt that many modern-day evolutionists would be pleased to hear that their theory began, not with Darwin, but with Greek mythology and its Phoenician prototype.

There are some striking similarities with the Biblical creation story. There is the darkness and chaos, destitute of form, which corresponds to Gen. 1:2 - *And the earth was without form and void; and darkness was on the face of the deep.* There is the appearance of light, and the sun, moon and stars, and the male and female animals. Then there is Protogonus (Adam) and his wife Aeon (Eve) who discovered food from trees, so we have an allusion to the fall. Then we have Genos and Genea (Cain and his wife), stretching their hands to heaven, and this may represent Cain's offering of vegetables which turned out to be unacceptable to the Lord.

Now we will look at the account of creation, given by Berosus, from the mouth of Oannes the fish-man who is one of the characters in his story:

There was a time in which there was nothing but darkness and an abyss of waters, wherein resided most hideous beings, which were produced of a two-fold principle. Men appeared with two wings, some with four wings, and two faces. They had one body, but two heads – the one of a man, the other of a woman. They were likewise, in their several organs, both male and female. Other human figures were to be seen with the legs and horns of goats. Some had horses' feet; others had the limbs of a horse behind, but before were fashioned like men, resembling hippocentaurs. Bulls, likewise, bred there with the heads of men; and dogs, with fourfold bodies, and the tails of fishes. Also horses, with the heads of dogs: men, too, and other

---

[21] Orelli supposes that Genos is Cain and Genea is his wife.
[22] Hodges, *Cory's Ancient Fragments*, pp.1-5.

animals, with the heads and bodies of horses and the tails of fishes. In short, there were creatures with the limbs of every species of animals. Add to these fishes, reptiles, serpents, with other wonderful animals, which assumed each other's shape and countenance. Of all these were preserved delineations in the temple of Belus at Babylon.

The person, who was supposed to have presided over them, was a woman named Omoroca; which in the Chaldee language is Thalatth; which in Greek is interpreted Thalassa, the sea: but, according to the most true computation, it is equivalent to Selene, the moon. All things being in this situation, Belus came, and cut the woman asunder: and, out of one half of her, he formed the earth, and of the other half the heavens; and at the same time he destroyed the animals in the abyss. All this (he says) was an allegorical description of nature. For the whole universe consisting of moisture, and animals being continually generated therein; the deity (Belus), above-mentioned, cut off his own head; upon which the other gods mixed the blood, as it gushed out, with the earth; and from thence men were formed. On this account it is that men are rational, and partake of divine knowledge. This Belus, whom men call Dis, (or Pluto,) divided the darkness, and separated the heavens from the earth, and reduced the universe to order. But the animals so recently created, not being able to bear the prevalence of light, died.

Belus upon this, seeing a vast space quite uninhabited, though by nature very fruitful, ordered one of the gods to take off his head; and when it was taken off, they were to mix the blood with the soil of the earth, and from thence to form other men and animals, which should be capable of bearing the light. Belus also formed the stars, and the sun and the moon, together with the five planets.

Eusebius, on Polyhistor, on Berosus.[23]

This account, like the account of Sanchoniathon, agrees with the Biblical description of darkness and chaos, but adds a description of hideous animals. A woman, representing the waters, is cut in half, and out of her is formed the heavens and the earth. While this is equally hideous, it is a figurative representation of the same story that is related in Genesis, that God made a firmament (the atmosphere which represents the lower part of the heavens) and *divided the waters which were under the firmament from the waters which were above the firmament...* (Gen. 1:7). So the Biblical account of the formation of heaven and earth is basically the same as the account of Berosus.

---

[23] Hodges, pp.58-60.

9

Then we have Belus cutting off his own head, so that the blood gushed out on the earth, and men were formed. This is clearly the Babylonian way of saying that men were formed *in the image of God* (Gen. 1:27).

The narrative then returns to the separation of heaven and earth, and associates with it the division of darkness, which means the separation of light and darkness. The animals, who were more accustomed to the darkness of the pre-creation chaos, could not bear the light and they died. All you have to do is omit these hideous animals and you have something that is quite close to the Biblical first day of creation.

Belus appears to be still alive, even after cutting off his own head (anything can happen in mythology) and he orders one of the other gods to cut off his head and pour the blood on the earth, to form "other men and animals". It isn't clear who are the "other men", but they must be of a lower order because they have been formed from the blood of a lesser god. Perhaps the ancient Babylonians, like the modern-day evolutionists, thought that apes were some kind of primitive men. This was certainly true of the Carthaginians who went on a voyage, past the Pillars of Hercules (Straits of Gibraltar) and down the coast of Africa. The *Periplus of Hanno*[24] tells us how they got as far as Ghana and found some gorillas who they thought to be some kind of savage humans. The end of the story is as follows:

> . . . we arrived at a bay called the Southern Horn;[25] at the bottom of which lay an island like the former,[26] having a lake, and in this lake another island, full of savage people, (the greater part of whom were women), whose bodies were hairy, and whom our interpreters called Gorillae. Though we pursued the men we could not seize any of them; but all fled from us, escaping over the precipices, and defending themselves with stones. Three women were, however, taken; but they attacked their conductors with their teeth and hands, and could not be prevailed upon to accompany us. Having killed them, we flayed them, and brought their skins with us to Carthage. We did not sail further on, our provisions failing us.

---

[24] Hodges, pp.36-40.
[25] Probably Cape Three Points, the southernmost point of Ghana.
[26] The Western Horn, probably Cape Palmas, Liberia.

So much for the Carthaginians. If the Babylonians took the same view, and the "other men" of their creation story were actually apes or gorillas, we have something similar to the fifth day of the Biblical creation story. *Let the waters bring forth abundantly the moving creature that has life,* ... (Gen. 1:20). The Hebrew word translated "life" is *nephesh* which literally means "breath" and in its context it means "breath of life". We therefore have animals created with the *breath of life* on the fifth day, and man created *in the image of God* on the sixth day. Although the Bible is consistently monotheistic, this concept of two different orders of life bears some resemblance to the Babylonian belief that animals and humans were respectively created by a lesser and a greater god.

Armorica, the Ancient Name of Brittany

To take a slight digression, we will now see how the Babylonian history affects our understanding of Western Europe and possibly America.

I used to wonder why there was a place called Brittany in the north-west corner of France. It wasn't part of Britain, so why was it called Brittany? Then I read Geoffrey of Monmouth's *History of the Kings of Britain* and discovered that during the 4th century AD, a British king called Maximianus, who was Roman on his mother's side, attacked the north-west corner of France which was then known as Armorica. He re-populated the country with Britons and called it a "second Britain". Then when the Roman Empire collapsed, the Saxons invaded and the Britons living on the mainland were driven into Wales. Some of them went to the "second Britain" as a place of refuge. It was known as "Little Britain", or "Brittany", and the mainland eventually became known as "Great Britain".

So, having resolved the question about "Brittany", I began to wonder why it was originally called "Armorica". Then when I began to read the Babylonian story of creation, it all became clear. Berosus tells us that a woman called Omoroca was cut in half, so that one half of her formed the earth and the other half formed the heavens. A footnote in *Cory's Ancient Fragments*[27] tells us that the name *Omoroca* is a Greek corruption of the Aramaic word *Amqia*, meaning the deep, or the ocean. It seems likely,

---

[27] Hodges, p.59.

therefore, that *Armorica* was so named because it was the farthest corner of Gaul, bordering on the Atlantic Ocean.

The ancient world had a profound respect for the sea. They would try any other solution, before setting sail and trusting themselves to the "mercy of the gods". The relatively shallow waters of the Mediterranean or the English Channel were easily capable of sinking ships, and only the bravest or the most suicidal would venture out into the Atlantic Ocean. It appears that the name *Armorica* was an expression of their respect for this fearsome place.

However, we should also consider that the ancient Norse compound word "omme-rike", in its simplest translation, means "the remotest land". Apparently, this is how the Vikings named America, or perhaps Columbus learned the name from them.[28] Armorica is also the remotest land in northern Europe, although it's doubtful that the name came from the Vikings. Whatever be the case, it is interesting that two similar words, *omme-rike* and *Omoroca*, respectively mean the farthest land and the deep ocean. Perhaps both of them, in different ways, originated from Babylon.

At this point, we can clearly see the value of relating the history of the world from the beginning. Place names are usually very ancient (unless it's something like Milton Keynes) and you have to wind the clock back as far as possible to find out what they mean. And now we come to the end of this digression and continue where we left off.

Ten Kings Before the Flood

Berosus identifies ten kings before the flood, who may be compared with the ten Biblical patriarchs from Adam to Noah. The following fragment is from Apollodorus:

> This is the history which Berosus has transmitted to us. He tells us that the first king was Alorus of Babylon, a Chaldean; he reigned ten sari;[29] and

---

[28] Wicken, D., *Did The Vikings Name America?*
[29] A sarus is 3,600 years. This, and a few other definitions, are given in the next fragment from Abydenus.

afterwards Alaparus and Amelon, who came from Pantibiblon;[30] then Ammenon the Chaldean, in whose time appeared the Musarus Oannes, the Annedotus, from the Erythraean sea.[31] (But Alexander Polyhistor, anticipating the event, has said that he appeared in the first year; but Apollodorus says that it was after forty sari; Abydenus, however, makes the second Annedotus appear after twenty-six sari.)[32] Then succeeded Megalarus, from the city of Pantibiblon, and he reigned eighteen sari; and after him Daonus, the shepherd, from Pantibiblon, reigned ten sari; in his time, (he says), appeared again, from the Erythraean (or Red) sea, a fourth Annedotus, having the same form with those above, the shape of a fish blended with that of a man. Then Euedoreschus reigned from the city of Pantibiblon for the period of eighteen sari. In his days there appeared another personage, whose name was Odacon, from the Erythraean (or Red) sea, like the former, having the same complicated form, between a fish and a man. (All these, says Apollodorus, related particularly and circumstantially whatever Oannes had informed them of. Concerning these appearances Abydenus has made no mention.) Then Amempsinus, a Chaldean from Laranchae,[33] reigned, and he, being the eighth in order, ruled for ten sari. Then Otiartes, a Chaldean from Laranchae, reigned, and he ruled for eight sari.

Upon the death of Otiartes, his son, Xisuthrus, reigned eighteen sari. In his time the great Flood happened. So the sum total of all the kings is ten; and the period which they collectively reigned amounts to one hundred and twenty sari.

Syncellus and Eusebius, on Apollodorus, on Berosus.[34]

---

[30] A footnote from Hodges, (p.51), says that Pantibiblon is the Greek rendering of Sippara, called Sepharvaim, and it appears in the Bible in 2 Kings 17:24. Sepharvaim appears in Biblical maps on the banks of the Euphrates north of Babylon.

[31] This signifies the Red Sea or the Persian Gulf. Hodges, (p.51), identifies it as the Persian Gulf.

[32] The text in brackets is from Syncellus or Eusebius, but neither Cory nor Hodges say which one.

[33] Larissa, or Larsa, about 20 miles south-east of Erech. The modern Arabic name is Tall Sankarah, in southern Iraq.

[34] Hodges, pp.51-52.

The following fragment is from Abydenus:

> So much concerning the wisdom of the Chaldeans.
>
> It is said that the first king of the country was Alorus, who gave out a report that he was appointed by God to be the Shepherd of the people: he reigned ten sari. Now a sarus is esteemed to be three thousand six hundred years; a neros, six hundred: and a sossus, sixty.
>
> After him Alaparus reigned three sari; to him succeeded Amillarus, from the city of Pantibiblon, who reigned thirteen sari; in his time a semi-daemon called Annedotus, very like to Oannes, came up a second time from the sea. After him Ammenon reigned twelve sari, who was of the city of Pantibiblon; then Megalarus, of the same place, eighteen sari; then Daos, the shepherd, governed for the space of ten sari, he was of Pantibiblon; in his time four double-shaped personages came out of the sea to land, whose names were Euedocus, Eneugamus, Eneuboulos, and Anementus. After these things was Anodaphus, in the time of Euedoreschus. There were afterwards other kings, and last of all Sisithrus (Xisuthrus). So that, in all, the number amounted to ten kings, and the term of their reigns to one hundred and twenty sari. And, among other matters not irrelevant to the subject, he continues thus concerning the deluge. After Euedoreschus some others reigned, and then Sisithrus (Xisuthrus). To him the god Kronus (*i.e.* Saturn) foretold that, on the fifteenth day of the month Desius[35] there would be a Deluge, and commanded him to deposit all the writings whatever he had in the city of the Sun, in Sippara. ...
>
> *Syncellus and Eusebius, on Abydenus, on Berosus.*[36]

Note: This passage continues with the exit of Sisithrus from the ark, see page 25.

Both of these fragments agree that there were ten kings before the flood. Apollodorus gives all the names, while Abydenus gives all except Amempsinus and Otiartes, but agrees with the number. These kings correspond to the Biblical patriarchs as shown in Table 1.

---

[35] The Macedonian month of Desius, corresponding to May or June.
[36] Hodges, pp.53-54.

Table 1 - Ten Kings Before the Flood

Bible	Berosus	Comments
Adam	Alorus	Alorus, or Adi-ur means "devoted to the god Ur"[37]
Seth	Alaparus	
Enos	Amelon	First appearance of the "fish-man".
Cainan	Ammenon	
Mahalaleel	Megalarus	Megalarus (Amegalarus), or Amil-ur-gal, possibly means "man (or servant) of Urgal".
Jared	Daonus	
Enoch	Euedoreschus	
Methuselah	Amempsinus	
Lamech	Otiartes	Otiartes (Ardates), or Ubara-Tutu, by comparison with the Assyrian *ardu* (servant) means servant of a god called Tutu.
Noah	Xisuthrus	Xisuthrus, or Si-sit, means "him who escaped the flood".

In the middle of a fragment from Alexander Polyhistor, we have a comment from one of the later historians. On page 8 we saw the account of creation, and the text continues with the comment in parentheses as follows:

> (In the second book was the history of the ten kings of the Chaldeans, and the periods of each reign, which consisted collectively of one hundred and twenty sari, or 432,000 years, reaching to the time of the Flood. For Alexander, surnamed Polyhistor, as from the writings of the Chaldeans, enumerating the kings from the ninth, Ardates, to Xisuthrus, who is called by them the tenth, proceeds in this manner:)
>
> *Syncellus or Eusebius, on Polyhistor, on Berosus.*[38]

The fragment then continues with the story of the flood (see page 26).

---

[37] The meanings of these names are given by Hodges (pp.48-49) by comparison with cuneiform scripts.

[38] Hodges, p.60. Syncellus (8-9th century) is credited with preserving some of the work of Eusebius (3-4th century), but neither Cory nor Hodges say which one of them inserted this comment.

King Noah

The Bible does not describe any of the pre-flood patriarchs as 'kings', although Josephus does, as follows:

> Seth begat Enos in his two hundred and fifth year;[39] who, when he had lived nine hundred and twelve years, delivered the government to Cainan his son, whom he had in his hundred and ninetieth year; he lived nine hundred and five years. . . Now Mathusala, the son of Enoch, who was born to him when he was one hundred and sixty five years old, had Lamech for his son when he was one hundred and eighty-seven years of age, to whom he delivered the government, when he had retained it nine hundred and sixty-nine years. Now Lamech, when he had governed seven hundred and seventy-seven years, appointed Noah, his son, to be ruler of the people, who was born to Lamech when he was one hundred and eighty-two years old, and retained the government nine hundred and fifty years.
>
> *Josephus, Antiquities, I,iii,4.*

In that case, if Noah was a king, did he build the ark with the help of his subjects? Josephus suggests that he did not. Instead he says the giants took over and Noah went into exile.

> But for what degree of zeal they had formerly shown for virtue, they now showed by their actions a double degree of wickedness; whereby they made God to be their enemy; for many angels of God accompanied with women,[40] and begat sons that proved unjust, and despisers of all that was good, on account of the confidence they had in their own strength, for the tradition is, that these men did what resembled the acts of those whom the Grecians call giants. But Noah was very uneasy at what they did; and, being displeased at their conduct, persuaded them to change their dispositions and their acts for the better; – but, seeing that they did not yield to him, but were slaves to their wicked pleasures, he was afraid they would kill him, together with his wife and children, and those they had married; so he departed out of that land.
>
> *Josephus, Antiquities, I,iii,1.*

---

[39] Josephus, although he was Jewish, sometimes gives chronologies that do not agree with the Bible. Compare this, for example, with Gen. 5:6.
[40] See Gen. 6:1-4.

Longevity

The Biblical patriarchs, before the flood, lived for hundreds of years, possibly for genetic reasons although the situation is not fully understood.[41] However, the longevity of the ten kings, according to Berosus, is truly astonishing. Each of their reigns is measured in sari, which are units of 3,600 years, so that their first king Alorus reigned 36,000 years. Even longer, we have Megalarus, Euedoreschus and Xisuthrus who reigned 64,800 years each. Altogether, these ten kings reigned for 432,000 years, compared with the Biblical calculation of 1656 years from creation to the flood.

Berosus is not always consistent. A fragment from Alexander Polyhistor (see page 19) describes the pre-flood period as 15 myriads of years. A 'myriad' is ten thousand, so the total period is 150,000 years.

We also find great longevity in the early Egyptian records of Manetho[42] and the Old Egyptian Chronicle.[43] Manetho describes the 'Dynasty of the Demigods', which is followed by 31 other dynasties. The first king is Hephaestus (Vulcan) who reigned 724½ years and four days. The second is Helios (the Sun) who reigned 86 years. If Helios began to reign only after his father Hephaestus had died or handed over the kingdom, this implies that Helios was also of great age.

However, these figures are small compared with the Old Egyptian Chronicle which describes the first two kings as follows:

To Hephaestus is assigned no time, as he is apparent both by night and day.
Helius the son of Hephaestus reigned three myriads of years.

This suggests that the reign of Hephaestus was semi-infinite, meaning his reign ended at a specific point in time, but before that he had always been king (or at least they did not know when he started). Helius reigned for three myriads, which is 30,000 years.

---

[41] For a discussion of how genetics might affect longevity, see Wieland, C., *Decreased Lifespans: Have We Been Looking in the Right Place?*
[42] Hodges, p.111.
[43] Hodges, p.136.

Comparing the Egyptian, Babylonian and Biblical accounts, we are given the impression that people genuinely lived a long time, but some of the accounts have become exaggerated.

Martin Anstey[44] suggests that a sarus is only ten years, by comparison with the Hebrew 'eser' which means 'ten', or a 'decad'. In that case, the total pre-flood period of 120 sari is 1,200 years, each containing 360 days, making up 432,000 days, but the Chaldeans later magnified it to 432,000 years to enhance their antiquity.

Oannes, the Fish-Man

During the reign of the ten kings, there were appearances of a fish-man, or a number of fish-men, called Annedoti, and their chief was Oannes. He taught the people about arts and sciences, including the knowledge of how to grow crops, and in post-flood paganism he was known as Dagon, the Mesopotamian god of vegetation. The worship of Dagon eventually gave way to the worship of the sun-god Baal, who represents the power of the sun over livestock and crops.

Sometimes Oannes, or Dagon, appears as a merman, and sometimes as a man clothed with a fish, as shown in figures 1 and 2.

Figure 1 - Oannes / Dagon the merman[45]

---

[44] Anstey, M., *The Romance of Bible Chronology*, Chapter 1, Section 2, *Ancient Literary Remains.* <www.preteristarchive.com/Books/anstey_chrono_01c.html>, Oct. 2002.

[45] Artist unknown, will acknowledge in a future edition.

Figure 2 - Oannes / Dagon represented by Assyrian priests, making an offering to the sun-god Baal in the presence of the king. [46]

The fragments of Berosus, from Apollodorus and Abydenus, describe Oannes as someone who appeared before the flood. The same theme is followed by Alexander Polyhistor. We have seen, on page 8, a description of the pre-creation chaos. This fragment begins with a description of Babylonia, and then introduces Oannes as follows:

> Berosus, in his first book concerning the history of Babylonia, informs us that he lived in the time of Alexander,[47] the son of Philip. And he mentions that there were written accounts preserved at Babylon with the greatest care, comprehending a term of fifteen myriads of years.[48] These writings contained a history of the heavens and the sea; of the birth of mankind; also of those who had sovereign rule; and of the actions achieved by them.
>
> And, in the first place, he describes Babylonia as a country which lay between the Tigris and Euphrates. He mentions that it abounded with wheat, barley, ocrus, sesamum; and in the lakes were found the roots called gongae, which were good to be eaten, and were, in respect to nutriment, like barley. There were also palm-trees and apples, and most kinds of fruits; fish, too, and birds; both those which are merely of flight, and those which take to the element of water. The part of Babylonia which bordered upon Arabia was barren, and without water; but that which lay on the other side had hills, and was fruitful. At Babylon there was (in these times) a great resort of people of

---

[46] Representation by Layard, *Bablyon and Nineveh*, p.343, from Hislop, p.215.

[47] Alexander the Great, the son of Philip II of Macedonia.

[48] A myriad is ten thousand, so this represents 150,000 years.

various nations, who inhabited Chaldea, and lived without rule and order, like the beasts of the field.

In the first year there made its appearance, from a part of the Erythraean sea[49] which bordered upon Babylonia, an animal endowed with reason, who was called Oannes. (According to the account of Apollodorus) the whole body of the animal was like that of a fish; and had under a fish's head another head, and also feet below, similar to those of a man, subjoined to the fish's tail. His voice, too, and language was articulate and human; and a representation of him is preserved even to this day.

This Being, in the day-time, used to converse with men; but took no food at that season; and he gave them an insight into letters, and sciences, and every kind of art. He taught them to construct houses, to found temples, to compile laws, and explained to them the principles of geometrical knowledge. He made them distinguish the seeds of the earth, and showed them how to collect fruits. In short, he instructed them in everything which could tend to soften manners and humanise mankind. From that time, so universal were his instructions, nothing material has been added by way of improvement. When the sun set it was the custom of this Being to plunge again into the sea, and abide all night in the deep; for he was amphibious.

After this, there appeared other animals, like Oannes, of which Berosus promises to give an account when he comes to the history of the kings. Moreover, Oannes wrote concerning the generation of mankind; of their different ways of life, and of their civil polity; and the following is the purport of what he said, - [*at this point begins the description of the darkness and abyss of waters, and the hideous animals, see page 8.*]

Syncellus and Eusebius, on Polyhistor, on Berosus.[50]

Considering that Oannes was amphibious, he must have been considered capable of surviving the flood, and is therefore not limited to the pre-flood world. In that case, who was he? The most obvious explanation is given by Cory,[51] in his Preface to the *Ancient Fragments* as follows:

The large extract preserved by Alexander Polyhistor, is extremely valuable; and contains a store of very curious information.

---

[49] This identification of the Erythraean sea, bordering on Babylonia, confirms that it must be the Persian Gulf.

[50] Hodges, pp.56-58.

[51] Cory, 1828, p.ix. This Preface is omitted from the 1876 edition by Hodges.

The first book of the history opens naturally enough with a description of Babylonia. Then referring to the paintings, the author finds the first series a kind of preface to the rest. All men of every nation appear assembled in Chaldea: among them is introduced a character, who is represented as their instructor in the arts and sciences, and informing them of the events, which had previously taken place. Unconscious that Noah is represented under the character of Oannes, Berosus describes him, from the hieroglyphical delineation, as a being literally compounded of a fish and man, and as passing the natural, instead of the diluvian, night in the sea, with other circumstances indicative of his character and life.

It seems that the ancient Chaldeans used to draw pictures of Noah, as if he was a man with the properties of a fish, because he had survived the flood, with his family and the animals whom he had preserved, while the rest of the world perished. Only the fishes were able to survive without the help of Noah, so he was typified as a "fish-man".

Cory's distinction between the natural and diluvian night is very appropriate. There was rain for forty days and forty nights, but the total period in the ark was a year and ten days, before it was safe to come out and disperse around the world. During that time, the animals would have had to hibernate to preserve food. The diluvian night, in the minds of the Babylonians, became confused with an ordinary night, so Noah was typified as the "fish-man" who went into the sea at night and came out in the daytime to teach people the arts and sciences.

Noah must certainly have been a teacher, being the only man of considerable age who had passed from the old world to the new (and we don't know the age of his wife). He was six hundred years old when he entered the ark, while his three sons, Shem, Ham and Japheth were only about one hundred years each. According to Gen. 5:32, Noah was five hundred years old when his three sons were born.

According to the chronology of Genesis, Noah was born when Enos, his seventh-generation ancestor was still alive, and he knew Enos for 84 years. Noah had known all the pre-flood patriarchs, except for Adam and his son Seth, and Enoch who was translated to heaven.

Curiously enough, the first appearance of Oannes the fish-man, according to the king-list of Berosus, is during the reign of Amelon who corresponds to Enos. In that case, Noah (Oannes) appears conversing with his oldest living ancestor, and he was not *teaching*, instead he was *learning*.

The ancient Chaldeans must have been awe-inspired by this old man, five hundred years older than any of his sons, who could pass on all the knowledge of the old world to the new, and who is credited with preserving both humanity and the animal world from destruction. As the knowledge of his fame passed from generation to generation, together with the distortions of time and the heathen corruptions of his teaching, he became deified as a fish-god.

Alexander Hislop, in his *Two Babylons*,[52] identifies Oannes with Noah, and also with his descendants, Nimrod and Osiris. Nimrod was the great-grandson of Noah who became the first king of Babylon. He is believed to have been killed, but came back to life as Tammuz, the posthumous child of his wife Semiramis. Either she was pregnant when Nimrod was killed, or else she became pregnant from another man, who is not identified. In like manner, the Egyptian Osiris was killed and cut in pieces, but came back to life as Horus, the posthumous child of his wife Isis. She claimed that she had gone down into the underworld and had intercourse with her dead husband, and then came back again and gave birth to Horus. In both of these cases, there is the death of a man, who comes back as a god, and in the process his wife is also deified. The re-birth of the man is a pagan corruption, based on the emergence of Noah from the ark, as he is considered to have been "re-born" after the flood.

Jonah, the Reluctant Fish-Man

We all know the story of Jonah, the reluctant prophet who went to sea to get away from Nineveh, the capital of Assyria, where he was supposed to preach and call on the people to repent of their sins, otherwise their city would be destroyed. There was a violent storm, and the sailors threw him overboard because they believed the storm was a consequence of his disobedience. He was swallowed by a big fish, and vomited up on dry land, from where he made his way to Nineveh.

The people of Nineveh, when they saw this man who had come out of the mouth of a fish, listened to his preaching and repented, so that their city was saved. Now it's unusual for people to listen to a prophet. Usually they kill him, and then their descendants a few generations later venerate him as a prophet. But in this case they listened to Jonah and obeyed him

---

[52] Hislop, pp. 114, 136, 243-244.

without question. The reason was because they were terrified. They thought that Jonah was Oannes the fish-man, and if they didn't listen to him, perhaps there would be another flood.

The Bishop's Mitre

Have you ever wondered why a bishop, in the Anglican or Roman Catholic church, wears a hat which is divided down the middle so that it looks like the open mouth of a fish? The hat is called a mitre, and according to Hislop,[53] it is derived from Oannes, the Babylonian fish-god. We have already seen, on page 19, how an Assyrian priest wears a fish-costume while making an offering to Baal, and we should notice that the headgear looks distinctly similar to a bishop's mitre.

The fish was used by the early church, as a secret symbol to indicate their presence, so they would know where to meet during times of persecution. They understood the meaning of the fish, as the symbol of a teacher who becomes hidden and then returns, but in this case they applied it to someone who genuinely died and rose again, as opposed to the fake resurrections of Nimrod and Osiris.

While the early use of the fish symbol seems fair enough, the church has probably gone a bit too far with the use of the mitre, making their bishops look like the priests of Babylonia and Assyria.

Location of the Ark

There are a number of theories about where the Ark might have landed, and the following possible locations have been suggested:

- Mount Ararat
- Durupinar
- North-West Iran, possibly Sahand or Sabalan
- Cudi Dagh (Eastern or Central)

Figure 3 shows the locations, together with the rivers leading to the Plain of Shinar where they eventually settled in Babylon.

---

[53] Hislop, p.215.

Figure 3 - Urartu, Kurdistan and Babylon

Mount Ararat

Most English translations of the Bible, including the King James Authorised Version, say that the ark landed on the "mountains of Ararat" (Gen. 8:4). Some people have supposed that this means Mount Ararat itself, in north-east Turkey. It is the highest mountain in the region at 16,945 ft. (5,165 m) and there have been expeditions to try and find the ark, but without success. There have been some alleged eye-witness accounts of a boat-like structure, but none of them can be confirmed, and there are no photographs.

The name 'Ararat' is the Hebrew name of Armenia, and it is only in relatively recent times that the name was applied to a specific mountain.

In the time of Moses, who is widely credited as the author of the first five books of the Bible, it was known as the ancient kingdom of Urartu. In Hebrew, the name is spelt אררט (RRT)[54] and it could just as easily be rendered Ararat or Urartu because there are no vowels.

The kingdom of Urartu is marked on the map, and the name is synonymous with Ararat and Armenia, although it represents a much larger area than Armenia today. The Biblical term "mountains of Ararat" could be anywhere in Urartu, since the whole region is mountainous.

Durupinar

At Durupinar, 18 miles south of Mount Ararat, at an altitude of about 6,300 ft (1,920 m) there is a boat-shaped mound which is thought to be an impression left behind by the ark. It is named after Captain Ilhan Durupinar who identified it from a Turkish Air Force aerial photograph in 1959. However, it could be purely geological, and there are other boat-shaped mounds in the region. This is a controversial site, and some people are convinced that it's genuine, while others dispute it.[55] A visitors centre has been built near the site, for the convenience of those who want to go there.

Urartu and Kurdistan

Having established that the ark is somewhere in Urartu, we will now see some fragments showing that it must be in the overlapping areas of Urartu and Kurdistan. At the same time we will look at some features of the Babylonian flood story to see how it compares with the Bible.

On page 14 we saw a fragment of Berosus, from Abydenus, giving a list of kings before the flood, and then it says how Noah (Sisithrus or Xisuthrus) was told that there would be a flood and he should deposit all his writings in the city of the Sun at Sippara. The fragment continues as follows:

> Sisithrus (Xisuthrus), when he had complied with these commands, instantly sailed to Armenia, and was immediately inspired by God. During the

---

[54] The Hebrew characters are read from right to left. The first aleph (א) is a silent character under which a vowel pointer may be placed.

[55] For the arguments for and against the Durupinar site, see <www.noahsarksearch.com/durupinar.htm>, Oct. 2002.

prevalence of the waters Sisithrus (Xisuthrus) sent out birds that he might judge if the flood had subsided. But the birds passing over an unbounded sea, and not finding any place of rest returned again to Sisithrus. This he repeated; and when upon the third trial he succeeded, for the birds then returned with their feet stained with mud, the gods translated him from among men. With respect to the vessel, which yet remains in Armenia, it is a custom of the inhabitants to form bracelets and amulets of its wood.

Syncellus and Eusebius, on Abydenus, on Berosus.[56]

This fragment has a striking similarity to the Bible, in that Noah sent out birds to find out if there was dry land. However, the Bible does not agree that Noah was taken away from the earth when the birds returned. Instead it tells us how he came out of the ark and offered a sacrifice, and then he built a vineyard and got drunk and was found naked in his tent. He lived for 350 years after the flood, so that he died at the age of 950. (Gen. 9:28-29). We will return to this question later, when we have seen some more fragments.

The location of the ark is in Armenia (Urartu), which agrees with the Bible, and there is the claim that it still existed during the time of Berosus, which was the third century BC.

On page 8 we saw the account of creation, according to Berosus, in a fragment from Alexander Polyhistor. This is followed by a brief comment on the second book of Berosus (see page 15). The fragment then continues with the story of the flood as follows:

After the death of Ardates, his son, Xisuthrus, succeeded, and reigned eighteen sari. In his time happened the great Deluge; the history of which is given in this manner. The Deity, Kronus, appeared to him in a vision, and gave him notice, that upon the fifteenth day of the month Daesia[57] there would be a flood, by which mankind would be destroyed. He therefore enjoined him to commit to writing a history of the beginning, progress, and final conclusion of all things, down to the present term; and to bury these accounts securely in the city of the Sun at Sippara; and to build a vessel, and to take with him into it his friends and relations; and to convey on board everything necessary to sustain life, and to take in also all species of animals that either fly, or rove upon the earth; and trust himself to the deep. Having

---

[56] Hodges, p.54.
[57] The Macedonian month of Desius, corresponding to May or June.

asked the Deity, whither he was to sail? he was answered, "To the Gods:" upon which he offered up a prayer for the good of mankind. And he obeyed the divine admonition: and built a vessel five stadia in length, and in breadth two. Into this he put everything which he had got ready; and last of all conveyed into it his wife, children, and friends. After the Flood had been upon the earth, and was in time abated, Xisuthrus sent out some birds from the vessel, which, not finding any food, nor any place to rest their feet, returned to him again. After an interval of some days, he sent them forth a second time, and they now returned with their feet tinged with mud. He made a trial a third time with these birds, but they returned to him no more; from whence he formed a judgement, that the surface of the earth was now above the waters. Having, therefore, made an opening in the vessel, and finding, upon looking out, that the vessel was driven to the side of a mountain, he immediately quitted it, being attended by his wife, his daughter, and the pilot. Xisuthrus immediately paid his adoration to the earth, and, having constructed an altar, offered sacrifices to the gods.

These things being duly performed, both Xisuthrus, and those who came out of the vessel with him, disappeared. They who remained in the vessel, finding that the others did not return, came out, with many lamentations, and called continually on the name of Xisuthrus. They saw him no more, but could distinguish his voice in the air, and could hear him admonish them to pay due regard to the gods. He likewise informed them that it was upon account of his piety that he was translated to live with the gods; that his wife and daughter, with the pilot, had obtained the same honour. To this he added that he would have them make the best of their way to Babylonia, and search for the writings at Sippara, which were to be made known to all mankind: and that the place where they then were was the land of Armenia. The remainder having heard these words, offered sacrifices to the gods; and taking a circuit, journeyed towards Babylonia.

The vessel, being thus stranded in Armenia, some part of it yet remains in the Gordyaean mountains in Armenia; and the people scrape off the bitumen, with which it had been outwardly coated, and make use of it by way of an alexipharmic[58] and amulet. In this manner they returned to Babylon; and having found the writings at Sippara, they set about building cities, and erecting temples: and Babylon was thus inhabited again.

Syncellus and Eusebius, on Polyhistor, on Berosus.[59]

---

[58] An antidote to poison, and an amulet or charm against the evil eye.
[59] Hodges, pp.60-63.

This passage, like the previous one, agrees with the Bible in a number of ways, but says that Noah, his wife and daughter, and the "pilot" (whoever he is) have been translated to live with the gods. Noah doesn't teach anything in person to those who remained, except that they could find his writings at Sippara.

The Gordyaean mountains can be identified as Kurdistan. The name 'Gordy' becomes 'Kurdi' and the ending 'stan' means a country or region so we have Kurdistan. So the ark has to be in the region where Urartu and Kurdistan overlap.

North-West Iran - Sahand or Sabalan

There are a few people who speculate that the ark landed in Iran, based on an alleged eye-witness report from Edward Davis who was in Hamadan during World War II. He was taken to a mountain to see the remains of the ark, but nobody seems to know where it was. It could be Sahand or Sabalan, or somewhere in the mountains of western Iran, along the border with Iraq.[60]

There is some support for this region in a Chaldean fragment, from Nicolas of Damascus, who lived at about the time of Augustus Caesar.[61]

> There is above Minyas, in the land of Armenia, a very great mountain, which is called Baris (i.e. a ship); to which it is said that many persons retreated at the time of the Flood, and were saved; and that one in particular was carried thither in an ark, and was landed on its summit; and that the remains of the vessel were long preserved upon the mountain. Perhaps this was the same individual of whom Moses, the legislator of the Jews, has made mention.
>
> *Eusebius and Josephus, on Nicolas of Damascus.*[62]

The place called 'Minyas', otherwise known as 'Mannai' is the area south of Lake Urmia, in north-west Iran. The people were known as the Manneans, although they probably occupied a large area around Lake Urmia, not just Mannai itself. The mountain called 'Baris', which very significantly means 'a ship' cannot be identified with any certainty.

---

[60] For speculation about the ark in Iran, see
<www.noahsarksearch.com/iran.htm>, Oct. 2002.
[61] Augustus Caesar, Roman Emperor, b. 63 BC - d. AD 14.
[62] Hodges, p.74. See also Josephus Antiquities, I,iii,6.

The 'very great mountain' in this Chaldean fragment could be Sahand (12,211 ft; 3,722 m) or Sabalan (15,827 ft; 4,824 m), since these are the highest mountains in the region. They are both in Urartu, but outside of Kurdistan, so there is uncertainty about their possible status as ark sites.

There are other high hills in the area, and if we set aside the requirement to look for the highest ones, we can identify the region of Mannai, to the south of Lake Urmia, as an area that satisfies the requirements for an ark site because it is within the overlapping areas of Urartu and Kurdistan. However, to make any real progress on ark research in this region, it is necessary to identify the mountain called 'Baris'.

Eastern Cudi Dagh

The site that appears to have the most historical support is the eastern Cudi Dagh, 6,920 ft high (2,110 metres), and about 200 miles south of Mount Ararat. The word 'Dagh' is Turkish for 'mountain', so it is called 'Mt. Cudi'.

This mountain is in the overlapping regions of Urartu and Kurdistan, and there is a historical reference that specifically names it. The Koran identifies the Cudi Dagh by it's Arabic name 'Al Judi' as follows:

A voice cried out: 'Earth, swallow up your waters. Heaven, cease your rain!' The floods abated, and His will was done. The ark came to rest upon Al-Judi, and a voice declared: 'Gone are the evil-doers.'

The Koran, Sura Hud, 11:44.

Muslim commentators are uncertain about whether this refers to Al-Judi in Kurdistan, or another Al-Judi in Saudi Arabia. It seems that Muhammad learned the name from Jews and Christians who knew the place in Kurdistan, but a tradition developed among Muslims, based on Al-Judi in Saudi Arabia which was more familiar to them.

The Muslim sources, and the arguments in favour of the Cudi Dagh as an ark site, are given in more detail by Bill Crouse.[63]

The Cudi Dagh location is verified by the existence of a monument to the Flood, on the top of the mountain. It is built of stone in the shape of a

---

[63] Crouse, B., *The Landing Place.*

29

boat and is called 'Sefinet Nebi Nuh' which means 'The Ship of the Prophet Noah'.

Figure 4 - 'Ship of the Prophet Noah' on Cudi Dagh

This photograph, by Gertrude Bell,[64] was taken in 1909 when she went on an expedition to the area. She also discovered a local tradition, where Christians, Muslims and Jews would meet on the site once a year, in the summer, to commemorate the Prophet Noah. There used to be a Nestorian monastery at the site, called the 'Cloister of the Ark', but it was destroyed by lightning in 766.

Central Cudi Dagh

The Central Cudi Dagh, marked on the map, is just a small hill 2,100 ft high (640 metres), but is identified as a possible ark site because the people at the nearby town of Urfa (otherwise known as Sanliurfa) believe that the ark landed there. It is outside both Urartu and Kurdistan, and there appears to be no supporting evidence for this site apart from the local tradition.

---

[64] Bell, G., *Amurath to Amurath*. See also:
<www.noahsarksearch.com/BellGertrude/CudiDaghCloisterOfTheArk003.jpg>, Oct. 2002.

Cudi Dagh Culture Trail

There is some interesting history and culture along the route between eastern and central Cudi Dagh sites.

Figure 5 - Cudi Dagh Culture Trail

The ancient city of Midyat dates back to the Hurrians who lived in the area in the third millennium BC. According to Edith Porada[65] the Hurrians or other related tribes were the ancient ancestors of the Manneans.

The city of Midyat is on a high plateau called Turabdin which means 'Mountain of the Servants of God'. The name refers to the monks who lived there in almost eighty monasteries that were founded since the fourth century. There are many churches there today, and also many mosques. There is also a Yezdi community, of Persian origin, and their religion is thought to be derived from Zoroastrianism. Strangely enough, the people of Midyat, and also the towns of Mardin and Urfa to the west, are very fond of pigeons, which are domesticated and kept in the courtyards of their houses.[66] Could this be derived from the memory of Noah, who sent out birds from the ark, to see if there was land?

---

[65] Porada, E., *The Art of Ancient Iran, Pre-Islamic Cultures,* Chapter 9, *The Finds of Hasanlu - The Art of the Manneans,*
<www.noteaccess.com/Texts/Porada/9.htm>, Oct. 2002.
[66] Celebi, E., *Midyat - City of Stone.*

Historical Sightings of the Ark

If the ark was on the Cudi Dagh, or some other site in the region, how long did it remain there? We have already seen how it was there in the third century BC, at the time of Berosus. According to Josephus, it was still there in the first century AD.

> After this the ark rested on the top of a certain mountain in Armenia ... Noah learned that the earth was become clear of the flood. So after he had stayed seven more days, he sent the living creatures out of the ark; and both he and his family went out, when he also sacrificed to God, and feasted with his companions. However, the Armenians call this place (Αποβατηριον) [Apo-ba-tay-reon] *The Place of Descent*; for the ark being saved in that place, its remains are shown there by the inhabitants to this day.
>
> *Josephus, Antiquities, I,iii,5*

The Place of Descent is not easily identified because of linguistic problems, discussed by Bill Crouse (see note 63). However, Crouse also gives a number of later sightings of the ark, as follows:

- Eusebius, in the 3rd century AD, wrote in his Chronicle that a small part of the ark still existed in the Gordyaean mountains.
- Al-Mas'udi, a Muslim scholar in the 10th century AD, wrote that the ark still existed on mount el-Judi. He identifies the place as about 25-30 miles from the Tigris, which conforms to the Cudi Dagh location.
- In 1949, two Turkish journalists claimed to have seen the ark on Cudi Dagh, although the story cannot be verified. There are Kurds in the area who say that wood was found on the site at that time.

What Happened to Noah?

We have seen some fragments of Berosus, saying how he never descended from the mountain after the flood, instead he was taken away to live with the gods.

- A fragment from Abydenus (see page 25), says he was taken away as soon as the birds returned with their feet stained with mud.
- A fragment from Alexander Polyhistor (see page 26) says that Noah came out of the ark, together with his wife, daughter and the 'pilot', and they offered a sacrifice, and then they were translated to the gods.

While these two accounts differ from each other in detail, they differ totally from the Bible, which says he planted a vineyard, and was found drunk and naked in his tent, and he lived for 350 years after the flood. The question is, which story should we believe? The answer is that we can only go so far, in reconciling the Biblical and Babylonian accounts with each other. A detail of this sort is trivial, compared with the many striking similarities between the Biblical and Babylonian accounts that we have already seen.

For the historian, there is little to choose between them, but we can ponder on which version of the story we would like to believe.

The Babylonian version portrays Noah as someone who is just too good. He is so good, he seems to be perfect, and it is hardly surprising that the Babylonians deified him.

The Bible also makes him appear faultless during the entire period of his epic drama, as he passed from the old world to the new. This is entirely feasible, as men are often known to display heroic qualities while under stress. However, when the drama is over, we see his human side. He planted a vineyard and got drunk. While this is regrettable, it is hardly surprising. He had faithfully built the ark on dry land while the rest of the world mocked. He didn't have much fun while building the ark, and the flood itself wasn't much fun either, and then the first few years after the flood must have been a tough survival exercise. When he at last got established somewhere, he built a vineyard for his own pleasure, the first pleasure he had enjoyed for many years. The character we see in the Bible is not so perfect, but much more believable.

Descent from the Ark

The descent from the ark, after the waters had subsided, must have been a difficult and dangerous task. According to the Bible, Noah removed the covering from the ark on the first day of the new year, and he saw that the land was dry all around him, but he stayed in the ark, or at least in the vicinity of the ark, for almost two more months before leaving it altogether. He wouldn't leave until God commanded him to do so (Gen. 8:15-16).

The reason for this delay (apart from the divine command) is because, although there was dry land around the ark, there was not enough land to support life, and some time was required for plants to grow. The ark was still the safest place, because they could continue to use their provisions.

Josephus gives the following account of the anxiety they felt as they went down from the mountain and tried to build settlements elsewhere:

> Now the sons of Noah were three, – Shem, Japhet, and Ham, born one hundred years before the Deluge. These first of all descended from the mountains into the plains, and fixed their habitations there; and persuaded others who were greatly afraid of the lower grounds on account of the flood, and so were very loth to come down from the higher places, to venture to follow their examples. Now the plain in which they first dwelt was called Shinar.
>
> *Josephus Antiquities, I,iv,1*

Josephus doesn't say who the 'others' were. We can only say that he must have been following the Babylonian account, which says Noah took his 'friends and relations' into the ark (see Berosus according to Alexander Polyhistor on page 26). Josephus makes it clear why they were afraid to go onto lower ground. They might have been concerned about the problems of building houses on recently waterlogged ground, but their real concern was the possibility of another flood.

> But as for Noah, he was afraid, since God had determined to destroy mankind, lest he should drown the earth every year; so he offered burnt offerings . . . When Noah had made these supplications, God, who loved the man for his righteousness, granted entire success to his prayers . . .
>
> *Josephus Antiquities, I,iii,7-8*

Although Noah himself was reassured, it seems that the others did not believe him. The place where they eventually came down to the plain is also very interesting. The plain of Shinar is central and southern Mesopotamia, from Babylon to the Persian Gulf. If they went directly down the mountain from Cudi Dagh, they would have arrived in northern Mesopotamia, known as Padan-Aram. They may have journeyed further to Shinar, before building settlements, but a more likely solution is given by Berosus. He says that '*taking a circuit*' they journeyed towards Babylonia (see the fragment from Polyhistor on page 27). This means they were unable or unwilling to go directly into the plain. It would have been waterlogged for some time, collecting the water that flowed down from the mountains and slowly dispensing it into the sea. Their most

likely route would be to go either east or west, following the coastline of
the receding waters, until they were able to proceed more directly towards
Babylon.

The Bible tells us how people came *'from the east'* towards Babylon.

> And the whole earth was of one language, and of one speech. And it came to
> pass, as they journeyed from the east, that they found a plain in the land of
> Shinar; and they dwelt there.
>
> *Genesis 11:1-2*

However, the Hebrew is difficult to translate, and instead of *'from the
east'* it could just as easily mean *'in the east'*. The Hebrew for *'east'* is
qedem and it is prefixed by *mi(n)* which means *'out of'*, or *'away from'*.
The two words come together to give *miqqedem*, but this is the same
word form that is used in Gen. 2:8.

> And the Lord God planted a garden eastward in Eden ...

In this case it describes a place that is in the east, from the point of view
of Moses who was in the Sinai desert, or somewhere near Israel, when he
wrote it. The passage about Babylon, in that case, simply means that
people in the east were in the process of migration, and does not imply a
direction of travel. The Hebrew is discussed in more detail by Stephen
Clothier.[67]

Since Berosus tells us that they travelled in a curved path, there are
two possible routes to Babylon from the eastern Cudi Dagh:

- East and then south, along the foothills of Kurdistan, then south-west
  along the River Divala until it meets the Tigris. Then they went a
  short distance across the plain to the Euphrates and south towards
  Babylon.
- West to Urfa and then south-east along the Euphrates to Babylon.
  This route passes alongside the central Cudi Dagh, and perhaps
  through some distortion of history, it might provide the basis of the
  local tradition that the ark landed there. The eastern Cudi Dagh is the
  more likely ark site, but possibly Noah might have stopped at Urfa
  for a while, before proceeding south along the Euphrates.

---

[67] Clothier, S., *The Possible Significance of Gen. 11:2 - Does it provide us with a
clue as to where the Ark landed?*

Was it Plagiarism?

Having considered these various fragments of Berosus and other ancient authors, and compared them with the Bible, we see that they agree with each other about many things. While this is reassuring, and gives the impression of a consistent history, we have to ask the question, were they just copying things from each other?

Bible from Babylon?

First we consider whether the Biblical creation and flood story could have been made up from Babylonian records. It is certainly possible that Moses, the author of Genesis, had access to Babylonian records, since he was brought up in the house of Pharaoh, and after he had fled from Egypt he spent some time with a Midianite priest and married his daughter Zipporah (strangely similar to Sippara where Noah's books were buried). Since the culture of ancient Egypt is derived from the earlier Babylon, it is very likely that Babylonian records were available.

However, even if Moses had the Babylonian records, he would not have needed to use them. The reason is that Abraham came from Ur of the Chaldees, and he would have known the history anyway. Abraham was the tenth generation descendant of Noah, of the line of Shem, and the Biblical chronology tells us that Shem was still alive during his time, in fact, Shem outlived Abraham by 13 years! Furthermore, Shem can be identified as Melchizedek, the priest-king who met with Abraham and offered him bread and wine, according to the Jewish literature.[68]

Babylon from the Bible?

Now we look at the question of whether or not Berosus could have taken his history from the Bible. He may have had access to a Bible, although it cannot be known for certain. He knew about Abraham, although he did not name him, and he wrote about him as follows:

---

[68] Midrash Rabbah - Genesis LVI:10, Leviticus XXV:6, Numbers IV:8; Talmud - Nedarim 32b.

After the Flood, in the tenth generation, there was a certain man among the Chaldeans, renowned for his justice and great exploits, and for his skill in the celestial sciences.

Eusebius, on Polyhistor, on Berosus.[69]

How did Berosus know about Abraham? Did he get it from the Bible? Not necessarily. Abraham came from Ur of the Chaldees, so he might have made his mark on society before he left. This quote from Berosus doesn't prove anything one way or the other.

The question we have to consider is, what would Berosus gain by taking the Hebrew scriptures and plagiarising them? He was highly respected among the Greeks, and they built a copper statue at Athens in his honour. He would never have gained any such honour by writing a boiled-down, corrupted version of the Bible and presenting it to the Greeks. If the Greeks wanted a Bible, they could have got one directly from the Jews, and be assured of much greater accuracy. Indeed, this is exactly what they did, because the Greek Bible (Old Testament) was available to the Early Church.

Berosus got his fame, not by re-processing the Hebrew Bible, but by making his Babylonian literature available to the Greeks. He was in a unique position to do this, having been a priest of Bel at Babylon with access to the temple records (until the conquest of Alexander the Great), and having knowledge of the Greek language.

The Babylonian history is not a corrupted Bible, and neither is the Bible a corrupted Babylonian history. Instead, they are separate accounts, made by two different cultures, based on a common memory of the actual events.

The Greek Story of Creation and the Fall

The Greek creation story identifies Ouranos as a pre-creation deity, although we will see later, in Chapter 2, that he also represents Noah. (See '*The Descendants of Noah*', page 45).

The first of all the gods was Chaos, who gave birth to Gaia (Earth) and Tartarus (the dark underworld), without the need for a mate. Gaia in turn gave birth to Ouranos (Heaven), also without the need for a mate.

---

[69] Hodges, p.63.

Ouranos became her mate and from him she gave birth to the Titans, Cyclopes and Hecatoncheires. The Cyclopes had one eye in their foreheads, and the Hecatoncheires were monstrous creatures with a hundred hands and fifty heads, and Ouranos hated them and cast them into Tartarus. Gaia was grieved that her children were imprisoned, so she persuaded the Titans to attack their father. She gave the adamantine sickle[70] to Kronus, one of the Titans, and he castrated Ouranos and dethroned him. Ouranos gave a prophecy, that there would be vengeance for this terrible deed and Kronus would be dethroned by his own son.

When Kronus became king, he was much the same as his father, and he shut up the Cyclopes and Hecatoncheires in Tartarus. He had children from his wife Rhea, who was also a Titan, but he swallowed them at birth, fearing that his father's prophecy might come true. Rhea was grieved at the death of her children, so when Zeus was born she wrapped a stone in a cloth and gave it to Kronus to eat, as if it was the new-born child. There were other children who survived and they were collectively known as the Olympians. There were other gods called Olympians, but the children of Kronus (Cronos) and Rhea were also called Cronides.

When Zeus grew up, he led the Olympians in a rebellion against the Titans which lasted for ten years. Then he took the Cyclopes and Hecatoncheires as his allies, and defeated the Titans and shut them up in Tartarus, and appointed the Hecatoncheires as their guards. Because of his exploits, he established himself as the 'king of the gods'. He is also known as the sky god, with lightning in his hand.

There are two stories about the creation of man:

- Prometheus was a Titan who did not oppose Zeus, and he moulded men out of water and earth. He also gave them fire, which he had stolen from Zeus, and he was nailed to a rock by Hephaestus (Vulcan), the son of Zeus.

- Persephone (Core or Cura), Queen of the Underworld and daughter of Zeus, formed a man out of mud, and Zeus gave him life (the spark of life, as in the Frankenstein story, not the breath of life).

---

[70] A sickle made of the hardest metal. This may be compared with *adamant* which means a person with a hard, unyielding opinion.

The first woman, Pandora, was made by Haephastus, by mixing earth and water. Athena, the daughter of Zeus, clothed her and taught her needlework. After that, the Olympians each gave her a gift (the name Pandora means 'all gifts'). Aphrodite put grace on her head, and Hermes gave her speech, shamelessness and deceit. The Charities (Graces) and Peitho (Persuasion) gave her gold necklaces, and the Horae (wardens of the sky and Olympus) put flowers on her head.

Up to this time, the world enjoyed a period called the 'Golden Age' where there was no sorrow or suffering, and no need to work because everything was available in abundance. There was death, but it was like falling asleep, and there was no such thing as old age. But it was all about to go wrong.

Epimetheus, one of the Titans, received a jar[71] from Zeus, contrary to a warning from his brother Prometheus never to take any gift from him. Pandora opened the jar and all sorts of evil came out, and the Golden Age came to an end. Pandora is clearly the Greek version of Eve who took the forbidden fruit.

Lamech and his Three Sons

In Genesis 4 we are told that Cain, the son of Adam, killed his brother Abel and fled to the land of Nod, east of Eden, where he built a city. His fifth-generation descendant Lamech had two wives, Adah and Zillah, and from them he had three sons:

- Jabal, from his wife Adah, was the father of those who lived in tents and kept cattle.

- Jubal, also from his wife Adah, was the father of those who played the harp and organ.

- Tubal-cain, from his wife Zillah, was a blacksmith, working with brass and iron, and taught his craft to others.

---

[71] This is more commonly known as *Pandora's box* although Hesiod calls it a *jar*. See Evelyn-White's translation of Hesiod's *Works and Days*, 11, 90-105, <sunsite.berkeley.edu/OMACL/Hesiod/works.html>, Oct. 2002.

These three sons have their counterparts in Greek mythology:

- Hermes, the son of Zeus and Maia, was a thief and cattle-driver. He was also musical and he made his own lyre. He stole cattle from his brother Apollo, and he denied the theft, but nobody believed him and eventually he had to agree to return the cattle. However, Apollo saw the lyre and asked if he could have it in exchange for the cattle. The deal was struck, so Apollo went off with the lyre and Hermes kept the cattle. Then Hermes made a shepherd's pipe for himself, and Apollo wanted it also, and he obtained it in exchange for a golden wand for herding cattle, and some lessons in divining by the use of pebbles. Hermes is also known as a messenger god, who introduced the idea of sending ambassadors in times of warfare, to seek terms of peace.

- Apollo, the son of Zeus and Leto, was a god of music, art, prophecy, archery and healing. He improved on the lyre that he had obtained from Hermes, increasing the number of strings from three to seven.

- Hephaestus (Vulcan), the son of Zeus and Hera, was a blacksmith, working with all kinds of metals.

From this comparison we have the result that Zeus must be Lamech, and we should also note that both of them were polygamists.

Who is Zeus?

If Zeus is the sky god who gave the spark of life to humans, how can he also be Lamech? Not only does he have a dual identity, but we shall soon see that he has a third identity, as a son of the Biblical Ham, most probably Cush or Mizraim. These multiple identities are a consequence of the migration of histories from one era to another, as the Greeks used the pre-flood histories to immortalise and deify their early post-flood kings. We will return to this subject later, on page 66, but first we have to look at the early post-flood world.

Chapter 2 - The Early Post-Flood World

They say that the first inhabitants of the earth, glorying in their own strength and size, and despising the gods, undertook to build a tower, whose top should reach the sky, upon that spot where Babylon now stands. But, when it approached the heaven, the winds assisted the gods, and overturned the work upon its contrivers, (its ruins are said to be at Babylon,) and the gods introduced a diversity of tongues among men, who till that time had all spoken the same language. And a war arose between Kronus and Titan; and the place in which they built the tower is now called Babylon, on account of the confusion of the languages; for confusion is by the Hebrews called Babel.

Syncellus and Eusebius, on Abydenus, on Berosus. [72]

The above fragment from Berosus is basically the same as the Biblical account, except that it is polytheistic and it tells us of a war breaking out. The war is undoubtedly a consequence of the confusion of tongues, since the people from different families and tribes could not understand each other, but it may also have been a clash between the paganism of *Kronus* and the monotheism of *Titan*. These characters will be identified later, in the section on '*The Descendants of Noah*', see page 45.

A footnote in *Cory's Ancient Fragments* explains that the word 'Babylon' is the Greek form of the Assyrian name 'Bab-ilu', meaning 'Gate of God', and it was regarded as a holy city. The Hebrew word 'Bilbool', sounds like 'Bab-ilu' and means 'confusion'. It is directly defined in the Biblical narrative of the dispersion as follows:

Therefore is the name of it called Babel; because the Lord did there confound the language of all the earth: and from thence did the Lord scatter them abroad upon the face of the earth.

Gen. 11:9

It is not surprising that the same name means two different things in Assyrian and Hebrew, considering that Babylon is the place where the languages originated. The Assyrians remembered the original purpose of

---

[72] Hodges, p.55.

the tower as the 'Gate of God' and the Hebrews remembered it as an act of folly, resulting in the confusion of tongues.

So much for the name, but we will now focus on the objective that the people were trying to achieve by building the tower. They could not have imagined that they could reach to the gods, merely on account of the height of their tower, considering that they had only recently descended from a range of mountains that were much higher than any tower that they could build. It is more likely that the tower was an observatory where they could study the stars, and somehow it would facilitate some kind of magic that could influence the gods. The specific purpose is not stated in any of the ancient fragments, but we can gain an insight into it from the story of one of their kings.

Gilgamesh

Gilgamesh was the fifth king of Uruk after the flood. The city of Uruk was on the Euphrates, to the south of Babylon, and from this city we get the name of the modern state of Iraq. He was the son of Lugulbanda, a shepherd god, and Ninsun, a goddess of Uruk who was noted for her wisdom. He had a companion called Enkidu, who had been made out of clay by Aruru, the goddess of creation and was of the essence of Anu, the sky god and Ninurta the war-god. Enkidu was a wild man of the forest, and lived with the animals, but he was tamed and humanised by a harlot who had been specially brought to him, to make him into a companion for Gilgamesh.

Gilgamesh was a strong and powerful giant, so that no man could match him, until he met Enkidu and they began to fight. They were enemies at first, but when it turned out that they were equally matched, they embraced each other and became friends, and together they embarked on a series of exploits.

The Battle Against Humbaba

The first exploit of Gilgamesh and Enkidu was a journey to the Cedar Mountain (possibly Lebanon), where they fought with the Monster Herdsman called Humbaba, a god of wild nature, capable of creating storms and causing volcanoes to erupt. This monster is too powerful for either Gilgamesh or Enkidu, and they have to enlist the help of Shamash, the sun-god, who also has power over nature and comes to their aid.

Gilgamesh and Enkidu first had to lure Humbaba out of the forest, which was very large, by cutting down trees. During this time, Enkidu had a dream about how the heavens and earth roared, there was darkness and flashes of lightning, fire blazed out, and the clouds lowered and rained down death. Clearly, he is seeing a vision of the flood, which had only recently wiped out almost the whole of humanity, and this battle is about control of the elements.

Earlier in the story, when Gilgamesh is discussing his intended journey with Enkidu, he says "Where is the man who can clamber to heaven" as if he is referring to the intended purpose of the tower of Babel. We therefore have an interpretation of the Forest Journey. It represents the hopes of the Babylonians, that somehow they would be able to ascend to the assembly of the gods, and would be able to influence them so that they would never again bring a flood upon mankind. In particular, they wanted to get rid of Humbaba, who appears in the role of the god who actually raises the storm, according to the will of the other gods.

The story also emphasises the importance of Shamash, the sun-god. To the Babylonians, the appearance of the sun meant the end of the diluvian night, so that the sun-god, under different names, became the primary object of worship throughout the ancient world, including the Egyptians and the Druids.

The Bull of Heaven

The next battle was against the Bull of Heaven, which represents drought. The Bull came and drank from the river at Uruk, and great cracks opened up in the ground so that men fell into them. Enkidu leapt onto the Bull and seized it by the horns, and then Gilgamesh drew out his sword and thrust it into the Bull, between the neck and the horns. When they had killed the Bull, they cut out its heart and offered it to Shamash.

This story, together with the battle against Humbaba, represents the dual fear of flood and drought. The pre-flood world had never seen rain, and instead there was a mist which came up from the earth and watered the ground (Gen. 2:5-6). After the flood they had rain but no mist. When it rained, they were afraid of flood, and when it didn't rain they were afraid of drought. So when Gilgamesh and Enkidu killed the Bull and offered it's heart to Shamash, they were asking for sunshine and rain in due season.

The Death of Enkidu and the Search for Immortality

After Gilgamesh and Enkidu had killed both Humbaba and the Bull of Heaven, the gods took counsel together and decided that one of them must die. Enkidu became ill, and greatly resented the fact that despite all his exploits, the gods were still capable of deciding his fate. He would much rather have died in battle, leaving for himself a great name, than to die of an illness which he considered to be a shameful death. Enkidu died, and Gilgamesh wept bitterly for him, and then set out on the search for eternal life, in case the same fate should overtake him.

He went off in search of Utnapishtim,[73] the Babylonian Noah, who had entered the assembly of the gods after the flood. Gilgamesh came to Mashu,[74] a mountain with twin peaks, which guards the rising and setting sun. At the gate there were Scorpions standing guard, half-man and half-dragon, so Gilgamesh told them about his mission and persuaded them to let him through. He passed through twelve leagues of darkness and then the sun streamed out. He went into the garden of the gods and met a young woman called 'Sidduri', who lived alongside the Ocean and made wine. He told her of his quest, and asked her how he could get to Utnapishtim, who was somewhere across the Ocean. She told him his quest was hopeless, but eventually she gave way and told him that down in the woods he would find Urshanabi, the ferryman of Utnapishtim, who might be able to take him across the Ocean, otherwise he would have to abandon his quest and turn back.

Gilgamesh, in his anger, smashed the tackle of the boat, apparently unaware that it was needed to make the boat seaworthy. He told Urshanabi of his quest, but Urshanabi replied that he had destroyed the equipment needed to get across the water. However, he could go into the forest and make long poles that he could thrust into the water to drive the boat. Gilgamesh made the poles, and the two of them set off across the Ocean. Gilgamesh drove the boat, using the poles, but when they came close to Dilmun, the place of the sun's transit, he had used up the last pole, so Gilgamesh removed his clothes and held them up against the wind, completing the journey. They found Utnapishtim, lying at ease, and

---

[73] Utnapishtim is the old Babylonian name of Noah, the same person who is called Xisuthrus by Berosus.

[74] Mashu is sometimes thought to be the Lebanon and Anti-Lebanon mountains.

Gilgamesh asked him what was the secret of eternal life. Utnapishtim replied that nothing is permanent, everything dies at the appointed time, and then he proceeded to tell him the story of the flood, which is much the same as what we have already seen from Berosus.

Utnapishtim was displeased with Urshanabi, because he had arrived in the boat without tackle and mast, and Gilgamesh was driving the boat. He banished him from the shores of Dilmun, so that he would have to return to Uruk with Gilgamesh, but then he told Gilgamesh a secret of the gods. He told him about a plant that grows under water, that can restore a man's lost youth. It was prickly, but he could try and take it in his hands. Gilgamesh went deep under the water and took the plant, and brought it to the surface. He showed it to Urshanabi the ferryman, and said he would take it back to Uruk and give it to the old men so that they would recover their youth, and then he would take it himself. However, as they continued on their journey, they stopped at a pool and Gilgamesh went in to bathe, and a serpent came up and snatched the plant out of his hand, and then it shed its skin. Gilgamesh lamented that all his efforts had come to nothing, and the two of them returned to Uruk.

At this point we realise that the tree of life, which appears in the book of Genesis, also exists in the Babylonian literature. Just as Adam and Eve were deceived by a serpent and were denied access to the tree of life, so also we see that Gilgamesh has hold of the prickly plant for just a short time, but before he has made any use of it, a serpent snatches it away.

The complete story of Gilgamesh, or at least the text that is available from excavations in Mesopotamia, is given by Sandars,[75] together with some explanations.

The Descendants of Noah

Noah had three sons, Shem, Ham and Japheth, who were with him in the ark, according to the Biblical account. When the nations were scattered after the tower of Babel, they went in three directions, each setting up their respective empires in different parts of the world.

- Shem went to Asia, including the Middle East and Arabia, but excluding Central Asia and India.

---

[75] Sandars, N.K., *The Epic of Gilgamesh.*

- Ham went to Africa.
- Japheth had a very large area, including Europe, the northern parts of the world, Central Asia and India. This is in accordance with Genesis 9:27 *"God shall enlarge Japheth, and he shall dwell in the tents of Shem . . ."*

These empires were further sub-divided among the grand-children of Noah, and their destinations are given by Josephus,[76] in a passage that is too lengthy to quote here, but copies are easy to obtain. I would also recommend Bill Cooper's book After the Flood,[77] which contains an appendix on each of the three patriarchs and their descendants.

The Babylonian history also mentions three patriarchs, according to the following Chaldean fragment.

> "The Sibyl says, that when all men formerly spoke the same language, some among them undertook to erect a large and lofty tower, in order to climb into heaven. But God, (or the gods), sending forth a whirlwind, frustrated their design and gave to each tribe a particular language of its own, which (*confusion of tongues*) is the reason that the name of that city is called Babylon."
>
> "After the Flood, Titan and Prometheus lived, and Titan undertook a war against Kronus."
>
> *Chaldean fragment - Syncellus, Eusebius and Josephus on Alexander Polyhistor.*[78]

These three patriarchs seem to correspond to Shem, Ham and Japheth, although they appear in this passage with different names. The question is, which way round are they?

Kronus can be identified as Ham, according to the following passage from Sanchoniathon:

> ... And Kronus coming into the country of the south, gave all Egypt to the god Taautus [or Thoth], that it might be his kingdom ...
>
> *Eusebius on Sanchoniathon.*[79]

---

[76] Josephus, *Antiquities of the Jews*, I,vi.
[77] Cooper, Bill, *After the Flood*.
[78] Hodges, p.75.
[79] Hodges, pp.18-19.

Also, Kronus appears in the Egyptian king lists as the Saturn of Egypt, in the so-called *'Dynasty of the Demigods'*.[80] According to Holinshed,[81] the name 'Saturn' is a title used throughout the ancient world, to represent the founder and first ruler of any new kingdom, as the people spread out around the earth. His son and successor would be called 'Jupiter' and the third in line was called 'Hercules'.

Although Kronus was the Saturn, he does not appear as first in the Egyptian king list. Manetho mentions three previous kings, Hephaestus (Vulcan), Helios (the Sun) and Agathodaemon. These could be pre-flood kings, or additional sons of Noah who were there before Ham became established. Alternatively, the entire dynasty could be pre-flood, according to a principle described on page 66 where histories migrate from one age to another. Whatever may have been the case, Ham was the recognised patriarch of Africa, in the post-flood world, and he set up his kingdom in Egypt and became known as the Saturn.

To identify Prometheus, we have to turn to Greek mythology. Ouranos (Heaven) and Gaia (Earth) have two sons called Kronus and Iapetus, and a number of other children. Iapetus has a son called Prometheus, who is best known from *Prometheus Bound*, the Greek tragedy by Aeschylus,[82] where he is sometimes referenced by his own name and sometimes as the 'son of Iapetus'. The name 'Prometheus' could be seen as representing Iapetus in the Chaldean fragment, so it becomes:

> After the Flood, Titan and Prometheus [son of Iapetus] lived, and Titan undertook a war against Kronus.

Clearly, the name Iapetus must be the Biblical Japheth, and the point is further emphasised by the fact that *Prometheus Bound* is set in Scythia, precisely the domain that was occupied by one of the sons of Japheth, namely Magog.[83]

---

[80] See Manetho and the Old Egyptian Chronicle, from Cory's Ancient Fragments. Kronus appears in the 1828 version (Cory pp.47,50) and in the 1876 version (Hodges pp.111,136), but only the 1876 version identifies him as Saturn.

[81] Holinshed's *Chronicles*, vol.1, p.38.

[82] Aeschylus (c.525 - c.455 BC). Greek dramatist.

[83] Cooper, Bill, *After the Flood*, Appendix 3.

Having identified Kronus and Iapetus as two of the three post-flood patriarchs, we come to the inevitable conclusion that Ouranos and Gaia must be Noah and his wife.

This leaves only the Chaldean Titan to be accounted for, so he must be Shem. The first-generation descendants of Ouranos and Gaia, in Greek mythology, are all called Titans, so it appears that the Chaldeans used it, as a generic name, to represent someone who was not named more specifically.

Here we have a strange contradiction in the interpretations of Greek mythology. The 'Titans' are sometimes considered to be the children produced by the union of rebellious angels and human women, according to Genesis 6:1-4.

> And it came to pass, when men began to multiply on the face of the earth, and daughters were born unto them, that the sons of God saw the daughters of men that they were fair; and they took them wives of all which they chose. And the Lord said, My spirit shall not always strive with man, for that he also is flesh: yet his days shall be an hundred and twenty years. There were giants in the earth in those days; and also after that, when the sons of God came in unto the daughters of men, and they bare children to them, the same became mighty men which were of old, men of renown.

These children are known as the 'Nephilim', according to the Hebrew word that is translated 'giants', and it means 'fallen ones'. They were the most evil creatures, half-devil and half-human, capable of corrupting future generations of humanity, so they had to be wiped out, and that is why God sent the flood.

Comparing this with the Greek mythology, the term 'sons of God' corresponds to Ouranos (Heaven), and 'daughters of men' corresponds to Gaia (Earth). Their children, the Biblical Nephilim are called 'Titans'.

In that case, if Noah is Ouranos, he is not a righteous man at all, he is a rebellious angel. Likewise, if Shem is called Titan, he is not the righteous son from whom the Israelites are descended. Instead he is one of the Nephilim.

How do we resolve this contradiction? The answer is that the Greek mythology, in all its complexity, is drawn from many different sources, a fact that is admitted by John Fleming.[84] This interpretation implies that

---

[84] Fleming, J., *Fallen Angels And The Heroes Of Mythology.*

the Greeks (and their Babylonian predecessors) were not satisfied just to tell the story of Noah. They wanted to spice it up a bit, so they took the rebellious angels and the Nephilim and used them to create the characters. It's a bit boring, having a nice little family of eight people in a boat, so they replaced them all with devils (except for Gaia who was always from the earth and remained compassionate toward her children while Ouranos wanted to kill them).

Returning to the Chaldean fragment, we see that Titan (Shem) goes to war against Kronus (Ham) and we need to consider what they might have been fighting about. The descendants of Ham, and particularly Nimrod the grandson of Ham, were primarily responsible for setting up the tower of Babel and the paganism that went with it. They were originally monotheistic, having been taught by Noah and the other pre-flood patriarchs, but rapidly descended into paganism.[85]

Shem, on the other hand, was the patriarch of a long line of descendants who were all monotheistic. He outlived many of his descendants, including Abraham who was the tenth generation after Noah, and he must have influenced all of them. His opposition to Ham and his paganism would easily have been enough to start a war, especially if the descendants of Ham had attempted to continue the ambitions of Nimrod from their new power base in Egypt.

Additional Children of Noah

Now that we have seen how the Greek Ouranos and Gaia represent Noah and his wife, we can look at some other ancient fragments that tell us about these two parents and their children, but first we have to understand what are the possibilities, regarding the number of children born to them. The ancient fragments do not all fit in nicely with the Bible, identifying three children and only three. Some of them identify additional children, including both sons and daughters. The Bible, while it only mentions the three children born before the flood, does not exclude the possibility that Noah and his wife might have had other children after the flood. In fact it implies quite the opposite.

---

[85] There is evidence of early monotheism in many pagan religions. See Hales, R.L., *The Original World Monotheism*, <www.creationism.org/csshs/v07n2p18.htm>, Oct. 2002.

> And God blessed Noah and his sons, and said unto them, Be fruitful, and
> multiply, and replenish the earth.
>
> *Gen. 9:1*

This command wasn't just to Noah's three sons, it was to the whole
family, including Noah himself. So we should expect Noah to continue
having children, if he and his wife were still capable of it. However, there
is no mention of additional children of Noah in the Bible. Instead, we
have the following:

> These are the three sons of Noah: and of them was the whole earth
> overspread.
>
> *Gen. 9:19*

Does this exclude the possibility of additional children of Noah? Not
necessarily. The three sons were given authority as emperors over three
parts of the world, and their authority was passed on to their sons and
heirs, but other descendants of Noah might have travelled with them.

Genesis 10 gives a list of descendants of Shem, Ham and Japheth,
and it ends as follows:

> These are the families of the sons of Noah, after their generations, in their
> nations: and by these were the nations divided in the earth after the flood.
>
> *Gen. 10:32*

In other words, the names listed in this chapter are all kings. If there were
additional children born to Noah, they are not listed because they are not
kings, or at least they were never intended to be kings, although some of
them might have tried to usurp a legitimate ruler.

There is nothing conclusive about the question of additional children
of Noah. It is not possible to prove anything one way or the other, but it
will help to keep an open mind about it as we look at the ancient
fragments.

> But from Sydyk[86] descended the Dioscuri or Cabiri, or Corybantes, or
> Samothracian deities. These (*he says*), first invented a ship. From these
> descended others who were the discoverers of medicinal herbs, and of the

---

[86] The name 'Sydyk' applies to more than one person. This passage is
immediately preceded by another passage in which Sydyk is a sibling of Misor
(Mizraim). The name seems to be used generically for anyone who is righteous.

cure of poisons, and of charms. Contemporary with these was one Elioun, called Hypsistus (*i.e. the most high*) and his wife named Beruth, and they dwelt about Byblus [*the Hebrew* Gebal]. By these was begotten Epigeus, or Autochthon, whom they afterwards called Ouranos (*i.e.* Heaven); so that from him that element which is over us, by reason of its excellent beauty, is named heaven. And he had a sister of the same parents, and she was called Ge (i.e., Earth), and by reason of her beauty the earth was called by the same name. The father of these, Hypsistus, [or ELIOUN], having been killed through an encounter with wild beasts, was consecrated [i.e. deified], and his children offered libations and sacrifices to him. But Ouranos succeeding to the kingdom of his father, contracted marriage with his sister Ge (the Earth), and had by her four sons, Ilus who is called Kronus, and Betylus, and Dagon, which signifies Siton (corn), and Atlas.

Eusebius on Sanchoniathon.[87]

At the end of this passage, Kronus appears as one of four sons instead of three. However, this passage reveals more than just the children of Noah. If we work back through the generations, we find something very interesting. The great-grandfather of Ouranos is called Sydyk, which corresponds to the Hebrew צדיק (Tzadik) and means *the righteous one*. This person is the Biblical Enoch, who never died. Instead he was translated to heaven because he "walked with God". (Gen. 5:24). The identification of Sydyk with Enoch confirms that Ouranos must be Noah.

We also see that people first started building ships during the generation of Methuselah, the grandfather of Noah. That means two generations of ship-building technology had accumulated before Noah was asked to build the mother of all ships.

Now we will look at a fragment from Euhemerus,[88] who was a Greek contemporary of Berosus. He believed that there was a historical basis for the Greek mythology, and the gods were just deified men. The Greek pagans considered him to be an atheist, and they hated him, but the Christians liked him because they could use his ideas to oppose paganism. From his name we get the term "Euhemerism", the practice of relating mythology to real historical events.

---

[87] Hodges, pp.10-11.

[88] Euhemerus (Euemeros, Euemerus, Evemerus) was a Greek mythographer who lived at the court of Cassander, king of Macedonia, from about 301 to 297 BC. His most important work was his *Sacred History*.

Here is a fragment from Euhemerus, where he writes about an island in the Indian Ocean called Panchaea.

> ... upon the brow of a certain very high mountain in it, there was a temple of the Tryphylaean Zeus, founded by him at the time he ruled over all the habitable world, whilst he was yet resident among men. In this temple stood a golden column, on which was inscribed, in the Panchaean characters, a regular history of the actions of Ouranos, and Kronus, (Saturn), and Zeus (Jupiter).
>
> In a subsequent part of his work, he relates that the first king was Ouranos, a man renowned for justice and benevolence, and well conversant with the motion of the stars; and, that he was the first who honoured the heavenly Gods with sacrifices, upon which account he was called Ouranos (Heaven). He had two sons by his wife Hestia, (Vesta), who were called Pan and Kronus; and daughters Rhea and Demetra. And Kronus reigned after Ouranos; and he married Rhea, and had by her Zeus, and Hera, and Poseidon. And when Zeus succeeded to the kingdom of Kronus he married Hera, and Demetra, and Themis, by whom he had children; by the first, the Curetes;[89] and Persephone, (Prosperine), by the second, and Athena, (Minerva), by the third. He went to Babylon, where he was hospitably received by Belus, and afterwards passed over to the island of Panchaea, which lies in the ocean, where he erected an altar to Ouranos (Heaven), his forefather. From thence he went into Syria to Cassius, who was then the ruler of that country, from whom Mount Casius (*on the borders of Egypt*),[90] receives its name. Passing thence into Cilicia, he conquered Cilix, the governor of those parts; and, having travelled through many other nations, he was honoured by all and universally acknowledged as a god.
>
> *Eusebius, on Diodorus Siculus, on Euhemerus.*[91]

In this passage we see that Ouranos and his wife Hestia have four children, two sons and two daughters. We always seem to have Kronus in every list of descendants, because he was the Saturn of Egypt and his name has been perpetuated as the Egyptian mythology was passed on to the Greeks. The family tree is shown in figure 6.

---

[89] A footnote from Hodges (p.173) says that the Curetes were priests of Jupiter on the island of Crete, and of the goddess Cybele (Rhea).
[90] A footnote from Hodges (p.174) says that Mount Casius could be *Ras Kasaroun* on the coast of Egypt, or *Jebel Okrah* on the coast of northern Syria.
[91] Hodges, pp.172-174.

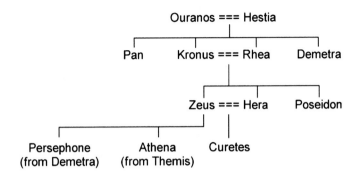

Figure 6 - Descendants of Ouranos, according to Euhemerus

This family tree is basically a variation of the Greek mythology. It names Hestia instead of Gaia as the wife of Ouranos, and there are other variations that we will not dwell on here.

The striking thing about this account from Euhemerus is the way that he strips the Greek gods of all their deity. None of them are gods in his opinion, not even Zeus. Ouranos is a king who offers sacrifices to the gods, so he cannot be a god himself. In any case, he is specifically described as a *"man renowned for justice and benevolence"*. He was the first to offer sacrifices, so he must be Noah, offering sacrifices as he came out of the ark.

Then we have Zeus offering sacrifices to his forefather Ouranos before he goes on a journey conquering other nations. He is eventually acknowledged as a god because of his military success.

We also have the '*Curetes*' who cannot be gods, even though they are the children of Zeus and Hera. According to Richmond Hodges,[92] they are the priests of Jupiter on the island of Crete, and of the goddess Cybele (Rhea).

The views of Euhemerus are of paramount importance, considering that he flourished about 300 BC and his criticism of the deification of kings was a thorn in the side of the Greek pagans for centuries afterwards, well into the Christian era. He may well continue to be a thorn in the side of modern-day evolutionists, who would like to hide the real history, just as the Greeks had done.

---

[92] Hodges, p.173, footnote.

The Egyptian Osiris and Greek Zeus

The Egyptian mythology is much the same as the Greek mythology. They have the same gods under different names. The family tree of the Egyptian gods is as follows:

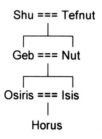

Figure 7 - Family tree of the Egyptian gods

The corresponding Greek mythology is as follows:

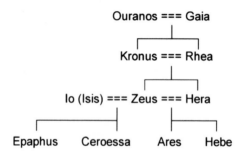

Figure 8 - Family tree of the Greek gods

These two mythologies have a number of things in common:

- The Egyptian Shu means 'air, or supporter of sky', while the Greek Ouranos means 'heaven'.
- The Egyptian Tefnut means 'moisture', while the Greek Gaia means 'earth'.
- The Egyptian Isis is sometimes seen wearing a crown with horns, while the Greek Io is a priestess of Hera and she turns into a cow. When Io goes to Egypt she becomes Isis.

This places the Egyptian Osiris in the same position as the Greek Zeus who is married to his sister Hera. Zeus had many other women, so that Hera became jealous, and there are two stories of what happened when Zeus seduced Io. One story is that Hera turned Io into a cow. The other story is that Zeus saw Hera coming, so he turned her into a cow to avoid detection, then he turned himself into a bull.

Clearly, the two mythologies are the same, except that the Egyptian Isis is the wife of Osiris, and in the Greek mythology she is the mistress of the same Osiris who is called Zeus.

Considering that Ouranos and Gaia are Noah and his wife, and Kronus is Ham, then we know that Zeus (Osiris) must be one of the sons of Ham. The four sons of Ham are Cush, Mizraim, Put and Caanan. Out of these four, Mizraim is most closely associated with Egypt, but Cush and Put were not far away. Cush was in Ethiopia to the south, and Put was in the coastal region to the west. Caanan was further away in Phoenicia, otherwise known as the land of Caanan where the Israelites settled when they came out of Egypt.

The identification of Osiris as one of the sons of Ham is confirmed by Sanchoniathon as follows:

All these things the son of Thabion, the first hierophant[93] of all among the Phoenicians, allegorized, and mixed up with the occurrences and passions of nature and the world, and delivered to the priests and prophets, the superintendents of the mysteries: and they, perceiving the rage for these allegories increase, delivered them to their successors, and to foreigners: of whom one was Isiris, the inventor of the three letters, the brother of Chna, who is called the first Phoenician.

Eusebius on Sanchoniathon.[94]

This is basically a statement that the work of Sanchoniathon represents real history, even though some of it is allegorised. To give just one example of an allegory, there are two separate genealogies that are stitched together to become one, so that they are incomprehensible except to those who know about the breakpoint between them (i.e. the specially initiated *'priests and prophets, the superintendents of the mysteries'*). The

---

[93] First initiating priest or expounder of sacred mysteries.
[94] Hodges, p.19.

breakpoint, in this case, is the beginning of the paragraph that mentions the 'Sydyk', referenced by footnote 86. Anyone interested in this subject should see how it is explained by Cory, in the 1828 version of his *Ancient Fragments*.

Anyway, returning to the passage from Sanchoniathon, we see that Isiris is the brother of Chna, who is identified as Caanan. According to Richmond Hodges,[95] the name 'Chna' appears on the Phoenician coins of Laodicea and Libanum. Osiris is one of the three brothers of Caanan, but we can probably discount Put because there is nothing obvious, in classical history, to identify him with Osiris. This leaves us with two candidates:

- Cush may be associated with Osiris, not directly, but as the father of Nimrod who is thought to have had a similar type of death and rebirth.
- Mizraim is the patriarch of Egypt, so he could be Osiris. This identity is supported by Cumberland.[96]

Since we have already associated Osiris with Zeus, according to their genealogy, we have the result that both Cush and Mizraim can be identified with Zeus.

Cory[97] makes an additional observation about the passage from Sanchoniathon, as follows:

> If the legends were handed down to Isiris, the son of Ham, they must have been handed down by one of the predecessors of this Isiris, that is by Noah, or one of his own sons: Thabion is derived from Theba the Ark, and in the phraseology of Bryant[98] is equivalent to the Arkite: it is a title of Noah: therefore the first hierophant of Phoenicia was a son of Noah, a predecessor of Mizraim and Caanan, an inhabitant also of Phoenicia, in short was Ham himself. And it is some confirmation, indirect enough it must be owned, of the very prevalent belief in the apostacy of that patriarch.

---

[95] Hodges, p.19, footnote 3.

[96] Hodges, p.19, footnote 2. Richard Cumberland (b.1631 - d.1718) was Anglican Bishop of Peterborough from 1691. He published a number of works, including *Sanchoniatho's Phoenician History* (1720). For details see *Encyclopaedia Britannica*.

[97] Cory, p.vi.

[98] Bryant, J., *New System, or, An Analysis of Ancient Mythology*.

In other words, regardless of any conclusions we may come to about Cush and Mizraim, we can be certain that their father Ham was the founder of the pagan religious system.

The Greek Dionysus and Roman Bacchus

Although we can associate Zeus with Osiris, according to their genealogies, we cannot do so from their life histories. They have a few things in common, as we have seen, but not enough to identify them as the same person.

There is a story about how Zeus fought against a winged fire-breathing monster called Typhon, who cut off the sinews from his hands and feet and hid them in a bearskin, but Hermes recovered the sinews and refitted them to Zeus, so that he recovered. However, this does not compare with the death and rebirth of Osiris. Zeus did not die in his battle with Typhon, he was just injured.

A much more comparable story is found in Dionysus. He was the son of Zeus, from either Demetra or Persephone who both appear in figure 6 (page 53). He was killed by the Titans and cut to pieces and boiled, but Demetra collected the pieces together. Zeus gave his heart to Semele to drink, and she became pregnant, so that Dionysus was reborn. Dionysus is known as a god of wine and pleasure. Semele was a descendant of Epaphus, who appears in figure 8 (page 54). Epaphus was an Egyptian king who was also a patriarch of the Ethiopians and Libyans. For details of these stories, see the *Greek Mythology Link*.[99]

If Zeus is Cush, then Dionysus must be Nimrod, who was killed and reborn as Tammuz as we have already seen on page 22. The Romans worshipped Dionysus under the name Bacchus, and according to Bill Cooper,[100] the name is derived from the Semitic[101] *bar-Cush*, meaning son of Cush.

At this point, an interesting suggestion emerges regarding the confrontation between Cush and Typhon. We have already seen, on page 49, that Shem might have been at war against Ham and his

---

[99] Parada, C., *Greek Mythology Link*.
[100] Cooper, Bill, *After the Flood*, p.190.
[101] The term *Semitic* applies to any of the nations descended from Shem, not just the Jews.

descendants, because of their paganism. In that case, the fire coming out of Typhon's mouth was the Word of God, although from the point of view of the pagans, he is typified as an evil monster.

We should now have enough evidence to convince us that the Babylonian, Egyptian and Greek mythologies are a representation of Noah and his wife, and their descendants. In particular, they describe the system of paganism that was initiated by Ham. But there is still more evidence, as we consider the alleged confrontation between Ham and his father Noah.

Castration of Ouranos

> In the thirty-second year of his power and reign, Ilus, who is Kronus, having laid an ambuscade for his father Ouranos in a certain place in the middle of the earth, and having gotten him into his hands, cuts off his private parts near fountains and rivers. There Ouranos was consecrated,[102] and his spirit was separated, and the blood of his private parts dropped into the fountains and the waters of the rivers; and the place is shown even to this day.
>
> *Eusebius on Sanchoniathon.*[103]

This is the pagan version of Ham's indiscretion against his father Noah. The Biblical version is as follows:

> And Noah began to be an husbandman, and he planted a vineyard: and he drank of the wine, and was drunken; and he was uncovered within his tent. And Ham, the father of Canaan, saw the nakedness of his father, and told his two brethren without. And Shem and Japheth took a garment, and laid it upon both their shoulders, and went backward, and covered the nakedness of their father; and their faces were backward, and they saw not their father's nakedness. And Noah awoke from his wine, and knew what his younger son had done unto him. And he said, Cursed be Canaan; a servant of servants shall he be unto his brethren. And he said, Blessed be the Lord God of Shem; and Canaan shall be his servant. God shall enlarge Japheth, and he shall dwell in the tents of Shem; and Canaan shall be his servant. And Noah lived after the flood three hundred and fifty years. And all the days of Noah were nine hundred and fifty years: and he died.
>
> *Gen. 9:20-29*

---

[102] *i.e.* deified.
[103] Hodges, p.15.

If Ham did nothing more than see his father naked and tell his brothers, then the story seems fairly innocuous. However, the whole story has probably not been told. It says *"Ham, the father of Canaan, saw the nakedness of his father..."* as if Caanan had something to do with it. Then we see that Noah curses Caanan instead of Ham. So it appears that Caanan did something that goes beyond the offence of Ham.

However, if the offence was to cut off Noah's genitals, it would be impossible for such an event to be left out of the Bible. It clearly could not have happened, and in any case Noah is supposed to have lived for 350 years after the flood. The pagan version says *"his spirit was separated"*, meaning he died, in clear contradiction to the Biblical version.

While the modern scientific mind may try and establish the facts, the fertile imagination of the ancient Greeks and other pagans was concerned with no such thing. All they wanted was some myths, so they could deify their ancestors and make themselves look good. To elevate a man into a god, you have to exaggerate all his deeds. His good deeds become very good, and his bad deeds become very bad. In this case, the seemingly minor indiscretion of seeing your father naked, and making a joke of it, is turned into a murder by castration.

There are two versions of why Kronus should castrate his father Ouranos:

- The Greeks say that Ouranos and Gaia had some children who were hideous monsters, and Ouranos cast them into Tartarus, the dark watery underworld. Then they had some more children who were called Titans. Gaia wanted to rescue her earlier children from Tartarus, and encouraged the Titans to attack Ouranos. She provided Kronus with the adamantine sickle and he castrated him.
- The Phoenician version, from Sanchoniathon, says that Ouranos had children by other women, so that Gaia became jealous, and Kronus rose up against his father to avenge his mother.

The Kings After the Flood

The books of Berosus, together with various other Chaldean fragments, give details of kings who lived after the flood in different parts of the world, in addition to those described here. I have chosen to describe only the early descendants of Noah, and to compare them with the Greek mythology, and on page 64 we will see how it leads to the foundation of Troy.

The other king lists are basically snapshots of world history, and are too fragmented to be put together into any common theme. However, they will be useful to anyone who wishes to study specific periods of early history, and anyone who is interested should obtain a copy of Cory's Ancient Fragments.

The list of ten kings before the flood has been preserved, probably because ancient historians took a special interest in these kings, since they lived in a world that was different from the world we know now. There are no continuous lists of kings after the flood, because historians have not preserved them with the same care, with the notable exception of the Hebrews who have given us the list of patriarchs from Noah to Abraham, then to King David, and the continuing history of Israel.

The Greek Flood Stories

There have been at least four floods in the ancient history of Greece, and possibly more, but we only have details of three of them.

- The flood of Atlantis.
- The flood of Ogygus, king of Thebes in Boeotia, in 1764 BC.[104] At this time Phoroneus was king of Argos.
- The flood of Deucalion, king of Thessaly, in 1503 BC.

The Flood of Atlantis

The story of Atlantis appears in Plato's Dialogues,[105] and is related by a participant called Critias, who describes what he had heard from his grandfather when he was a boy. A man called Solon, who was a relative of his grandfather, had been to Egypt and talked with the priests. He struck up a conversation about Phoroneus, and the flood that occurred later in the days of Deucalion, hoping to find out what the Egyptians

---

[104] The dates of the two floods of Ogygus and Deucalion are given by Eusebius, according to the *Wall Chart of World History* (Hull, E.).

[105] The story of Atlantis is taken from Plato's Dialogues with Timaeus and Critias (see Jowett, Benjamin). You need to read both dialogues to get the whole story.

knew about ancient times. One of the priests replied that the Greeks were like children when it comes to matters of antiquity, and they don't know anything that is really old. Then he proceeded to tell them the story of Atlantis.

He said that nine thousand years earlier there was a great island in the Atlantic Ocean, called Atlantis. They invaded Libya and part of Europe, but the Athenians had resisted them valiantly and defeated them. Then there were violent earthquakes and floods, so that the whole island of Atlantis disappeared into the sea in a single day. He calls it the "great deluge of all" as if it was greater than any of the floods that the Greeks knew about, and it seems very plausible that this was an Egyptian account of Noah's flood. He says it was the third flood before Deucalion, so this is how we know there were at least four floods altogether (unless the counting is inclusive, in which case there are three).

He also talked about natural disasters generally, that they are caused by heavenly bodies moving about the earth, implying that the great flood was caused by one of these. This is in accordance with modern creationist thinking, although most of the water of the flood is thought to have come up from under the ground, rather than down from the heavens. There are problems with the so-called 'vapour canopy' theory which suggests that before the flood, there was a large amount of water vapour in the upper atmosphere, and the flood occurred because the water canopy collapsed. If there was so much water in the pre-flood atmosphere, it would have caused intolerable global warming, so that life would become impossible. It is much more feasible that most of the water came up from the ground, and indeed the Biblical account says that the *"fountains of the great deep"* were broken up. (Gen. 7:11). It is very likely that a large object appeared in space and passed close to the earth, so that the tidal forces caused a disturbance of the earth's crust releasing large amounts of water.

The Flood of Ogygus

From this record, therefore, we affirm that Ogygus, from whom the first flood (in Attica) derived its name, and who was saved when many perished, lived at the time of the exodus of the people from Egypt along with Moses. (*After a break*): And after Ogygus, on account of the vast destruction caused by the flood, the present land of Attica remained without a king till the time of Cecrops, 189 years. Philochorus, however, affirms that Ogygus, Actaeus, or whatever other fictitious name is adduced,[106] never existed. (*After another break*): From Ogygus to Cyrus, as from Moses to his time, are 1235 years.

Julius Africanus.[107]

There are other fragments about the flood of Ogygus, but the above fragment tells us most of what is known. Ogygus has no known ancestry, but he had two daughters, Aulis and Alalcomenia, and it is thought that he had a son called Eleusis.

The Flood of Deucalion

This is the best known of the Greek flood events, and some of the details resemble Noah's flood, although it's possible that the story of Noah could have migrated forward to the time of Deucalion, according to the principle described on page 66.

Deucalion is the son of Prometheus, who we have already seen on page 47, identified as the son of Iapetus (Japheth). Deucalion's mother is either Clymene, an Oceanid,[108] or else Pronoia who is of unknown parentage.

Zeus sent the flood because of the impiety of the human race, and in particular because of Lycaeon, the son of Pelasgus, who offered a human baby as a sacrifice. For his offence he was turned into a wolf. Zeus took counsel with the other gods, and at first he thought of destroying the world with thunderbolts, but then he remembered that the world was already destined to be destroyed by fire, so he sent the flood instead.

The flood was caused by the combined influence of the Winds that lifted water to the clouds, and the River Gods[109] who burst their banks and flooded the plains. All the animals were drowned, or died of starvation (so it couldn't have been a global flood, otherwise they would have all drowned).

---

[106] *Adduce* means to offer as proof or evidence.
[107] Julius Africanus, Five Books of Chronography, fragment XII. Christian Classics Ethereal Library, <www.ccel.org/fathers2/ANF-06/anf06-50.htm#P2303_646305>, Oct. 2002.
[108] The Oceanids are the daughters of Oceanus and Tethys, son and daughter of Ouranos and Gaia.
[109] The River Gods are the sons of Oceanus and Tethys.

Deucalion was warned by his father Prometheus, that there would be a flood, so he built a chest and stored provisions, then he got into it with his wife Pyrrha. They floated in the chest for nine days and nights, then the rain stopped and they landed on Mount Parnassus, in Phocis. When the waters subsided, Deucalion and Pyrrha worshipped the Corycian Nymphs who lived in the mountain, and Themis who kept the oracles.

Deucalion was concerned about how he could live in a world that was empty of both men and women (although he had his wife Pyrrha), so they prayed to Themis and on her advice they threw stones behind them, over their heads. The stones that Deucalion threw became men, and the stones that Pyrrha threw became women. After that, they started having children in the usual way. They had a number of sons who became kings, including Hellen, who gave his name to the Hellenes.[110]

It is said that other people survived the flood of Deucalion.

- Megarus, a son of Zeus by a Nymph, survived the flood by swimming towards the cry of the birds and climbing Mount Gerania.

- Cerambus was taken up into the air on wings by the Nymphs.

- In Phocis, some people followed the howls of wolves and reached the top of Mount Parnassus.

The animals were completely wiped out, but they were spontaneously regenerated from the earth, restoring the original species and creating new ones. This regeneration occurred by the combination of the water left by the flood, and heat from the sun, according to the belief that life is generated spontaneously from fire and water. Now, where have we heard that before? Was it the Stanley Miller experiment, where useless amino acids with no structure were formed by zapping a gas mixture with electric sparks, or was it Frankenstein, robbing graves and stitching body parts together, then trying to bring the assembled corpses to life during a thunderstorm? We can make jokes about it, but those who believe in the spontaneous origin of life from the primeval soup will not be pleased to hear that it comes from Greek mythology (or its Phoenician prototype, see page 8).

---

[110] It is sometimes said that Hellen was the son of Zeus and Pyrrha.

From Noah to Dardanus

While the Greek mythology might seem like pure fiction and fantasy, it is widely recognised that as the generations progress, real human kings descend from the god-like figures of their ancestors. Actually, they are all human, beginning with Ouranos and Gaia who represent Noah and his wife, and we will now see how Dardanus, the founder of Troy, descended from them.

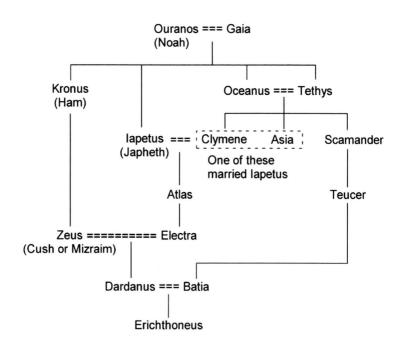

Figure 9 - Descent of the Kings of Troy, from Ouranos.

According to the Bible, Noah and his wife had three sons called Shem, Ham and Japheth. The Greek mythologies don't say anything about Shem because he was monotheistic and never got involved with their paganism, so in the above diagram he is missed out (although the Chaldeans identify him as 'Titan', see page 48). The Greek mythologies mention Ham and Japheth, under the names Kronus and Iapetus, and there are other children, including a son called Oceanus and a daughter called Tethys. All the children of Ouranos and Gaia are collectively known as 'Titans'.

Oceanus and Tethys got married and had both sons and daughters. Their sons were called 'River Gods' and their daughters were called 'Oceanids'. It seems appropriate that some of these early descendants, born after the flood, should have names associated with water.

One of the Oceanids, either Clymene or Asia, married Iapetus (Japheth) and they had a son called Atlas who had a daughter called Electra. She married Zeus who, as we have seen, is either the Biblical Cush or Mizraim. Zeus and Electra had a son called Dardanus, who became the first king of Troy.

According to Virgil,[111] Dardanus came from Corythus, in Etruria in north-west Italy. The people were called Etruscans and it is thought that they might have come from Asia Minor. Virgil says that Dardanus went on a voyage to Samothrace in Phrygia, so he was going back in the direction that his ancestors came from. (Silly man, the nations were supposed to disperse around the world from Babylon, but he was going in the wrong direction. No wonder Troy was doomed.)

He married Batia, the grand-daughter of Scamander the River God, who represents the river near Troy. Her father was Teucer, king of the Teucrians. Dardanus and Batia had a son called Erichthonius who succeeded him as the next king of Troy, and the lineage continues as far as the Trojan war.

The story of Troy provides some illustrious heroes who were immortalised by Homer[112] and Virgil, giving us much of the Greek and Roman history. The Greeks love the story, because it shows their valour, and the Romans love it because even in defeat, their hero Aeneas was able to flee from the burning city and establish his kingdom elsewhere in Italy.

Some of the nations of Europe claim that their royal families are descended from the scattered remnants of Troy, although not all of it can be proved. However, there is good reason to believe that Brutus, the great-grandson of Aeneas, came to Britain and was the founder of the Welsh monarchy, despite claims to the contrary, and I will deal with this in Chapter 4.

---

[111] Jackson Knight, W.F., *Virgil - The Aeneid*, p.181.
[112] Rieu, E.V., *Homer: The Iliad*; *Homer: The Odyssey*.

Longevity Within the Greek Mythology

The line of descent from Noah to Dardanus indicates great longevity, a matter we have already seen in relation to other histories (see page 17). The flood occurred during the 24th century BC, according to Biblical chronology, but the reign of Dardanus was in the 15th century BC, so we have nine centuries from the flood to Dardanus. Considering that Dardanus was the great-grandson of Noah on his father's side, and he was the great-great grandson of Noah on his mother's side, there must have been great longevity among these early patriarchs. This should be no great surprise, considering that Noah lived for 950 years, and his son Shem lived for 600 years. However, the subsequent generations did not live so long, and there might be a problem spanning this long period in a traditional dynasty where each king is succeeded by his eldest son, because the son would already be quite old when he begins to reign.

Dardanus was a contemporary of Moses, who was the 16th generation after Noah, so either there are some generations missing in the line from Noah to Dardanus, or else we are not looking at a traditional dynasty as we would normally understand it. During this early period, when an empty world was being repopulated, new kingdoms were being set up. It is very likely that each successive son was given a kingdom, somewhere in the empire of his father, regardless of his age. If Zeus was a younger son of Kronus, and Dardanus was a younger son of Zeus, then it might be possible to span this time period.

However, it is not possible to be exact with any of this. We have to remember that we are dealing with mythologies that are huge exaggerations of the real histories that lie behind them, and there must be many forgotten details that we will probably never know.

Migration of Pre-Flood History to Greek Mythology

One of the problems of Greek mythology is that information appears to be sometimes borrowed from one era and transported to another. In particular, fragments of pre-flood history seem to have been re-cast into a later period, and sometimes into the post-flood world.

Roy Hales[113] has described it as an 'open system' where things are moved around, as opposed to a 'closed system' where everything is static. The Bible is the key to the migration of events, as it gives them in their correct order.

How to Make a God

We have already seen, in the section beginning on page 37, that Zeus is the sky god with the thunderbolt in his hand, who zaps the first human into life. Then we saw that he appears as Lamech, a descendant of Cain. Now we see that he appears after the flood, as either Cush or Mizraim, one of the grandsons of Noah. So who is he?

The answer is that anyone can be Zeus. In all probability, the Greeks felt the need to spice up the memories of their early post-flood kings, so they borrowed a few events from the pre-flood period. They must have been feeling despondent about their relatively short lives, and the knowledge that everything was so much better before the flood. So they credited their kings with the deeds of their earlier ancestors, or even a modified version of the deeds of the One True God, so that there would be something respectable to hand down to posterity.

From Adam to the Welsh and English Monarchies

At this point we need to consider the implications of what has been said so far.

- The Babylonians have given us the ten kings before the flood, corresponding to the Biblical patriarchs from Adam to Noah.
- The Greeks have given us the genealogy from Noah to Dardanus, the founder of Troy. This assumes that the deeds of Zeus were attributed to either Cush or Mizraim, and if not, they were most probably attributed to another king of the same period.
- The kings of Troy are well known from Homer and Virgil, as far as Aeneas and his son Ascanius who went to Italy.

---

[113] Hales, R.L., *Mythology, The Bible and the Postflood Origins of Greek History*, <www.creationism.org/csshs/v07n4p20.htm>, Oct. 2002.

- The story continues up to the arrival of Brutus in Britain and the succession of British (Welsh) kings.

If all of this can be believed, then we have a continuous line of descent, or at least a continuous succession, from Adam to the Welsh kings.

The lineage can be taken even further, to the English monarchy. On page 105, we begin a discussion of the British history, from the Saxon invasion to the death of Cadwallader. Henry VII, the first Tudor king of England, was a Welshman descended from Roderick the Great, king of Wales from 843 to 877, the fifth king after Cadwallader.

Henry is descended from Roderick along two separate lines:[114]

- His great-great grandfather, Tudor Fychan of Pemmynydd, is descended from Cadell, king of South Wales and second son of Roderick.
- His great-great grandmother, Margaret, wife of Tudor Fychan, is descended from Anarawd, king of North Wales and eldest son of Roderick.

The history of the English monarchy is well known, so we have a continuous line of descent or succession from Adam to the present Queen Elizabeth II.

---

[114] For Roderick, Anarawd and Cadell, see Caradoc of Llancerfan, *Historie of Cambria*, pp.24-37. For the ancestry of Henry VII, see Tompsett, B., *Directory of Royal Genealogical Data*, <www.dcs.hull.ac.uk/cgi-bin/gedlkup/n=royal?royal00773>, Oct. 2002.

Chapter 3 - Dubious Histories

The information in Chapters 1 and 2 is taken from sources that are widely believed to be authentic. In this chapter we will look at something that is more difficult to substantiate, but is important because of its influence on the Renaissance and Tudor periods. Any serious researcher into early history is likely to come across this literature and will need to recognise it.

Annius of Viterbo

A Dominican Friar, called Giovanni Nanni, lived in the town of Viterbo about 65 miles north of Rome. He was otherwise known as *Annius of Viterbo*. In 1498 he published a set of fragments, attributed to Berosus and Manetho, together with a commentary, and the complete work was called the *Antiquities*. There were two editions, both published in 1498, one in Venice and the other in Rome. The text and translation of the fragments attributed to Berosus and Manetho, from the Rome edition, have been made available by Asher.[115]

These fragments describe the history of the ancient world, giving much more detail than had ever been known before. It contained numerous events that were flattering to the nations of Europe, but especially Italy and France. For example:

- Noah went to Italy and ruled the country for a while.

- Hercules, the son of Osiris, married a Scythian lady called Araxa, and they had a son called Tuscus who became king of Italy. Hercules also married a Celtic princess called Galathea and they had a son called Galatheus who became king of France (Celtica).

- Iasus, king of Italy, was later given the kingdom of France because their royal line had failed. He married a noble and rich lady called Ipitus Cibeles, and they had a very honoured guest at the wedding. Isis, the widow of Osiris was there, and she was at least 450 years old at the time.

---

[115] Asher, R.E., *National Myths in Renaissance France*, Appendix 1.

- According to an embellishment of the tale, which does not exist in the alleged Berosus and Manetho fragments (at least not in the Rome edition), some of these events occurred in the home town of Annius. The appointments of Tuscus and Galatheus as kings of Italy and France were both made at the same time, at a great ceremony held in Viterbo. The wedding of Iasus and Ipitus Cibeles, with Isis in attendance, was later held in the same city.

The story contains great acts of valour, in Italy and in other parts of Europe. It was well received, because it was flattering to people who wanted to read something good about themselves. This was the Renaissance period, when people could get hold of printed books for the first time, but they lacked the skills required to evaluate what they were reading.

Annius lived for only four years after he had published his book, and died in 1502. Then in 1504 his work was criticised by Petrus Crinitus, who claimed that it was fraudulent, that it never came from either Berosus or Manetho, and he made it all up. This was followed by similar claims from other people, but Annius was unable to answer any of them because he was already dead. The main cause for complaint was that the source documents that he was supposed to have used could never be found.

The supposed fragments of Berosus and Manetho, that came from the hand of Annius, became known as *pseudo-Berosus* and *pseudo-Manetho*. For a discussion of the entire affair, together with some of the text from Annius, see Asher.[116]

In addition to the alleged forgeries, there is another complaint against Annius. Sometime before he wrote his *Antiquities*, he was accused of carving inscriptions on stone and burying them, and then digging them up again. He took the stones to the local magistrates to try and prove that Viterbo had been founded by Osiris and Isis, before the foundation of Rome. Of course his supporters flatly denied that he was involved in any such forgery.

---

[116] Asher, R.E., *National Myths in Renaissance France*.

Is Fake History Worth Anything?

Most of us would respond intuitively that fake history has no value whatsoever, except to be put in a museum of fakes, for purposes of amusement, and to encourage aspiring historians to be careful what they read. But this is to over-simplify the question.

So-called 'fake' histories have a real value, because they are rarely if ever entirely fake. They have to contain some elements of truth, to make them plausible. To emphasise the point, we have to consider that the police talk to fraudulent people all the time, in the hope that they might discover some small but important details that might lead to the truth. There is one such detail in the *pseudo-Berosus* that needs to be noted. It says that one of the names of Noah was Arsa, and cities were named after him. Now it just happens that the city of Urfa, in south-east Turkey, is near the central Cudi Dagh, which is one of the possible ark sites discussed on page 30. So, regardless of his claim to be in possession of ancient documents, we have to ask ourselves, did Annius know anything about the city of Urfa?

Lost Works of Berosus

The loss of ancient literature is always a cause of lament among historians, and if the works of Berosus are ever found, they will be considered priceless. We can only speculate on where they were last seen, and what might have happened to them. They obviously survived the Roman invasion of Athens in 146 BC because Apollodorus and Alexander Polyhistor were using them. In any case, the Romans had respect for the Greek culture and would be unlikely to destroy their books.

Rome itself fell in AD 476, but this is unlikely to have caused the destruction of the works of Berosus. Constantine the Great had already moved the centre of his administration to the city of Byzantium, and re-named it 'Constantinople'. The Eastern Roman Empire, otherwise known as the Byzantine Empire, survived for almost another millennium.

Constantinople became an important centre of learning and trade, but in 1453 it fell to the Ottoman Muslims and they called it 'Istanbul'. Unlike the Romans, they had no regard for the Greek culture, and many books were burnt. Presumably, some copies of Berosus might have been destroyed at this time. The fall of Constantinople is still a sore point for the Greek people today, and they continue to call it 'Constantinopolis'.

After the fall of Constantinople, many Greek intellectuals migrated to Italy, and they made a significant contribution to the Renaissance. Some of them might have told Annius what they knew about the lost works of Berosus, or the ancient traditions that were preserved by their fallen empire. But to speculate about these things would be over-generous. Annius never claimed to have picked up just a few scraps of knowledge from Greek migrants. He claimed to be in possession of the lost books of Berosus, which neither he nor his supporters could ever produce.

History of the World According to Annius and Friends

The work of Annius provided the starting point for other authors to write their own histories, and some of these turned out to be more fantastic[117] than the work of Annius himself. We will look at two of these, from Tudor period historians in Britain.

- *Travels of Noah into Europe* by Richard Lynche.[118]
- *Chronicles of England, Ireland and Scotland* by Raphael Holinshed.[119] (See page 81).

Travels of Noah into Europe

Richard Lynche was writing his books from 1596 until he died in 1601 and he is thought to be the same person who wrote *Fountaine of Ancient Fiction* and *Sonnets to Diella*. His *Travels of Noah* was his last book, published in 1601, and although it was published in London, it says nothing about Britain. He wrote the story as if he really believed it and was not attempting to flatter anyone, not in his own country anyway. His dedication to his patron, Peter Manwood,[120] is rather like a death-bed note.

---

[117] The words 'fabulous' and 'fantastic' are used by historians to describe things that are made up of fables and fantasies. They don't mean 'good' as in the modern usage.

[118] Lynche, R., *An Historical Treatise of the Travels of Noah into Europe.*

[119] Holinshed's *Chronicles.*

[120] Peter Manwood is best known as the antiquary who published *The Actions of the Lowe Countries*, written by Sir Roger Williams, updated by Sir John Hayward and with an epistle dedicatory to Sir Francis Bacon.

It says:

> "... I judged it irrequisit by dedication of these few lines unto you **(disabled by Fortune for any other fashion)** to let you know how much I desire to be found thankful to an assured friend. The matter handled, challenges no great worth, the manner in the dressing of it less, and yet my endeavours to deserve the continuation of your love, not to be rejected: as Time shall beget a more opportune occasion, my industry shall not slack to apprehend the same, from which it may be produced a better-shaped issue : **till when and ever after I rest**". [*emphasis mine*]

It is unusual for people to make up fables, passing them off as fact on their death-bed, and we can be reasonably sure that he believed what he wrote, whatever the actual truth might be.

The genealogy from Noah to Dardanus, according to Richard Lynche, is illustrated in figure 10, and he tells the story as follows:

Noah and his Family

Noah and his wife Tytea had three sons, Shem, Ham and Japheth, who were with them in the ark, together with their wives, eight people altogether. After the Flood, they had at least 30 additional children, including two daughters, Rhea and Araxa the Great. (Araxa is identified as the mother of Scythia in the Rome edition of Annius).

The children of Noah and Tytea are not arranged in the diagram in the order of their birth. Instead they are arranged in a way that is easy to draw, considering the intermarriages within the family.

The Mischief of Ham

Ham was into magic art, and was called Zoroast. He hated his father, because he thought himself least loved by him. (Is this the well known "second child syndrome"?). By his magic he bewitched his father in the "places of generation" (genitals), to prevent him from having more children. For these and his other impieties, he incurred the wrath of God, and was banished from his father, but was given his allotted part of the world as his inheritance.

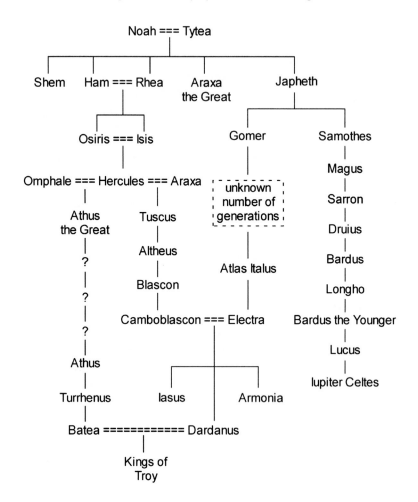

Figure 10 - Descent of the Trojan and Celtic (Samothean) Kings

This part of the story is clearly a compromise between the castration of Ouranos, which appears in the Greek mythology, and the confrontation between Noah and Ham that appears in the Bible, when Ham saw Noah naked in his tent. The Greek account says that Kronus cut off the genitals of Ouranos completely and threw them into the sea, an action that would be fatal if applied to a mere mortal. The Annius Rome version says that Ham charmed his father and castrated him, but not fatally. The magic "charm" was supposedly a means of anaesthetic, as if the wine that Noah had drunk was not enough. Lynche does away with the castration altogether and just tells us about magic. These variations are basically an attempt to create a story that fits the Bible. Fatal castration is no good because Noah is supposed to have lived for 350 years after the flood. Then the castration story is abandoned altogether because it's so outrageous. If it actually happened, it would have been impossible to leave it out of the Bible.

Ham and Rhea

Ham married his younger sister Rhea, and this was a second marriage in both cases. Ham was married to Noegla (or Noela) who had been with him in the ark, and she was still living at the time of his second marriage. Rhea had been married to Hammon, the great-great grandson of Ham, a union that might seem incredible to us, but it was possible in those days because of their great longevity. Rhea left Hammon because he was having an adulterous affair with another woman called Almanthea, and she went to Sicily and married Ham. (He was in Sicily at the time because he had invaded Italy but his father Noah had thrown him out.)

No date is given for the marriage of Ham and Rhea, but it must have been quite late because of the generations between Ham and Hammon.

Osiris and Isis

Ham and Rhea had a son called Osiris and a daughter called Isis, who subsequently married. Isis was born in the year 302 after the Flood, in the first year of Semiramis queen of Babylon. She was 50 years old when she married Osiris, so the date of their marriage was 352. Osiris was about 60 years old at the time, but both of them were still youths. Together they ruled Egypt, and they taught the people agriculture.

Their eldest son was called Hercules, surnamed Lybidicus or Lybicus, and he appears as "Lehabim" in Genesis 10:13. This means his father Osiris must be the Biblical Mizraim, a possibility that we have already seen from the authentic fragments.

Hercules and Araxa

Osiris had many other children, from Isis and from other women, and when they were grown up he assembled an army and went around the world overthrowing giants. During these campaigns, Osiris went to

Scythia and found that his son Hercules had become "greatly enamoured with a lady called Araxa". This is unlikely to be 'Araxa the Great', the daughter of Noah, because Lynche would not have introduced her in this way. Whenever he returns to a previous character, he identifies them as "the aforementioned" or something similar. Araxa is more likely to be a descendant of Araxa the Great.

Strangely enough, Herodotus[121] tells a story about a how Hercules went to Scythia and while he was sleeping his mares went astray. He met a strange hybrid creature who was a woman from the buttocks upwards, but her lower part was a snake. She was the queen of that country, and she had found his mares, but would not return them until he had intercourse with her. She continued to delay returning his mares, so that he stayed with her for a long time, until he had given her three sons, then she returned his mares and he went on his way. The three sons were called Agathyrsus, Gelonus and Scythes. The youngest one, Scythes, was the first of the line of Scythian kings. Perhaps the "lady called Araxa" is a sanitised version of the Scythian snake-woman.

Returning to the story as it is told by Lynche, we find that Hercules and Araxa had a son called Tuscus who "much later" became king of Italy, and the province of Tuscany was named after him. As the details of the story unfold, we find out how much later. Osiris, after subduing giants in many countries, was killed in his home country of Egypt by a rebellion from within his own family that was led by his brother Typhon. Hercules, assisted by some of his brothers, avenged the death of his father by killing Typhon, then he went around killing other giants as his father had done. He lived peaceably in France for a while, then he went to Italy and fought with the Lestrigones for 10 years, eventually defeating them. He ruled over Italy for 20 years, then he appointed Tuscus as king of Italy in the year 625 after the Flood, at a great ceremony in Viterbo, the capital of Tuscany.

The appointment of Tuscus was 273 years after the marriage of his grandparents Osiris and Isis, and is another indication of great longevity.

---

[121] Godley, A.D., *Herodotus: The Histories*, 4.8.3-4.10.3.

Hercules and Omphale

While Hercules was going around killing giants, before he went to France, he went to Phrygia and overcame a tyrant called Tipheus. He appointed his son Athus as governor, who had been born to him from a lady called Omphale. Later in the story, we find that Athus had become known as "Athus the Great", and Dardanus was welcomed and entertained in Phrygia by another Athus who was his fourth-generation descendant.

Hercules and Galathea

When Hercules went to France (otherwise known as Celtica or Samothea), he married into their royal family and contributed to their line of descent as shown in figure 11.

Figure 11 - Kings of Celtica (France) and the Italian succession.

77

He was received by their king, Iupiter Celtes, who had a daughter called Galathea, a good and virtuous giantess. Iupiter Celtes was very proud of her and would not offer her to any man in marriage until he found someone who was worthy of her. He was impressed with the exploits of Hercules and offered her to him in marriage, and they had a son called Galatheus. Hercules became king of France for a while, then he appointed Galatheus as king, at the same ceremony in Viterbo where Tuscus was appointed king of Italy. The two of them were good friends, and Tuscus offered Galatheus the island of Sicily. Then when a government was set up, Galatheus returned to France. It was in the days of Galatheus that the kingdom of Celtica was first called Gaul.

Some time later, after the death of Belgius, the line of Celtic kings failed and Iasus, king of Italy, succeeded to the kingdom of France, so that he ruled both countries. This became a matter of discontent for his younger brother Dardanus, a matter we shall return to later.

From this point onwards we have to refer to both figures 10 and 11 because they both tell different parts of the same story.

The Troubled History of Italy

Gomer, the eldest son of Japheth, otherwise known as "Comerus Gallus", was the first king of Italy and the country was called "Kytim". (Note that Lynche says nothing about Kittim the son of Javan, who is commonly associated with Cyprus.). The kingdom was usurped by Ham, after the death of Gomer, and was corrupted with all sorts of impiety. Noah went there for a visit, thinking that Gomer was still alive, and found the country in disarray. He banished Ham from the kingdom and began to govern it himself, setting things in order, and called the country Ianingenes after his own surname Ianus. He appointed his daughter Crana as queen of the country north of the Tiber. He was then joined by Sabatius Saga, surnamed Saturn, a brother of Nimrod who had fled from Armenia because of a threatened assassination attempt by Jupiter Belus and Ninus, the son and grandson of Nimrod. Noah and Saturn reigned together in Italy, and then when Noah was getting old, he appointed his son Cranus as king.

Noah died in the year 346 after the Flood when he was 950 years old. This is in agreement with the Biblical age of Noah, which is also 950, but the Biblical date of his death is 350 years after the Flood, not 346 (Gen. 9:28-29).

78

Italy fell into disarray again after Noah's death, and came under the tyranny of giants who continued to rule the country, until Hercules eventually overcame them and appointed Tuscus as king, as we have seen earlier.

When Tuscus died, Altheus his son reigned in his stead, but was overthrown by Atlas Italus, a descendant of Gomer. Atlas had already overthrown his brother Hesperus, king of Spain, and then went to Italy and deposed Altheus. He re-named the country Italus after himself, and it became known as Italy.

Altheus had a son called Blascon and a grandson called Camboblascon. Atlas deprived Altheus and his family of all authority, but did not throw them out of the country altogether. Before he died, he compensated them by giving his daughter Electra to Camboblascon in marriage, together with a dowry consisting of all the towns and countries around the Alps. He was succeeded by his son Morges, who recognised all the wrong that had been done and handed over his crown to Camboblascon.

Camboblascon and Electra had two sons called Iasus and Dardanus, and a daughter called Armonia who never married. Iasus became a powerful ruler of two kingdoms, being appointed king of Italy while his father was still alive and then appointed king of France a year later. The reason for his appointment in France was because their royal line had failed, as we have already seen. He was considered the most favourable successor, being a descendant of Hercules, and the French royal family was also descended from Hercules.

The status of Iasus was increased even further when he married a noble and rich lady called Ipitus Cibeles, at a great ceremony held in Viterbo, where Isis the widow of Osiris was present. They had a son and heir called Corybantus.

Departure of Dardanus and the Foundation of Troy

Iasus, in spite of his good fortune and status, gave nothing to his younger brother Dardanus and made him look like a slave by comparison. Dardanus became jealous and fought against Iasus, and many of the population were drawn into an inconclusive civil war. Dardanus killed his brother Iasus while he was washing at a spring, an act that was considered reprehensible throughout the kingdom. Dardanus had no choice but to sail off, together with some of his followers, and he went to Asia Minor and built up the kingdom of Troy. In the meantime, Corybantus, the son of Iasus, became king of Italy but not of France. There was no king in France for a while, until they appointed Allobrox who was also descended from Hercules.

Dardanus stayed for some time in Samothrace, hoping to be called back to Italy, but it never happened. Then he went to Phrygia and was welcomed by Athus, the fourth generation descendant of Athus the Great, who we have already mentioned. Since Athus was descended from Hercules, there was a possibility that someone in his family might be offered the kingdom in Italy that Dardanus had been denied. So Dardanus resigned his right to a kingdom in Italy and offered it to one of the sons of Athus, in return for the right to build a kingdom of his own somewhere in Phrygia. They drew lots to choose between two sons of Athus, called Lydus and Turrhenus. The lot fell to Turrhenus, who went to Italy and was received by Queen Cibeles and her son Corybantus, king of Tuscania. Corybantus appointed twelve dukes to govern his country, and Turrhenus was one of them.

Dardanus and his people went to a place on the coast of Phrygia, at the Hellespont, and built the city of Dardania, so that it was founded 833 years after the Flood.

Turrhenus, who had gone to Italy, returned to Phrygia to visit Dardanus, but he never went back to Italy. Instead he stayed with Dardanus and they ruled together as neighbours. Turrhenus gave his daughter Batea in marriage to Dardanus, and their descendants succeeded them as heirs to the kingdom. It was in the days of their grandson Troas that the city of Dardania was first known as Troy.

How Much of This is New?

This story begins with things that we already know about, from the Bible, the Greek mythology, and the authentic Chaldean fragments. For example:

- We know about Noah and his three sons, Shem, Ham and Japheth, and Gomer the son of Japheth.
- We know about the possible existence of additional children of Noah and his wife, born after the flood.
- We know about Rhea, because she appears in the Greek mythology as the wife of Kronus (Ham).

- We know about Osiris and Isis from the Egyptian mythologies, and the possible identification of Osiris with Mizraim.
- We know that Electra was the daughter of Atlas.
- We know that Batea (Batia) was the daughter of Teucer, and his name appears corrupted to Turrhenus.
- We know about the marriage of Dardanus and Batea, and the descent of Trojan kings.

This genealogy starts off more or less correct with Noah and his children, although his wife's name Tytea is something new. It ends correctly with the marriage of Dardanus and Batea, but there is a considerable amount of new material in between, and in one place it contradicts the Greek mythology. Instead of Electra marrying Zeus, she marries Camboblascon, his great-great-great grandson!

Holinshed's Chronicles

Holinshed's *Chronicles* were written during the Tudor period, containing a comprehensive history of England, Scotland and Ireland, from the earliest times to shortly before the publication date (first edition 1578, second edition in 1587). This is a large six-volume work, but is relatively easy to obtain, compared with other sources of the same period, because it was used by Shakespeare.

The work was expanded to such great length because Holinshed used to write about everything he could find, and would then leave the reader to judge its authenticity. Such is the case with his treatment of early Britain, known as Samothea. After writing about it at length, he finished the section with the following paragraph. [122]

Upon these considerations I have no doubt to deliver unto the reader, the opinion of those that think this land to have been inhabited before the arrival here of Brute, [123] trusting it may be taken in good part, since we have but showed the conjectures of others, till time that some sufficient learned man shall take upon him to decipher the doubts of all these matters. Nevertheless,

---

[122] Holinshed's *Chronicles*, Vol.1, p.436.
[123] Brutus the Trojan, who came to Britain, and from whom the country is thought to be named. This subject will be dealt with in Chapter 4.

I think good to advertise the reader that these stories of Samothes, Magus, Sarron, Druis, and Bardus, do rely only upon the authority of Berosus, whom most diligent antiquaries do reject as a fabulous and counterfeit author, and Vacerius[124] has laboured to prove the same by a special treatise lately published at Rome.

Although Holinshed appears to be denouncing Berosus, I do not think that he means it that way. He is referring to the controversy over Annius of Viterbo, and the fragments that have become known as *pseudo-Berosus*. The real Berosus has always been respected as an authentic author, and the only question that arises is the separation of the authentic works from the alleged forgeries.

The Samothean Kings

Volume I of Holinshed's Chronicle describes Celtica, or Samothea, as an empire that included both Britain and France, stretching across Europe from the Rhine to the Pyrenees. This is in contrast to Richard Lynche who says nothing of Britain and appears to limit the kingdom only to France.

Sometimes the name Samothea is applied only to Britain, and sometimes to the whole empire. The name 'Celtica' usually denotes the whole empire, and the name 'Gallia' denotes France. However, the names are used so interchangeably that the Samotheans, Celts and Gauls are considered to be one people. This is not surprising, considering that the modern French word for Wales (a Celtic nation) is 'Pays de Gaule'.

There was a succession of Samothean kings, who ruled the empire until they were invaded by a giant called Albion. They were liberated by Hercules, and then the succession of kings continued until the arrival of Brutus the Trojan.

The island of Britain was first called Samothea, until Albion came and re-named it after himself. When Albion was defeated, it did not revert to Samothea, but retained the name of Albion, until Brutus arrived and called it Britain.

---

[124] Possibly Giorgio Vasari (1511-1574), but uncertain.

The succession of kings was as follows: [125]

Samothes
Magus
Sarronius
Druiyus
Bardus
Longho
Bardus Junior
Lucus
Celtes

> Albion (invaded Samothea)
> Hercules (defeated Albion)

Celtes (continued after defeat of Albion)
Galates
Harbon
Lugdus
Beligius
Iasius
Allobrox
Romus
Paris
Lemanus
Olbius
Galates II
Nannes
Remis
Francus
Pictus

> Brutus (invaded and set up a new succession of kings)

Holinshed's Chronicle gives more than one possible date for the arrival of the first inhabitants of Samothea. In one place it says that they arrived

---

[125] Holinshed's *Chronicles*, Vol.1, p.31.

200 years after the Flood. In another place (in Volume VI, Ireland) it gives the date of the Flood as 1650 AM (Anno Mundi - Year of the World from Creation). Going back to Volume I we have the arrival of Samothes in 1910 AM which is 260 years after the Flood. Without getting bogged down with the detail, we get the impression that the dispersion was not a gradual process. People travelled large distances in a very short time (probably to get away from Nimrod who had become a tyrant).

Samothes to Bardus - The First Five Kings

The first five kings of Samothea maintained the true religion that they had learned from Noah and Japheth. They are each described as follows:

- **Samothes** was a man of great learning, and he taught about astronomy, moral values and politics. He founded a sect of philosophers called the Samothei, who were skilful in the law of God and man. He delivered his knowledge in Phoenician letters, from which the Greek alphabet is derived.

- **Magus** was a man of great learning, like his father Samothes, and the Magi of Persia derived their name from him.

- **Sarronius**, otherwise known as Sarron, founded public places of learning, to encourage people to study and not to indulge in uncivilised behaviour. He was the founder of a group of philosophers called the Sarronides, who were able to offer sacrifices. Sarron believed that sacrifices should only be made by people who were skilled in divine mysteries.

- **Druiyus**, otherwise called Druis, was the founder of the Druids. At first, this was the true religion taught by his predecessors, but after his death the Druids fell into pagan superstitions.

- **Bardus** was a poet and musician, and from him we get the word 'Bard'. He established an order of poets or heralds called 'Bardi', and they were held in such high esteem that if two armies were engaged in battle, and the Bardi walked among them, the battle would stop until they had gone.

After Bardus, the Celts departed from the strict ordinances of their former kings and fell into idleness and decadence, so that they were quickly subdued by the giant Albion.

The Egyptian Family Feud

Ham, the son of Noah, had four sons:

- **Cush**, who had six sons, including the notorious Nimrod who was the founder of the worst features of idolatry and paganism, and instigated the rebellion at Babylon. After the dispersion, the descendants of Cush inhabited Ethiopia.

- **Mizraim**, who succeeded his father Ham as king of Egypt.

- **Put**, who inhabited the North African coastal region to the west of Egypt.

- **Caanan**, whose descendants occupied the land on the eastern coast of the Mediterranean, until they were driven out by the Israelites. One of his sons, called Heth, founded the Hittite empire in Turkey and Carthage, but they were eventually defeated by the Romans and totally wiped out.

Mizraim had seven sons, known as Ludim, Anamim, Lehabim, Naphtuhim, Pathruhim, Casluhim and Caphtorim. Two of these are of interest in this study:

- **Naphtuhim** was considered to be Neptune and was given the surname Marioticus because his dominions were among the islands of the Mediterranean sea.

- **Lehabim** was considered to be Hercules and was given the surname Lybicus.

The Egyptians adopted the practice of deifying their kings, just as the Babylonians had deified Nimrod. The same practice was passed on to the Greeks and Romans and to all the pagan world, until it was subdued by Christianity. There were no unique characters called Neptune or Hercules, instead there could be any number of them, depending on how the pagans deified their kings. In the case of these two sons of Mizraim, they were called Neptune Marioticus and Hercules Lybicus. Their father Mizraim was also deified, and was called Osiris.

85

This account from Holinshed, based on Annius of Viterbo, says that Neptune was the son of Osiris,[126] although in Greek mythology he is the son of Kronus and Rhea, and he is the brother of Zeus. However, these discrepancies occur elsewhere[127] and we do not need to be concerned with them. We just continue with the story. Neptune sailed the seas with his 33 giant sons, leaving each of them in a different place to overthrow the kingdoms that already existed and bring the world under their own tyrannical rule. The sons that feature in this story are:

- **Albion**, who invaded the island of Samothea with an army descended from Cush.

- **Bergion**, who invaded the island to the west of Samothea. It became known as Hibernia and is now called Ireland.

- **Lestrigo**, who invaded Italy.

- The king(s) from whom the **Lomnimi** or **Geriones** of Spain derived their name.

Osiris was opposed to their ambitions, so the giants held a judicial council, with the support of their father Neptune, and put him to death. This event was a cause of great lamentation that was regularly observed in the religion of ancient Egypt, and the practice was passed on to the Greeks and Romans who respectively lamented the deaths of Dionysus and Bacchus. It is also thought that Nimrod met a violent death. He may have been killed by Shem, or torn to pieces by wild beasts, but nobody seems to know for sure.

Hercules Lybicus was infuriated by the murder of his father Osiris and set out to kill the giant sons of Neptune wherever they could be found. He went to Spain and defeated the Lomnimi or Geriones, then he passed through Gallia on his way to Italy, to do battle with Lestrigo.

---

[126] Holinshed's *Chronicles*, Vol.1, p.432.

[127] Holinshed gives some contradictory accounts of the Egyptian genealogy, in which Hercules is sometimes the uncle of the giants and sometimes their cousin. This is typical of medieval literature, where terms representing family relations are frequently mixed up. The most common mix-up is the use of 'nephew' to mean 'grandson', and it becomes obvious when a so-called 'nephew' is third in line to the throne.

When Albion and Bergion heard that he was on his way to Italy, they set off to defend their brother Lestrigo, and fought against Hercules on the banks of the Rhine (it seems that Hercules must have gone further north to meet Albion and Bergion).

The battle was going badly for Hercules, and his army had used up all their weapons, but Hercules called on them to pick up stones which were available in abundance and throw them at the enemy. This way they killed both Albion and Bergion, and most of their army, so that the remainder were put to flight and the battle was won. After that, Hercules went throughout Gallia, overthrowing tyrants in every place.

It is thought that Hercules came to the island of Albion, arriving at a headland which Ptolemy[128] calls Promontorium Herculis, now known as Hartland Point in north Devon.

Holinshed gives a succession of Celtic kings who reigned after the defeat of Albion, beginning with the reinstatement of Celtes, although very little is said about them and there is doubt about what sort of rule they had. There are accounts of complete disorder as the other giants continued in a state of lawlessness. The British history that we will deal with in chapter 4, (which doesn't depend on Annius) says that when Brutus arrived, the island was empty except for a few giants. Whatever may be the case, we are told that the island retained the name of Albion until Brutus arrived and called it Britain.

There is a religious theme in this story, that the Samotheans had fallen because they had departed from the true religion of Noah and turned to paganism. When Albion came in 1721 BC (according to a rough calculation), the paganism got worse and continued after his death. It got no better when Brutus came, because Brutus himself was a pagan, and it was not subdued until the arrival of Christianity in the first century AD. The same theme is picked up by Gildas (c.AD 540) in his *Ruin of Britain*,[129] where he laments that Britain had been invaded by the Saxons because they had departed from the true Christian faith.

---

[128] Claudius Ptolemaeus, flourished AD 127 –145, Alexandria, Egypt.
[129] Winterbottom, M., *Gildas: The Ruin of Britain*.

Fables and Endless Genealogies

> Neither give heed to fables and endless genealogies, which minister questions, rather than godly edifying which is in faith ...
>
> *1 Tim. 1:4*

A great deal of mischief is caused by people who study genealogy for the wrong reasons, and then invent fables because they are unable to accept the results. There is great value in finding out about our ancestors, because it defines who we are, and this becomes apparent when we consider the problems of orphans who know neither their father nor mother and cannot trace any of their ancestors.

You only need to spend a few hours at a public records office, where people are looking for their ancestors, and you become aware that they are happy or sad about what they have found. Sometimes you hear moans and groans such as "Oh no, none of them were married!". People expect to find the birth of the first child at least nine months after the wedding, but I always advise people to start searching earlier. We can be moralistic about how we live our own lives, and how we bring up our children, but there is no point being moralistic about our ancestors. If they didn't do what they did, we wouldn't exist.

Sometimes I hear the occasional anecdote about how someone went to the public records office, hoping to find an ancestor who was a titled aristocrat, or maybe an archbishop, only to discover that the person they were looking for was a thief and a robber and spent most of his time in jail.

However, the worst problem is the political and religious wannabes who are so determined to find what they want, they are prepared to create fake histories.

We have already seen, in this chapter, the activities of Annius and those who have followed him, creating histories that have never been proved after more than 500 years and are widely regarded as fake.

Among the religious wannabes, we have people who wannabe Jewish (from the tribe of Judah) or wannabe Israelite (from the twelve tribes of Israel). These are the people who Paul was complaining about in his letter to Timothy, because if they couldn't find the right ancestors, they would invent fables, and claim to have gained some spiritual credit. The modern-day equivalent are the British Israelites, who claim that the British are descended from the lost tribes of Israel. There is some evidence of an early Jewish (or Israelite)[130] community in Cornwall, and I will deal with that on page 154, but it's important not to create spurious arguments to try and bolster up the case. For example, some British Israelites say that the word "Saxon" means "Isaac-son" and they are all descended from Isaac. They forget that Isaac is just an Anglicised version of "Yitzak", and the Hebrew for "son of Isaac" is "ben-Yitzak" which doesn't sound anything like "Saxon". Also they can't tell us at what stage in their history they stopped writing from right to left, and started writing left to right instead. These problems, and a few others, are discussed by David Williams.[131]

Now, there might have been some Jewish or Israelite ancestry in the history of the Saxons. If we go back ten generations, each of us has a total of 2046 ancestors, and these might include people from all the nations of the world. It may be that the British royal family has an ancestor from among the ancient Israelites, but it doesn't prove anything, it's pure chance.

As I study ancient history, I sometimes get enquiries from people who ask about the descent of their nation from ancient Israel. I know where the idea comes from, and I always explain that even if it can be proved, it's not so important. When the Israelites came out of Egypt they were a "mixed multitude" (Exodus 12:38). There were people among them from other nations, and possibly some Egyptians who had endured the first nine plagues and knew what was coming, so they threw in their lot with the Israelites and spread the blood of the Passover lamb around the door. The angel of death passed over, not when he saw the Israelites, but when he saw the blood.

I have to explain, that as I study ancient history I am not trying to gain credits for any religious or political group. I am only trying to find secular evidence for something that we already know from the Bible, that we are all descended from Adam and then from Noah. I believe that we have seen it, in Chapters 1 and 2. We have seen the ten kings before the

---

[130] The Jews derive their name from Judah, one of the twelve sons of Jacob. The name 'Israelite' applies more generally to the descendants of all twelve tribes, after their patriarch Jacob who is called Israel. The kingdom became divided in the time of Rehoboam, son of Solomon, so that the northern kingdom was called Israel and the southern kingdom was called Judah.

[131] Williams, D., *British Israelism - An Expose.*

flood, who are clearly the ten pre-flood patriarchs from Adam to Noah. We have also seen the genealogy from Noah to Dardanus, but only by looking through the fog of Babylonian, Egyptian and Greek history and mythology. It isn't a clear picture, but we can see it all the same, and we don't need fables to make it better.

Chapter 4 - From Dardanus to the Welsh Kings

Setting aside the dubious histories of Chapter 3, and returning to the genealogy from Noah to Dardanus that we saw earlier on page 64, we see that Dardanus married Batia and they had a son called Erichthonius. The Trojan royal line continues to Aeneas who fled the burning city of Troy and set up his new kingdom in Italy, then it continues with the descendants of Aeneas as far as Alba and Iulus. This is all documented by the Greeks and Romans, but other authors pick up the story and continue to the birth of Brutus, his marriage to a Greek princess, and his arrival in Britain where he was the first of a long line of kings.

Dardanus to Aeneas

The genealogy from Dardanus to Aeneas, and the first few generations of his descendants, is given by Homer, Virgil, Hesiod and various other ancient authors, and is documented in the Greek Mythology Link.[132] The royal line is shown in figure 12.

The kingdom of Troy continued until the reign of Priam, who gave his daughter Creusa in marriage to Aeneas and they had a son called Ascanius. Aeneas was the son of Anchises and Aphrodite (the Roman Venus), and he was considered to be half-human and half-god.

During the reign of Priam, the city was attacked by the Greeks and we have the epic drama of the Trojan horse. The Trojans thought they had defeated the Greeks, and they found a large wooden horse that had been left outside the city wall, so they brought it into the city as a trophy, not knowing that it was full of Greek soldiers. During the night, the soldiers came out of the horse and opened the city gate, letting the Greek army in.

The city was set on fire and the inhabitants were killed, although some escaped, including Aeneas, his young son Ascanius, and his elderly father Anchises. His wife Creusa got lost in the confusion and was killed.

---

[132] Parada, C., *Greek Mythology Link: Aeneas* <homepage.mac.com/cparada/GML/Aeneas.html>, Oct. 2002.

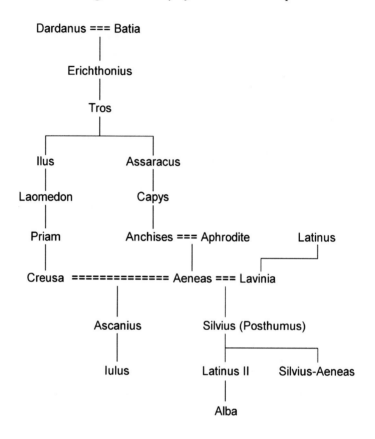

Figure 12 - Dardanus to Aeneas and the Kings of Alba-Longa

Aeneas and many others who escaped with him set off in ships, intending to go to Italy, but they were shipwrecked and landed at Carthage in North Africa. They were welcomed by Dido, queen of the Carthaginians, who wanted to marry Aeneas in the hope that the Trojans and Carthaginians would unite and become a great empire. Aeneas stayed there for a while, but he believed that his destiny was in Italy, so he repaired his ships and set off. When Dido realised that they had gone, she killed herself and the funeral pyre could be seen from the ships as they sailed away.

After many other adventures, Aeneas arrived in Italy and was received by king Latinus who recognised that he was of the same stock as the Italians and wished to give him his daughter Lavinia in marriage. Dardanus, the ancestor of Aeneas and founder of Troy, had originally come from Italy. However, Lavinia was already betrothed to Turnus, king of the Rutulians, so a battle was fought between Aeneas and Turnus. Aeneas was victorious, and he married Lavinia[133] and set up his kingdom in Italy.

Aeneas and Lavinia had a son called Silvius, which means "born in the woods", the circumstance arising because Lavinia was in exile, hiding in the woods. Aeneas had died before Silvius was born, so Silvius was also called "Posthumus". There is some uncertainty about the sons of Silvius-Posthumus. There may have been two of them, one called Latinus and the other called Silvius-Aeneas, or they might have both been the same person.

Ascanius succeeded Aeneas to the kingdom, and he founded the city of Alba-Longa in the Alban Hills about twelve miles south-east of Rome (although Rome did not exist at the time).

Ascanius was also called Iulus, and he had a son called Iulus who should have succeeded him. However, Silvius-Posthumus was also a contender for the kingdom, because he was a small child when his father Aeneas had died but was now grown up. There was an election and the people voted for Silvius-Posthumus, but Iulus was given a position of spiritual authority and his descendants were called the Julii, or Julians.

The British History from Brutus to Cadwallader

From the descendants of Aeneas onwards, the story is picked up by the twelfth century British historian, Geoffrey of Monmouth, who wrote a book called *The History of the Kings of Britain*. It was based on a number of ancient sources, although he claimed that it was a translation from a single source which he calls his *very ancient book*.[134] There have been claims that his very ancient book has never been found, although there is evidence that it existed. Most notably there is a document attributed to

---

[133] Tysilio's *Chronicle* (Roberts, P., pp.2-3) gives two separate accounts. One says that Aeneas married Lavinia (in agreement with Virgil's *Aeneid*) and the other says that his son Ascanius married her. They both agree that Aeneas fought against Turnus, for the hand of Lavinia, so we have to assume that the former is correct.

[134] Thorpe, L., *Geoffrey of Monmouth*, p.51.

Tysilio[135] which is believed to be an extant copy or closely related to it. We will return to this issue later, but we can be sure that we are not into another Annius of Viterbo controversy.

Note: When considering early British history, the term 'British' means the Celtic-speaking people who are now known as 'Welsh'. The Celtic Britons used to occupy the whole island, but were eventually pushed into Wales by the Saxons.

Aeneas to Brutus

The genealogy, from Aeneas to Brutus and his sons, is as follows:

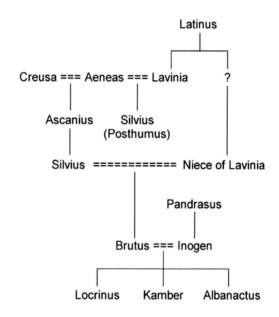

Figure 13 - Aeneas to Brutus and his three sons.

Ascanius had a son called Silvius, named after his uncle Silvius-Posthumus. Lavinia had a niece, who is not identified, from a brother or sister who is also not identified. Silvius had his way with Lavinia's niece, although they were not married, and she became pregnant. Ascanius

---

[135] Roberts, P., Tysilio's *Chronicle*.

consulted the soothsayers about the child and they told him he would cause the death of both his father and mother, but later he would become a great king. His mother, the niece of Lavinia, died in childbirth. The child was called Brutus, and when he was fifteen years old he was out hunting with his father Silvius. Brutus was standing under one tree, and his father under another, and a deer passed between them. Brutus shot an arrow at the deer, but it bounced off and killed his father. Thus he was considered to have killed both his father and his mother, although unintentionally, and was banished from Italy.

Brutus went to Greece where his royal lineage was recognised by Pandrasus,[136] king of the Greeks, and by the downtrodden Trojans who had escaped from Troy and were living as an under-class among the Greeks. The Trojans adopted him as their leader and assembled themselves into an army. He went to Pandrasus and asked for their liberty, so that they could live as equals among the Greeks, or else be given assistance to go to other lands. Pandrasus was enraged by this request and went to war against the Trojans, but Brutus prevailed against him. Pandrasus was anxious to achieve a peace of some sort, but he recognised that the war had led to feelings of resentment that would make it impossible for the Trojans to continue living among the Greeks. He therefore decided that the departure of the Trojans was the only possible option, and he furnished them with ships so that they could leave. He also gave his daughter Inogen to Brutus, to be his wife.

Brutus and his army sailed away and stopped in a few parts of Africa, then they sailed through the Pillars of Hercules (Straits of Gibraltar) and arrived in Gaul where they picked up some Trojan exiles, including a heroic figure called Corineus who was so strong that giants were like putty in his hands. They fought some battles against the Gauls, then returned to their ships and sailed to their intended destination, an island to the north of Gaul known as 'Alban' (Albion), which means 'White Island'.[137] Those who came with Brutus were called 'Britons', and the

---

[136] According to Cooper, in his translation of the *Chronicle of the Early Britons*, footnote 34, the name *Pandrassys* is probably derived from pan Doris, i.e. the king of all Dorians. The period, 12th-11th century BC, would be right for such a title.

[137] The name 'Alban' is probably derived from the white cliffs of Dover which could be seen from the coast of Gaul.

island became known as 'Britain'. The date of their arrival, according to Holinshed, is 1116 BC.[138]

When Brutus arrived in Alban, he found the island uninhabited except for a few giants, and he slew them with the help of his friend Corineus. However, if the story of the Samotheans is to be believed, the island was already populated before the arrival of Brutus. Also there is a Welsh account that the descendants of Gomer arrived in from France, 300 years after the flood (see page 143). These discrepancies might be resolved by considering the Irish history (see page 134). Ireland was occupied by giants called the Fomores, but a Scythian colony arrived from Greece, called the Firbolges, led by five sons of Dela, and in 1252 BC they threw the giants out. The question is, where did the giants go? They might have gone to Alban and wiped out the population, prior to the arrival of Brutus in 1116 BC.

Returning to our story, Corineus went to Cornwall because there were many giants there and he wanted to fight them. There was one especially big giant called Gogmagog, and on one occasion when Brutus and his men were killing giants, he commanded that Gogmagog should be spared for combat against Corineus. The contest duly took place, and Corineus threw Gogmagog over a cliff which became known as Gogmagog's Leap. The place is traditionally thought to be Plymouth Hoe.

When Brutus and his company became settled in the land, he founded a city on the Thames and called it 'Troia Newydd' (New Troy). It retained its name for a long time, but later it became corrupted to 'Troynovant' or 'Trinovantum'.[139] King Lud (73 BC), fortified the city and annexed lands to it, and re-named it 'Caer-Ludd' (Lud's Town). It later became known as Kaerlundein and finally the Saxons called it London. When Lud died, he was buried near a gateway called Porthlud, and the Saxons called it Ludgate.

---

[138] Holinshed's *Chronicles*, Vol. 1, p. 443. The date of 1116 BC is also given as 2850 AM (Anno Mundi = year of the world after creation), and in a number of other formats.
[139] A Celtic tribe called the Trinovantes or Trinobates is also thought to have been in Colchester, Essex.
See <www.britainexpress.com/History/prehistory/trinovantes.htm>, Oct. 2002.

There are a few street names in London that still perpetuate the name of Troy:

- Troy Town, in Peckham Rye;
- Troy Road, in Norwood;
- Troy Street and Troy Court, in Woolwich.

From the Death of Brutus to the Arrival of the Romans

I will not attempt to describe the whole history of this period, or any of the subsequent periods, because this is all available in the source material. Instead I will just describe a few highlights.

When Brutus died, the kingdom was divided between his three sons:

- Locrinus, the eldest son, took the area now known as England, as far north as the Humber, and it was called Loegria.
- Kamber took the area now known as Wales, and it was called Cambria.
- Albanactus took the country north of the Humber, including what is now known as Scotland, and it was called Albany.

Some time after the country had been divided, Humber, the king of the Huns invaded Albany and drove the people into Loegria. Locrinus and Camber combined their forces and defeated Humber. He was drowned in the river, and that's how the river got its name.

In the 9th century BC we have King Lear, who had three daughters and he wanted to know which one loved him the most. He divided his kingdom between his two eldest daughters because they said they loved him dearly, although they didn't really mean it, and he gave nothing to his youngest daughter, who refused to speak flattery, even though she was the only one who really loved him. In the end, his two eldest daughters left him destitute and he had to make amends with his youngest daughter who had married Aganippus, king of Gaul. The story of King Lear was later immortalised by Shakespeare.

In the 7th century BC there were two brothers called Ferrex and Porrex who disputed over the kingdom. Porrex laid a plot to assassinate his brother, but Ferrex discovered it and went to Siward, king of Gaul, and came back and defeated Porrex in battle and killed him. But their mother was enraged at the death of her son, so she went to Porrex's bedroom at night and killed him. After that there were two centuries of civil war.

In the early 4th century BC there were another two brothers, called Beli and Bran, who fought over the kingdom. They were appeased by the nobles, and it was agreed that Beli would have Loegria and Cambria, because he was the eldest, and Bran would have the land to the north of the Humber and would have to be subject to his brother. The arrangement was agreed and there were five years of peace, but then Bran was instigated by others to claim equal rights. He went to Llychlyn (which denotes Norway and Sweden) and married Elsing, the king's daughter, hoping to gain a political alliance that would defeat Beli. But on the way back he was pursued by Gwychlan, king of Denmark who wanted the princess for himself. Gwychlan successfully captured the princess, but was then driven by a storm onto the northern coast of Britain. They were seized by the country people and brought to Beli. Bran complained that he wanted his wife back, otherwise he would ravage the whole country. Beli went to war against him, and defeated him, so that he fled to Gaul. Some time later, he came back with an army, but as the two brothers were about to engage battle, their mother came between them and persuaded them to make peace. Beli and Bran remained together in London for a year, then they set out on a conquest of Gaul and Italy, which ended up with Bran as the Roman 'Emperor'.

It's an exaggeration to call him an Emperor, because the Roman Empire had not begun at that time, although it is well known that about 390 BC the Gauls invaded Rome and defeated them at the Battle of Allia, under a leader called Brennus. The only question is, did this Brennus come from Britain, or was it an army of Gauls in which a British king participated?

Beli was succeeded by his son Gwrgant, who went to war against the king of Denmark, and killed him, for refusing to pay tribute. On his return journey, he was passing through the Orkney islands and came across thirty ships, full of men and women. He seized their chief, who was called Bartholme, but the chief pleaded for his protection, explaining that they were called 'Barclenses',[140] and had been driven out of Spain, and they had been at sea for a year and a half, looking for somewhere to

---

[140] The Barclenses could be the ancestors of the Basque people of southern France and northern Spain, but it's only a possibility. Nobody knows for sure what is the origin of the Basques.

settle. Gwrgant was unwilling to let them settle in Britain, but he directed them to Ireland, which was at that time uninhabited. However, this story is denied by the Irish, who say that they never needed permission from the Britons to settle in Ireland.

From the Roman to the Saxon Invasion

King Lud who re-named Troia-Newydd to Caer-Lud, as we have already seen, had two sons called Avarwy and Teneuvan. They were both under age when he died, so his brother Caswallon succeeded him. Caswallon gave to each of his nephews a part of his territory. He gave London and the Earldom of Kent to Avarwy, and Cornwall to Teneuvan, but they were subject to him as the king of the whole nation.

During the reign of Caswallon, Julius Caesar made his first attack on Britain, in 55 BC. He landed at the Castle of Doral (probably on the Isle of Thanet) but was repelled by the Britons. He lost his own sword when it got stuck in the shield of Nyniaw (Nennius), Caswallon's brother, who used it to great effect. Caesar returned to Gaul in defeat, and then paid money to their chiefs and released all the prisoners, in case they should rise against him.

Two years later, Caesar attempted a second invasion, sailing up the Thames, but his ships were sunk as they ran into stakes that the Britons had driven into the river bed.

There were great celebrations in London, where many animals were sacrificed to the gods. There were also some sporting events, and in the course of these, Cyhelin, the nephew of Avarwy, killed Hirlas, the nephew of the king. The king was enraged, and insisted that Cyhelin be tried in his own court, but Avarwy, fearing the outcome, left the court with his nephew Cyhelin and withdrew to his own territory (probably the Isle of Thanet). The king complained to his chiefs, that Avarwy should not have left his court without his permission, and went out with his troops to ravage his territory. He then returned and attacked London, presumably to put down a rebellion by people who believed that he should not have attacked Avarwy.

The next objective for Avarwy was to resist Caswallon, so he invited Caesar to come and help him. Caesar landed at Dover and was received by Avarwy while Caswallon was still in London. Then Caswallon mobilised his troops and engaged Caesar in battle, but it ended with the British troops being surrounded on a hill, deprived of provisions.

Eventually, after some diplomacy from Avarwy who did not want the king to be overthrown, they made peace with the Romans and agreed to pay them an annual tribute of three thousand pounds of gold and silver. Thus the Britons were subdued, not because of their lack of valour, but because of their own internal divisions.

When Caswallon died, Teneuvan succeeded him as king, because Avarwy had gone to Rome. He had a peaceful reign and was succeeded by Cynvelin (Cymbeline) his son. Cymbeline also had a peaceful reign, having been educated by Julius Caesar, and did not withhold the tribute from the Romans.

Cymbeline had two sons, Gwydyr (Guiderius) and Gweyrydd (Arviragus). Guiderius succeeded him as king and refused to pay the tribute, so the Romans sent Claudius Caesar to Britain with a great army. They attacked Portchester and laid it under siege, so Guiderius went there and engaged battle. He was killed by a Roman who had disguised himself as a Briton, but his brother Arviragus quickly put on his armour and continued the battle, giving the impression that the king was still alive, and routed the Romans so that they fled. However, the Romans made a comeback, but the outcome was indecisive, so they concluded a peace in which Claudius gave his daughter to Arviragus in marriage. Claudius built a city on the River Severn and called it Claudii-castra and it became known as Gloucester.

The succession of Arviragus as king, upon the death of his brother Guiderius, can be dated AD 43 by comparison with the Roman records of the Claudian campaign against Britain.[141]

Claudius returned to Rome, and when Arviragus had strengthened his kingdom in Britain he followed the example of his brother Guiderius and refused to pay tribute to Rome. Claudius sent Vespasian to Britain, and he landed at Totnes and then went to Exeter and defeated Arviragus. It was during this period, in another battle, that Caradoc (Caractacus), chief of the Silurians, was captured and taken to Rome, a matter that is discussed later on page 170. Arviragus continued as a puppet king, under Roman rule, after his Queen who was a Roman had made peace.

When Arviragus died, his son Meurig succeeded him, and from that point onwards the monarchy was half-British and half-Roman, so there

---

[141] Birley, A.R., *Tacitus: Agricola and Germany*, Chronological Table, p.xlvi.

was peace by assimilation. Meurig was succeeded by his son Coel,[142] who was educated in Rome, and Coel was succeeded by Lles (Lucius) who was either his son[143] or his brother.[144]

Lucius, as we will see later (page 179), was the first Christian king, and he asked Eleutherius, the Bishop of Rome, to send teachers of the Christian faith to Britain.

Lucius left no children to succeed him,[145] and there was a series of wars between the Romans and Britons, with different people taking the kingdom:

- The Roman Senate sent Severus,[146] with two legions who subdued most of the Britons, and the rest fled north, but frequently came back and attacked the Romans. In response, the Romans built a wall to keep them out, along the border between Deira and Albania. This is known as "Hadrian's Wall",[147] from Tyneside to the Solway Firth, and Tysilio's *Chronicle*[148] credits Severus with building it, although it was probably a later improvement.

---

[142] Morgan, R.W, *St. Paul in Britain*, pp.158,192. Quotes the *Triads of the Isle of Britain*, identifying Coel as the son of Cyllinus, the son of Caractacus.

[143] Roberts, Tysilio's *Chronicle*, p.90.

[144] Lomax, F., *William of Malmesbury*, p. 62.

[145] This comes from Tysilio's *Chronicle*, (Roberts p.91). An alternative view is given by Morgan, p.192, who says that Lucius had a daughter called Gladys who married Cadvan, prince of Cambria, and they had a daughter called Strada who married Coel, king of Colchester. Coel and Strada had a daughter called Helen, who married Constantius and they had a son called Constantine who conquered Rome. In that case, Coel, king of Colchester, appears in the place of Coel, Earl of Gloucester.

[146] Septimius Severus, Roman Emperor AD 193-211.

[147] The Emperor Hadrian came to Britain in AD 122 and commanded Aulus Platorius Nepos, his Governor in Britain, to build the wall. It was completed in 132 when Sextus Julius Severus was Governor, but repairs and improvements were carried out for a long time afterwards. The Emperor Antoninus Pius, in AD 142, ordered another wall to be built further north, from the Firth of Forth to the Firth of Clyde. It was known as the Antonine Wall, and it became the new Roman frontier, but it was abandoned in 161 and the Romans moved back to Hadrian's Wall.

[148] Roberts, Tysilio's *Chronicle*, p.92.

- Severus had a Roman wife who gave him a son called Geta, and a British wife who gave him a son called Bassanius. He was killed in a battle against the Britons and was buried at York. The Romans made Geta their king, and the Britons made Bassanius their king, but Bassanius killed Geta and took the whole kingdom. According to Bede,[149] Bassanius also became Roman Emperor and was called Antoninus.[150]

- Caron, a Briton who had been to Rome, came back and raised an army of Britons to fight against Bassanius who was supported by the Romans and Picts. They engaged battle, but the Picts changed sides and joined Caron, so that the Romans were put to flight. Bassanius was killed and Caron took over the kingdom.

- The Roman Senate sent Allectus with three legions to Britain and defeated Caron, so that Allectus became king.

- The Britons would not accept Allectus, because of his cruelty, so they appointed Asclepiodotus, Earl of Cornwall, as their king. They marched on London and fought against the Romans, killing many of them. The Romans closed the city gates, but many more Britons came from all over the country and stormed the city, defeating the Romans. Asclepiodotus reigned for ten years, but during his time the Emperor Diocletian sent Maximian Herculius to Britain to persecute the Christians.

- Coel, the Earl of Gloucester (not to be confused with the previous Coel, son of Meurig),[151] went to war against Asclepiodotus and killed him.

- Constantius Chlorus, a Roman senator who had been involved in the conquest of Spain, came to Britain to make war against Coel, but when the day of battle arrived, they made peace. Coel died five weeks later, having reigned ten years. Constantius took the kingdom and reigned for eleven years, and was buried at York.

---

[149] Hurst, W., *Bede's Ecclesiastical History*, 1,v.

[150] Marcus Aurelius Antoninus, not be confused with the earlier Antoninus Pius who built the Antonine Wall.

[151] One of these Coel's might be the subject of the rhyme "Old King Coel was a merry old soul".

At some time during his reign, Constantius married Helen, the daughter of Coel and they had a son called Constantine who conquered Rome and became known as 'Constantine the Great'. He was the first Christian emperor and he ordered that all persecution of Christians should cease.

When Constantine went to Rome, he was accompanied by his three maternal uncles, Llewelyn, Trahaern and Meurig, and also Maxentius (Maximus) who is thought to be a son of Llewelyn although it is not certain. This Maximus later became known as 'The Cruel' because of his activities in Armorica (Brittany), but we will return to that later.

With Constantine in Rome, Eudaf (Octavius), the Earl of Erging and Euas,[152] took Britain. He was opposed by Trahaern, who returned from Rome to bring the country back under Roman rule. Octavius fought a successful battle against Trahaern at Urien, near Winchester, but Trahaern went to Albany and renewed the war. Octavius fled to Godbert, king of Scandinavia to ask for help. He also urged his friends in Britain to assassinate Trahaern, and the deed was done by the 'Earl of the Strong-Castle'[153] together with a hundred horsemen who lay in wait for him.

This left Octavius decisively in control of the country, and he continued until the time of the two Roman Emperors, Valentian and Gratian.[154] However, he had no sons, and only one daughter, called Helen, so there was a problem with the succession. Some of his council advised that his nephew, Cynan Meiriadawg, should succeed him, while others advised that Helen should marry Maximus and he would become king. Maximus was (it is supposed) the son of Llewelyn, and his mother was a Roman. He was a Roman Senator, and it was thought that his marriage to Helen would enable the Senate to protect Britain against foreign invasion. The council agreed on Maximus, who was in Rome at the time, and they sent him an invitation which he accepted. He came to Britain, married Helen, and became king.

Cynan, deprived of the sovereignty, went to Albany and raised an army, and came back and ravaged the country, but he was driven back by

---

[152] A footnote in Tysilio's *Chronicle* (Roberts p.97) says that Erging and Euas are two small districts (Hundreds) of Monmouthshire.

[153] It is not certain who this is.

[154] In AD 367, Gratian was appointed co-Augustus of the Western Empire, together with his father Valentian.

Maximus and fled to Scandinavia. Then he returned and made peace with Maximus, and five years later the two of them went to Gaul and slew Hymblat, chief of the Gauls. Maximus then told Cynan that he would give him Armorica, since he had been deprived of Britain. The Britons began to settle there and they called it 'Little Britain'[155] It later became known as 'Brittany'.

Maximus went to Rouen (Rennes) in Normandy and the Gauls fled from their towns. It was there that he earned his title 'Maximus the Cruel' because he wiped out every man in the land, leaving only the women and children. He then went to war against Rome, with the result that Gratian was killed, and Valentian was driven from the city.

The Britons who had settled in Little Britain complained that there were no women among them, so they sent to Britain for women to be despatched in ships. The number of women who set sail is uncertain, either 1100 daughters of men of rank together with 6000 others, or ten times as many in each case. However, there were adverse winds and the ships were scattered, and some of them sank.

The settlement of Britons in Little Britain, and the exploits of Maximus in Rome, meant that Britain was drained of troops, and the north of the country was invaded by the Picts and Huns. Maximus, who was in Rome at the time, sent troops back to Britain to defend it, and the Picts and Huns fled to Ireland.

About this time, Maximus was killed, together with other Britons in his party, and Gratian Municeps[156] assumed the sovereignty of Britain, but he was cruel to the Britons and was killed by his own supporters. When the Picts and Huns heard of this, they joined together with the Scots, Norwegians and Danes, and attacked Britain.

The Britons asked for assistance from the Romans and obtained a legion under the command of Severus[157] (not the Severus mentioned

---

[155] The term 'Great Britain' distinguishes the mainland from 'Little Britain'.

[156] Gracianus Municeps, not to be confused with the Emperor Gracian. He was a Briton with Roman citizenship and municipal responsibility, during the time of Emperor Honorius (AD 383-423). He is mentioned in *Bede's Ecclesiastical History*, 1, xi. See Hurst.

[157] This could possibly be the Emperor Libius Severus (AD 461-465). Little is known about him, and these events must have occurred long before he became Emperor.

earlier, on page 101). Together they drove out the invading armies and made improvements to Hadrian's Wall, to prevent further incursions.

From this point onwards, the Britons received no more help from the Romans. The Empire was in a state of decline, and they considered the defence of Britain to be more trouble than it was worth. The Romans returned to London and announced that no more tribute was required, then they set off in ships and returned to Rome.

This left the Britons in the position of having to defend themselves without assistance, and they did so successfully for a while, but could not resist the invasion of the Saxons.

From the Saxon Invasion to the Death of Cadwallader

This part of the story begins with the death of a British king called Constantine, not to be confused with the previous Constantine who became the Roman Emperor. Constantine had three sons called Constans, Aurelius Ambrosius and Uther who later became known as Pendragon.[158] Constans, the eldest son, was a monk at the time, with no knowledge about how to rule a country, and the other two were under age.

Vortigern, the son of Constans, had the greatest influence within the king's council, and took his father out of the monastery and made him king, and at the same time made himself superintendent of the country. He then sought to make himself king instead of Constans and sought help from forty chiefs of the Picts, offering them great favours if they could help him become king. They set about the task according to their own design, and entered the kings chamber, cut off his head, and gave it to Vortigern. This was not exactly what Vortigern wanted, and he sent the murderers to prison while the council in London decided what to do with them. The council ordered them to be hanged, and committed the care of the state to Vortigern while they decided on a rightful king. Vortigern didn't wait for their appointment of a king, and instead he assumed that there was no opposition and appointed himself as king without their consent.

Meanwhile, the Picts were enraged that their forty chiefs had been hanged, and they went to war against Vortigern. The nation was

---

[158] Pendragon means a military chief who had other chiefs under him. Each chief was a ruler of his own realm, but they appointed one of their number as Pendragon for the purpose of warfare.

unwilling to fight alongside Vortigern, because of his treachery, and instead his two uncles, Uther and Ambrosius, prepared a fleet to attack him from Brittany.

Vortigern was becoming increasingly desperate, until one day he was going over the hills of Kent and he found that three ships had landed. He went to enquire about them, and met two Saxon chiefs, Hengist and Horsa. They offered him their support and went with him to London. The date of this event was AD 454.

Soon, more Saxons began to arrive, and Hengist gave his daughter Rowena to Vortigern in marriage, in return for the Earldom of Kent. This was done without informing Gwrgant, the existing Earl of Kent, and it displeased the Britons, including the three sons of Vortigern from his first wife. These were called Vortimer, Katigern and Paschent. After he had obtained Kent for himself, Hengist persuaded Vortigern to give Scotland to his son Offa and his uncle Ossa, so that they could protect it from foreign enemies.

The Britons complained about the introduction of so many Saxons to Britain, and they appointed Vortimer, the son of Vortigern as king, and they made war on the Saxons and drove them out of the country. During one of the battles, Katigern and Horsa slew each other.

Rowena, distressed at the defeat of the Saxons, prevailed on some of the attendants of Vortimer so that they poisoned him, and Vortigern once again became king. She then invited Hengist to come back, and he arrived with sixty ships. The Britons were alarmed at so great a number, but Hengist made the excuse that he didn't know that Vortimer was dead, and they had come prepared in case he should oppose them, but they didn't mean any harm. However, their real intent becomes apparent in the next incident.

On May Day, there was a meeting between the British and Saxon chiefs, to decide how many Saxons could stay in the country. It was agreed that no-one should be armed, but Hengist commanded that each of his chiefs should hide a long knife in his boot. When the parties met together, and the Britons were unsuspecting, Hengist gave out a great shout '*Nehmt ihre Saxes*'[159] and each Saxon drew out his knife and killed

---

[159] A footnote in Tysilio's *Chronicle* (Roberts p.117) says that in the Welsh copy the words are '*owd iwr Saxes*' probably means '*out with your Saxes*'.

the Briton nearest to him. Four hundred and sixty British chiefs were killed that day. Hengist seized Vortigern and took him captive. The only Briton who escaped was Eidiol, Earl of Gloucester, who found a pole lying on the ground and killed seventy men. The Saxons then took the whole of Loegria from Vortigern and banished him from Loegria so that he fled to Wales.

Vortigern began to build a fort at Snowdon, but whatever he built by day fell down at night. At this point begins the myth and magic of Merlin, and the mysterious events at Tintagel castle that led to the secret marriage of Uther Pendragon to Ygerna and the birth of King Arthur. We will not get into the details of any of this here, because a multitude of books are already available on the subject. Suffice it to say the following:

- The British history says nothing about the knights of the round table or the holy grail. Arthur had a sword called 'Caliburn' which he used quite effectively, but it had no magic powers like the mythical 'Excalibur' and there was no lady of the lake. These are all later embellishments of the story.
- Although there are myths surrounding the birth of Arthur, we can be sure that Arthur himself is not a myth. He was a real person, the son of Uther Pendragon and Ygerna.

Arthur was crowned king when his father died. He was only fifteen years old at the time, but very capable. He immediately set about fighting the Saxons, Picts and Scots on many different fronts, and when the country was secure, he married Guinevere, the daughter of Gogfran the hero. Her mother was from a noble Roman family and she had been educated by Cador, Earl of Cornwall.

After that, Arthur went on conquests of Ireland and Iceland. The kings of Scotland and Orkney submitted to him of their own accord and paid tribute. Then he enjoyed twelve years of peace and invited men of ability to his court to show off the courage and skill of his soldiers. Encouraged by the praise he received, he set out to conquer all of Europe. First he conquered Norway and Denmark, and then Gaul, and finally returned to Britain and held a great festival attended by the nobles of many nations.

While they were all enjoying themselves, a delegation arrived with a message from Lucius, the Roman general, demanding that Arthur should appear in Rome, because he had not paid tribute to them, and the Senate wanted to pass judgement on him. Arthur responded by assembling an army, recruited from many nations, and he sent a message to Rome saying that he would appear in Rome at the appointed time, not to pay tribute, but to demand tribute from them. The Romans responded by assembling their own army, also from many nations, and marched towards Britain. Arthur went out to meet them, and after a series of battles, with losses on both sides, the Romans were routed and Arthur had the victory. Lucius, the Roman general, was killed in battle and Arthur sent his body to the Senate with a note warning them not to seek any more tribute from Britain.

Arthur began to make his way towards Rome, but he received a message from Britain saying that his nephew Medrod had taken over his kingdom and taken his wife Guinevere to his bed. Arthur returned to Britain, leaving the conquest of Rome to one of his chiefs, Howel of Brittany. On arrival in Britain, Arthur was opposed by Medrod, with an army made up of Saxons, Picts, Scots, Irish and other nations. There was a series of battles, and Medrod was killed, together with many of his chiefs, but Arthur received a wound which turned out to be fatal. He was taken to the Isle of Avalon[160] to have it taken care of, but he died.

Clearly, these tales of Arthur and his conquests are an exaggeration of what actually happened. He may have held back the Saxon advances in Britain for a while, or even driven them back, and he might have made some conquests in Europe. He might even have participated in the downfall of Rome, in alliance with other nations, but he could not have been the Emperor of all Northern Europe as this story claims, otherwise the histories of those nations would tell us about him.

The embellishment of history has always been a popular pastime, not just among the Britons but throughout the entire world. What nation has not embellished their history to make themselves look good? How many nations have conquered other nations and at the same time burned their books and libraries, causing them to forget their past? If some of the history of Europe can also be denounced as embellishment, there might be some empty holes that can be filled by the exploits of Arthur.

Returning to the history, we find that Constantine, the son of Cador,

---

[160] Glastonbury, see page 155.

succeeded Arthur to the throne in AD 552. He resisted the Saxons, and so
did a number of kings after him, but in the days of Caredig the Saxons
made advances throughout the land, so that the Britons gave up England
and migrated to the west, to Wales and Cornwall.

In AD 596, Augustine came to England, sent by Pope Gregory, and
with great success he converted the Saxons to Christianity. Then he went
to Wales, expecting to have the same success among the Britons, but was
disappointed. The Britons had already received Christianity, from much
earlier times, and Augustine was preaching a different kind of
Christianity that required submission to the Pope. He considered himself
to be the highest episcopal authority in the land, and he wanted the
Britons to submit to him, but they refused. From this point onwards there
are two different versions of the story. The Britons say that he
"instigated" a massacre, while the English say that he "prophesied" it.
Whatever may be the case, the event duly took place. Two Saxon kings,
Ethelbert of Kent and Ethelfrid of Northumbria, joined together to attack
the monastery at Bangor-is-y-Coed[16] near Wrexham, and punish the
churchmen who had opposed Augustine. They marched as far as Chester
and were opposed by Brochwel Ysgythrog, the local commander, but he
only had a small army and was forced to retreat to Bangor. The Saxons
continued on their way to the monastery and slaughtered 1200 monks.
The activities of Augustine are discussed in more detail later, on page
187.

The Britons were enraged, so that a number of regional kings joined
together and fought against the Saxons. Then they went to Chester and
appointed Cadvan, king of North Wales as their chief, and pursued
Ethelfrid and his army until they crossed the Humber. Ethelfrid obtained
reinforcements, to oppose Cadvan, but a peace treaty was concluded so
that Ethelfrid would have the country north of the Humber, and Cadvan
should have the country to the south.

Some time later, Ethelfrid put away his wife because he was having
an affair with another woman. His wife was pregnant at the time, and she
asked Cadvan to mediate with Ethelfrid, and he did so but without
success. She remained in Cadvan's palace and gave birth to a son, called

---

[16] This Bangor should not be confused with the other Bangor on the Menai Strait
near Anglesey.

Edwin. Cadvan's wife also gave birth to a son, called Cadwallon and the two boys were brought up together.

When Cadvan and Ethelfrid died, the two sons each succeeded to their father's kingdom, and renewed the terms of peace that were previously concluded by their fathers. However, after two years, Edwin asked Cadwallon for permission to make a crown for himself, so that he could be acknowledged as an independent king. Cadwallon was advised by Braint, his nephew, that they could not trust the Saxons, since they had showed so much treachery and deceit in the past, and upon this advice Cadwallon refused to allow Edwin to wear a crown. Edwin said he would make one anyway, and Cadwallon replied that he would cut off his head when he was crowned. Both of them assembled their armies and there was a great battle, and Cadwallon was defeated and fled to Ireland, while Edwin ravaged his territory.

Cadwallon attempted to return to Britain, but he found that wherever he tried to land, Edwin's army was there to oppose him. Edwin always knew where Cadwallon was, because he was informed my a magician from Spain, called Pelidys. Cadwallon sailed to Brittany to ask for help from Solomon, who was king at that time. Solomon was sympathetic to him, but was not in a position to help, and there was a dialogue between them in which they lamented that the decadence of the nation had brought them low.

Cadwallon spent the winter in Brittany, and during that time he sent Braint to Britain, to enquire about Pelidys, the magician. Braint went in disguise and killed the magician with a staff which had a concealed blade, then he went to Exeter and summoned the Britons to join him, and sent a message to Cadwallon asking him also to come.

A Saxon prince called Penda came with a large force and besieged Exeter, but then Cadwallon arrived from Brittany with an army of ten thousand men, given to him by Solomon, and they slaughtered the Saxons. Penda, to save his life, changed sides and offered hostages as a guarantee of his loyalty, and then marched with Cadwallon against the Saxons. They went across the Humber and slew Edwin, and routed his army. Oswald succeeded Edwin, but Cadwallon and Penda pursued him also, and killed him.

Oswald was succeeded by his brother, Oswy Whitebrow, and there was civil war among the Saxons. They tried to persuade Penda, who was king of Mercia, to break his loyalty to Cadwallon, but he refused and with

Cadwallon's consent he went to war against Oswy. Penda was killed, and his son Olfryd succeeded him. Olfryd continued the war, assisted by Edbert, prince of Mercia, but in the end, Cadwallon ordered them to make peace with Oswy.

Cadwallon died, after reigning for forty-two years as king of England and Wales. He was succeeded by his son Cadwallader who reigned in peace for eleven years, then he fell ill, and there were disturbances among the Welsh because Cadwallader's mother was a Saxon, the sister of Penda.

During these disturbances there was a famine, which they believed was sent by God as a punishment for their sins, and many people died of hunger, and those who remained alive were so weak they could not bury the dead. Cadwallader sailed to Brittany and was received by King Alan, the nephew of Solomon. The famine continued in Britain for eleven years, and the only people who survived were those who went to the forest and lived by hunting.

When the famine ceased, the Saxons who survived it sent word to Germany, saying they should come and take possession of the land, since it was almost empty of inhabitants. A large number of Saxons arrived, and Cadwallader wanted to go and dispossess them, but an angel appeared and told him to go to Rome instead and enter the religious life. Cadwallader sent his son Ivor, and his nephew Ynyr, to Britain to try and regain it, or at least to prevent the Welsh from being annihilated. Then he went to Rome as instructed and after five years he died there, in AD 688.

Ivor and Ynyr raised a large force and went to Britain, and for 28 years they fought against the Saxons without success. From that time onward they were no longer called Britons, but were called Welsh, and the Saxons had sovereignty of all England.

At this point we come to the end of the history that is related by Tysilio and Geoffrey of Monmouth. The rest of the story is given by Caradoc of Llancerfan and Humphrey Lhuyd.[162]

According to Caradoc, the Welsh held on to Cornwall for a short while, but were soon confined to Wales. They had their own local princes, and sometimes they went on raids into England, for the purpose of pillage and harassment, rather than to gain territory.

---

[162] Caradoc of Llancerfan, *Historie of Cambria*.

Humphrey Lhuyd gives the history after 1270, and tells us that when Edward I was King of England, Welsh independent rule came to an end. Lhewelyn ap Gruffyth was the last Welsh Prince to hold out against the English. He was killed in 1282 while some of his men were trying to defend a bridge. For the Welsh, this marked the end of a long period of self-government which had always existed, in some part of Britain, for 2418 years since the arrival of Brutus in 1136 BC.

Although Edward had subdued the Welsh, and begun to implement English law, he never had the goodwill of the common people and they would not accept him as their Prince. They said they would accept a Prince, appointed by the King of England, only if he was a Welshman. The King resolved the situation by sending his Queen Eleanor to Caernarfon while she was pregnant. When the time for the birth came near, he assembled the Barons of Wales, and hesitated for a while until he knew that the Queen had given birth to a son, then he asked them a question. He asked them if they would accept a Prince, named by the King of England, if he was born in Wales, could not speak a word of English, and whose life and conversation was without blemish. They agreed that they would, and Edward promptly named his own son, also called Edward, born in Caernarfon Castle a few days earlier.

Since then, the King of England has always appointed a Prince of Wales, and the tradition remains to this day.

Sources of British History

The history given above, from Aeneas and his great-grandson Brutus, to the death of Cadwallader, is taken from a body of literature consisting primarily of the following sources:

- Gildas, about 540.
- Tysilio, date uncertain, last recorded event 688.
- Nennius, date uncertain, about 800.
- Geoffrey of Monmouth, 1136.

The most complete and detailed history is from Geoffrey of Monmouth, but because of questions regarding the accuracy and authenticity of his work, I have, for the most part, followed Tysilio instead. Gildas and Nennius give useful fragments, rather than complete histories.

We will now look at each of these authors in detail.

Gildas

Gildas was a monk, born in the north, in the kingdom of Clyde, but thought to have been educated in South Wales where he wrote his works. In later years he is thought to have gone to Brittany where he died in 570.

His main work is *De Excidio Britonum* (The Ruin of Britain),[163] written about 540 or slightly earlier. It was not written as a history, but as a lamentation on the calamities that had befallen Britain since the fall of the Roman Empire and the arrival of the Saxons. He believed that the misfortunes of Britain were a consequence of their decadence, indulgence, and lack of Christian faith. Although he was not writing history, he nevertheless mentions numerous events and circumstances, providing us with much historical information.

Tysilio

Tysilio (*Sulio*) was born about 548, the second son of Brochfael Ysgythrog,[164] King of Powys. He fled from his father's court at an early age and became a monk at Meifod. Brochfael sent troops to bring him back, but he was eventually persuaded to allow him to stay. Tysilio was concerned about further trouble, so he moved to Church Island in the Menai Strait and preached to the people in Anglesey. He was there for seven years, then returned to Meifod and was appointed as Abbot. He rebuilt the Abbey Church and lived in peace for a while, until his brother died. Then his sister-in-law, Queen Gwenwynwyn, wanted to marry him, so that he would succeed to the kingdom of Powys. He refused both the marriage and the kingdom, and fled to Brittany with a few followers because his monastery was being persecuted. He founded another monastery there, at St. Suliac.

In the relative safety of Brittany, he wrote his '*Chronicle of the Kings of Britain*' (as it is now called), although he was not the sole author. He died in 640, but the history continues to the death of Cadwallader in 688,

---

[163] Winterbottom, M., *Gildas: The Ruin of Britain.*
[164] This Brochfael Ysgythrog should not be confused with Brochwel Ysgythrog who fought against the Saxons at Chester, in an attempt to defend the monastery at Bangor-is-y-Coed.

so it appears that the work was started by Tysilio and continued by the monks at St. Suliac.

Tysilio never mentions himself, and there is no surviving manuscript with a Dedicatory Epistle that would identify him, so there is no certainty that Tysilio actually wrote it. However, it is believed to have come from his monastery at St. Suliac and is therefore attributed to him.

The best surviving Welsh manuscript, representing this work, is held in Jesus College, Oxford, and is known as the *Jesus College MS LXI*. This is a 15th century copy of a 12th century original, and according to Flinders Petrie[165] it represents a body of literature from a much earlier period which is known to have existed in Breton (the language of Brittany) at least as far back as 940. English translations are available, by Peter Roberts[166] and Bill Cooper.[167]

The Chronicle ends with a colophon by Walter of Oxford as follows:

> I, Walter, Archdeacon of Oxford, translated this book from the Welsh into Latin, and in my old age have again translated it from the Latin into Welsh.

Peter Roberts, editor of the 1811 edition which Flinders Petrie was unable to find, adds a footnote as follows:

> Probably because he had given the original Welsh copy to Geoffrey of Monmouth.

In medieval literature, a colophon is sometimes added at the end of a book, to say who wrote it, or where it comes from, and is sometimes in decorative handwriting to distinguish it from the rest of the book. In modern times, we use a title page instead.

Flinders Petrie argued that the original Welsh copy was the "very ancient book" that Geoffrey of Monmouth used to produce his *History of the Kings of Britain*. The argument is based on the comparison of the text with other ancient sources, and particularly Julius Caesar, to show that it is an independent British history, and not derived from other well-known classic works. If this is the case, then there is every reason to suppose that

---

[165] Flinders Petrie, W.M., *Neglected British History*.
[166] Roberts, Peter, Tysilio's *Chronicle*.
[167] Cooper, Bill, *Chronicle of the Early Britons*.

Geoffrey of Monmouth must have used it. Those who are interested in the details of this argument should consult the paper presented by Flinders Petrie, to the British Academy, in 1917. (see note 165).

In addition to the detailed argument, Flinders Petrie expressed his dismay at the difficulty he experienced, finding a copy of Tysilio's Chronicle that he could work on. He knew about the English translation by Peter Roberts, published in 1811, and a second edition in 1862, but in 1917 they had both become so rare that he had to get one of the British Museum copies typed out. When he gave his lecture to the British Academy, he appropriately called it *Neglected British History*. Fortunately, Tysilio's Chronicle is much easier to obtain today because facsimile reprints are available.

Regarding the colophon by Walter of Oxford, the question arises about why he should have gone to the trouble of translating the Latin back into Welsh, when the original Welsh copy already existed? There could be two reasons:

• If the original Welsh copy was indeed the 'very ancient book', used by Geoffrey of Monmouth, it would have been in ancient Welsh or possibly Breton, and Walter might have wanted to produce a copy in the Welsh that was more familiar to him.
• Walter had retired from his duties as an Archdeacon and he might have translated the Latin into Welsh simply for his own pleasure.

Nennius

Nennius was a pupil of Elvodug, bishop of Bangor (the one near Anglesey, not Bangor-is-y-Coed), and he lived on the borders of Mercia. He was concerned about the poor state of Welsh scholarship and the loss of documents that had occurred since the Saxon invasion. The most severe blow was the massacre of the monks at Bangor-is-y-Coed and the destruction of their books.

His most important work was his *Historia Brittonum* (British History), completed about 800. It is not a continuous history, instead it is a collection of fragments from various sources. He begins by saying that he had "*undertaken to write down some extracts that the stupidity of the British cast out; for the scholars of the island had no skill, and set down no record in books*". He uses the word "stupidity", not as an insult, but to mean "lack of knowledge". They had lost their best scholars, and those that remained were disheartened and had lost their desire to work with books.

He made no attempt to prove the authenticity of his sources, some of which were contradictory, but that did not concern him. His primary objective was to preserve what remained of the Welsh literature, and to preserve some oral traditions that had not yet been committed to writing. He describes his objective by saying *"I have therefore made a heap of all that I have found..."*. An English translation is available, by John Morris.[168]

Geoffrey of Monmouth

Geoffrey always associated himself with Monmouth, probably because of his Welsh origins, but he seems to have spent most of his working life elsewhere. From 1129 to 1151 he appears to have been in Oxford, at St. George's College, and he might have been a Canon there. The college came to an end in 1149, and in 1151 he became Bishop Elect of St. Asaph in North Wales. In 1152 he was ordained priest at Westminster, and it is thought that he died in 1155.

He completed his '*Historia Regum Britannie*' (History of the Kings of Britain) in 1136. It was widely distributed and translated into a number of European languages, and it had considerable influence on subsequent historians. It was especially popular in Wales where it became a source of national inspiration.

However, he came in for criticism, because of his claim, in his Dedication to his patron, Robert, Earl of Gloucester, that he had obtained a "very ancient book written in the British language" from Walter, Archdeacon of Oxford, and he had translated it into Latin. He is accused of failing to identify the book, and there have been claims that he was making it all up, although there is plenty of evidence that the ancient book existed, as we have seen from the discussion of Tysilio's Chronicle.

The claim that he didn't identify the book is rather unfair, considering that in those days it was perfectly acceptable to name a book according to who owned it, or where it was held. For example, the Welsh manuscript of Tysilio's Chronicle used to be called the *Book of Basingwerke Abbey*. There were few books in those days, compared with the number of books

---

[168] Morris, J., *Nennius: British History and the Welsh Annals.*

available today, so a generalised description based on ownership would have been adequate. Geoffrey might have thought that the "very ancient book" from "Walter of Oxford" was all that he needed to say.

However, the problem is not just the identification of the book. It is also the claim that he *translated* it. Geoffrey's *History of the Kings of Britain* is larger than Tysilio's Chronicle, it has additional material, but it also has some material missed out. It cannot be considered in any way a translation of Tysilio. Instead, it appears to be a history that uses Tysilio as one of its sources.

So why was Geoffrey claiming to have translated something, and what did he actually mean? Was he being dishonest, or was he just being vague? He could have meant that he had translated his "very ancient book" into Latin, and then used it as source material for his history. But why should he make a translation if Walter of Oxford was already making one, as we have seen from Walter's colophon? The answer to that might be the nature of the book itself. If it was in ancient Welsh, or possibly Breton, it might have been necessary for both Geoffrey and Walter to work on it together, and they were both in Oxford at the time.

Whatever we may say about Geoffrey's claim, there is no way of escaping the fact that he failed to explain himself correctly and left himself open to criticism. This is regrettable, because it has caused some critics to reject the British history altogether, so that Gildas, Nennius and Tysilio have all been consigned to the same rubbish bin. The scarcity of Tysilio, as we have seen, is the reason why Flinders Petrie complained about *Neglected British History*.

A Political Perspective

Although Geoffrey identified his source adequately according to pre-Renaissance standards, it is nevertheless curious that he never mentioned Tysilio, and he never identified Brittany as the place where Walter's "very ancient book" originally came from. The reason for this is possibly because Tysilio was no ordinary monk. He was an absconded prince and a political exile, as we have already seen. Geoffrey might have been anxious to avoid controversy that would jeopardise his position as a Canon of the church, or might embarrass his patron, Robert, Earl of Gloucester.

117

The Good Book of Oxford

Further evidence of the "very ancient book" is provided by Geffrei Gaimar, who was a contemporary of Geoffrey of Monmouth and wrote a poetic book in Anglo-Norman,[169] called *L'Estoire des Engleis*.[170] This was published shortly after Geoffrey of Monmouth's *History of the Kings of Britain* and is complementary to it.

Gaimar ends his poem with an Epilogue which describes his sources, and a number of people who were involved with them. An English translation of the Epilogue is available, by Ian Short.[171]

Gaimar talks about how he obtained a large number of books in English, French and Latin, and he was helped by a noble lady called 'Constance'. He says how she sent to Helmsley for a book belonging to Walter Espec, about the kings of Britain. Robert, Earl of Gloucester had commissioned this book to be translated from the Welsh. He sent the translation to Walter Espec, who lent it to Ralf FitzGilbert, who in turn lent it to his wife, Lady Constance. Since Robert, Earl of Gloucester was Geoffrey of Monmouth's patron, this must be Geoffrey's *History of the Kings of Britain*, written in Latin, or at least a draft version.

Gaimar goes on to say how he had *"previously obtained, be it rightfully or wrongfully, the good book of Oxford which belonged to Archdeacon Walter"*. The term *"rightfully or wrongfully"* suggests that it was a book of great importance, and he had obtained it from Walter, in an effort to speed things up, at a time when other people wanted to see it. It could be an earlier version of Geoffrey of Monmouth's *History of the Kings of Britain*, or it could have been Walter's Latin translation of the "very ancient book" that Geoffrey was using. In any case, it confirms that Geoffrey's source must have existed.

He also mentions the *Winchester History* which came from Washingborough, and it is believed to be the Anglo-Saxon Chronicle, written in English. It is probably an early copy that originated in Winchester but found its way to Washingborough, a town outside of Lincoln which was of some importance during the 12th century. He

---

[169] Anglo-Norman is the Old French language that was used in England after the Norman conquest in 1066, in court circles, schools, universities, parliament etc.
[170] Bell, A., *Geffrei Gaimar: L'Estoire des Engleis*.
[171] Short, I., *Gaimar's Epilogue and Geoffrey of Monmouth's Liber vetustissimus*.

probably also had the Anglo-Saxon Chronicle from Winchester itself.

Gaimar mentions a number of influential people who had supplied him with his sources, and he would have been in serious trouble if any of these sources had never existed. The people are:

- Robert, Earl of Gloucester, the eldest son of Henry I. Although he was illegitimate, he was one of the most powerful men in the land.
- Walter Espec, the founder of Helmsley Castle in Yorkshire. He is thought to have been given his Yorkshire estates by Henry I, to strengthen the Scottish border. He also founded monasteries at Rievaulx and Kirkham in Yorkshire, and Warden in Bedfordshire.
- Ralf FitzGilbert, who lived near Washingborough. He also had estates in Hampshire and was a founder and benefactor of a number of monasteries.
- Lady Constance, the wife of Ralf FitzGilbert.
- Walter, Archdeacon of Oxford.

According to Gaimar, all of these people, except Walter of Oxford, had been in possession of the Latin text that clearly came from Geoffrey of Monmouth. All of them, *including* Walter, would have been implicated in any false claims that Geoffrey had made, about being in possession of a "very ancient book". Walter himself had been in possession of the 'Good Book of Oxford', which is either a translation or derivative of the "very ancient book".

Gaimar was name-dropping all these people in an effort to enhance the credibility of his *L'Estoire des Engleis*, and he would have invited their certain disapproval if he had implicated them in a conspiracy to create fake histories. It is impossible to imagine that any of them would want to tarnish their reputations in that way.

Polydore Vergil

Polydore Vergil, a Roman Catholic priest, was one of the most outspoken critics of Geoffrey of Monmouth, and the British history generally, during the time of Henry VIII. He published his *Anglica Historia* (English History),[172] in 1534, and it had considerable influence. It went through

---

[172] Ellis, H., *Polydore Vergil's English History*.

several editions and became required reading in English schools in 1582, by order of the Privy Council. However, it was not very complementary towards the Welsh, denouncing their entire history with the following words:[173]

> Truly there is nothing more obscure, more uncertain, or unknown than the affairs of the Britons from the beginning.

Obviously this did not please the Welsh, and they began writing rebuttals. One of these, by John Price and Humphrey Lhuyd,[174] denounces Polydore on account of his ignorance of Wales, and they give two examples:

- The Welsh name for Wales has always been 'Cambria'. It was the Saxons who first called it 'Wales', and they called the people and language 'Welsh', meaning 'strange' or 'not understood'. Similarly, there were people in various other places who referred to the French and Italians as those who speak 'Walsh'. Polydore Vergil thought that he was the first to find out the origin of the name of Wales,[175] when in fact it had already been documented by various historians, including Sylvester Giraldus 380 years earlier.

- The Welsh name for Anglesey is 'Môn' and the name for the Isle of Man is 'Manaw'. Polydore Vergil confused the names,[176] and produced his own corrupted version of a story that comes from Cornelius Tacitus.[177] He wrote about an army swimming across the sea to the Isle of Man, when in fact they had only gone across the Menai Strait from the Welsh mainland to Anglesey. This is not just a misprint in Polydore's history. He clearly describes it as an island in the sea between England, Ireland and Scotland, and he says that in ancient times it was possible to go there without ships at low tide.

---

[173] Ellis, *Polydore Vergil*, Book 1, p.33.
[174] Caradoc of Llancerfan, *Historie of Cambria*, Section on *History of Wales* by John Price and Humphrey Lhuyd, pp.xx-xxii.
[175] Ellis, Book 1, p. 12.
[176] Ellis, Book 1, p. 17.
[177] Church & Brodribb, *Tacitus: Annals*, Book 14, para. 29-30.

Polydore Vergil was an Italian priest, living in England. It is easy enough to understand that he could mix up two names that sounded similar in Welsh, but no Welshman would make that mistake and they were right to reject his incompetence. Consider, for example, what it would be like if someone came from China and wrote a history which says that London is the capital of Brittany. We would immediately denounce such a person as incapable of writing British history.

Polydore Vergil was given various appointments in England. In 1502, after his ordination, he was appointed as a sub-collector of Peter's Pence (a contribution to the Pope). He was favoured by Henry VII, who invited him to write a history of England. Henry VIII began to reign in 1509, and Cardinal Wolsey rose to a position of power as the administrator of the affairs of both state and church. By 1515, Vergil had fallen out of favour with Wolsey, probably because he didn't support Wolsey's ambitions, and he spent some time in prison, but he was released and his position was restored. He disliked the confrontation between Henry VIII and the Pope, and he chose a very significant date for the publication of the first edition of his *Anglica Historia*. The year 1534 was the very same year when Parliament passed the Act of Supremacy, declaring Henry to be Supreme Head of the Church of England.

In an early draft of his Epistle Dedicatory to Henry VIII,[178] he says that he was working intensively on his *Anglica Historia* for six years. That means he started working at a leisurely pace, with no great sense of urgency, when Henry VII first asked him to write a history. Then it suddenly became urgent when Henry VIII made up his mind, in 1527, to get rid of his first wife, Katherine of Aragon, and marry Anne Boleyn. The six years of intensive work covers almost the entire period of Henry's confrontation with the Pope.

Polydore might have realised that his days in England were numbered, and he had better get on with it quick while he still had the chance. He might have also felt that the problems between England and Rome were all the fault of the Welsh, because Henry VII had come from Wales and it was always his ambition to establish an independent church, an ambition that he passed on to his son, Henry VIII. Polydore was much

---

[178] Gasquet, F.A., *Polydore Vergil*, TRHS n.s. XVI (1902), 11. Referenced from McKisack, M., *Medieval History in the Tudor Age*, p.100.

too sensible to criticise Henry VIII directly, so it seems that he vented his frustration by denouncing the Welsh history.

He might have also had some objectives that would benefit the church of Rome. By discarding the Welsh history he was, in principle, also discarding the first-century British church that existed long before the arrival of Augustine. However, he was capable of generosity, and we will see on page 168 that he affirms his belief that Joseph of Arimathea came to Glastonbury.

Whatever his motivation, his work was not just for consumption in England. It was written in Latin, for the benefit of his native Italy. He made periodic visits there, and finally returned to his home town of Urbino in 1550.

Chapter 5 - Anglo-Saxon Genealogies

So far, we have looked at the history of the Britons, as far as the Saxon invasion, but who were these people called the Saxons? They came from northern Germany, along the Baltic coast, and they were allied with the Angles so that they became known as the Anglo-Saxons. The Angles came either from Angeln, a district which is now called Schleswig-Holstein, in Germany on the border with Denmark, or from Denmark itself. The Saxons were also allied with the Jutes, who came from the area of northern Denmark known as Jutland.

England is named after the Anglo-Saxons, and the English language has become known as the 'International Language' as it is most widely spoken all over the world. The Scots refer to the English as 'Sassinacs' because they are Saxons.

England is full of Saxon names, including many of the counties. Some of the counties directly reference the Saxons as follows:

Essex	East Saxon
Wessex	West Saxon
Sussex	South Saxon
Middlesex	Middle Saxon

The Saxon royal families in England, Norway, Denmark and Iceland all trace their ancestry back to Woden. Going further back, they all have a common ancestry going back to Sceaf (pronounced "Sheaf") who is thought to be either of the following:

- Japheth, the son of Noah.
- A descendant of Priam, king of Troy.

Anglo-Saxon Descent from Noah

Bill Cooper,[179] has demonstrated the descent of the Anglo-Saxons from Noah, on the basis that Sceaf is Japheth, by comparing six different king

---

[179] Cooper, Bill, *After the Flood*, Chapter 7, *Descent of the Danish and Norwegian Kings*.

lists. Each list has a few names missing, but they are sufficiently complete to be placed alongside each other to give a single comprehensive list, shown in figure 14.

Noe (Noah)
|
Sceaf (Japheth)
|
Bedwig
|
Hwala
|
Hrathra
|
Itermon
|
Heremod
|
Sceldwea
|
Beaw
|
Taetwa
|
Geata
|
Godwulf
|
Fodepald
|
Finn
|
Frithuwulf
|
Freawine
|
Frealaf
|
Frithuwald
|
Woden === Frigg (Frigida)
|
At least 10 sons

Figure 14 -Anglo-Saxon genealogy, from combination list.

The manuscript details are given by Cooper, but the six lists that make up this combination list can be summarised as follows:

- Three lists of Anglo-Saxon origin (Winchester Chronicle, Asserius, and Ethelweard).
- One Danish list (Langebek)
- One Icelandic list (Prose Edda)
- One British list (Nennius 31)

Three of these lists (Winchester Chronicle, Asserius and Langebek) identify Noah as the father of Sceaf (Japheth). Two of the lists (Ethelweard and Prose Edda) omit the name of Noah, but they have Sceaf in the correct position. Nennius omits both of them, as it starts the genealogy only from Geata.

An important observation must be made from the inclusion of Noah in some of the lists and his omission from others. These lists were not made up by medieval monks who were trying to insert the name of Noah into the Saxon genealogies. Otherwise, they would have inserted his name everywhere. The omission of such an illustrious character from some of the lists means that they represent real histories, and they have not been changed for the purposes of convenience.

Woden appears in all the lists, as the king whose name represents the most important of the Saxon gods. He is thought to have lived on the Island of Finn (Fyn) to the east of Jutland in Denmark, during the second century AD.[180] In that case, there is a problem with this genealogy. There are not enough generations to stretch all the way back to Noah, even allowing for the great longevity of the early patriarchs after the flood. We have already seen, on page 66, that there are problems getting from Noah to his great-grandson Dardanus over a period of about nine centuries. If we make the very generous assumption that it's possible, and we also assume that Hwala in the Saxon list is contemporary with Dardanus, then we can assume for the sake of argument that Hwala began his reign in 1480 BC.[181]

---

[180] *Angles in Jutland: from Woden to Cerdic*, <www.medievalhistory.net/page0004.htm>, Oct. 2002.

[181] This is the date when Dardanus began to reign, according to the *Wall Chart of World History* (Hull, E.).

Woden was the 15th generation after Hwala, and if we assume a mid-second century date of AD 150, there are 1630 years from Hwala to Woden. Dividing this by 15 we get 109 years between each generation, which is far too much.

Anglo-Saxon Descent from Priam, King of Troy

The Icelandic Prose Edda[182] contains all the names in the combination list, except Noah, Fodepald, Freawine and Frithuwald. Instead of Noah, there is a line of descent to Sceaf, from Priam, king of Troy, as follows:

```
            Priam, High King of Troy
                      |
   Munon, King of Troy === Troan
                      |
           Tror (Thor) === Sibil (Sif)
                      |
                   Loridi
                      |
                  Einridi
                      |
                 Vingethor
                      |
                 Vingener
                      |
                   Moda
                      |
                   Magi
                      |
              Seskef (Sceaf)
```

Figure 15 -Priam to Sceaf, from Prose Edda.

This genealogy does not in any way deny that Sceaf descended from Noah. We already have the genealogy from Noah to Dardanus (see page 64) and from Dardanus to Priam (see page 92), so we have the descent of Sceaf from Noah after a larger number of generations.

---

[182] Tompsett, Brian, *Directory of Royal Genealogical Data*, University of Hull. Lineage is from Icelandic prose Edda, <www.dcs.hull.ac.uk/cgi-bin/gedlkup/n=royal?royal14277>, Oct. 2002.

The reign of Priam is dated 1220 BC[183] giving 1370 years until the time of Woden (based on the date of AD 150 used earlier). Woden was the 26th generation after Priam, so we have 53 years between generations. Still a bit long by our standards, but much better, and certainly feasible if the great longevity of the early patriarchs continued among the kings of Troy.

Troan, the daughter of Priam, married Munon who was a provincial king of Troy with authority in his own realm, subject to Priam. Their son Tror married Sibil, the author of the well known Sibylline Oracles.

Which One Is Right?

The Prose Edda stands on its own, identifying Priam as the ancestor of Sceaf, while the other chronicles identify Noah as his father, or else they miss out his genealogy altogether. The only thing we can conclude from this is that the Saxons were vaguely aware of their descent from Noah, but they didn't know how far back it was. In that case, we need not be concerned about the number of generations, or which list is right. We just have to accept that Noah appears in the Saxon genealogy.

The most important question raised by the Prose Edda is not the descent from Noah, but the validity of the document itself and the suggestion that the Saxons descended from Troy. We have already seen that the Britons, or at least some of them, came from Troy (subject to the controversy over Geoffrey of Monmouth), and now we have to consider the possibility that both the Britons and the Saxons have the same ancient origin.

Early Saxon History

Viktor Rydberg in his *Teutonic Mythology*[184] gives an account of the early history of the Saxons, based on the Prose Edda and various other sources. He says that the Saxons believe that they are descended from Troy, although we have to consider the popular allegation that the story could have been made up by medieval monks who wanted to denounce the Saxon gods as deified kings, and they might have invented the history to go with it.

---

[183] Hull, E., *Wall Chart of World History*.
[184] Anderson, R.B., *Viktor Rydberg: Teutonic Mythology*.

The question is, how could they succeed in convincing the Saxons that they came from Troy if they never knew anything about it already? The invention of history from nothing is no easy task. It was attempted by Annius of Viterbo, on the basis of documents that could never be found, and he succeeded for a while, but eventually his fraud was discovered and nobody took him seriously any more. The same cannot be said of the Prose Edda which is considered to be a valuable collection of Saxon history, mythology and folklore.

In this case, the best approach is to set aside the arguments about medieval inventions, and present the history as it has been given.

There are two versions of the *Edda*:[185]

- The *Poetic Edda,*[186] or *Elder Edda,* is a collection of 34 mythological and heroic plays, mostly composed during the period AD 800-1200, probably in Iceland or Western Norway. They were collected together in the late 13th century.
- The *Prose Edda,*[187] or *Younger Edda,* was written by Snorri Sturluson, about 1222, as a guide to the poetry of Iceland.

Snorri Sturluson also wrote a saga called the *Heimskringla,*[188] giving the history of Norway to 1177.

Asgard - The Saxon Troy

Rydberg, in his chapter on the *Medieval Migration Sagas,*[189] first considers the *Prose Edda* and *Heimskringla* and deduces the following:

- Asgard, the home of the Norse gods, is the ancient city of Troy.
- Odin (Woden), the chief of the Norse gods, is Priam the High King of

---

[185] Columbia Encyclopaedia, <www.bartleby.com/65/ed/Edda.html>, Oct. 2002.
[186] Bellows, H.A., *The Poetic Edda*; Thorpe, B., *The Edda Of Sæmund The Learned*; <www.northvegr.org/lore/main.html>, Oct. 2002.
[187] Anderson, R.B. , *The Younger Edda. Also called Snorre's Edda, or the Prose Edda;* Brodeur, A.G., *The Prose Edda by Snorri Sturluson*; Young & Sigurdar, *Snorri Sturluson: The Prose Edda*. Anderson & Brodeur translations available at <www.northvegr.org/lore/main.html>, Oct. 2002.
[188] Laing, S., *Snorri Sturluson: Heimskringla,* <www.northvegr.org/lore/heim/>, Oct. 2002.
[189] Anderson, R.B., *Viktor Rydberg: Teutonic Mythology*, Chapter 2, *Medieval Migration Sagas*, <www.hi.is/~eybjorn/ugm/ugm2.html>, Oct. 2002.

Troy. *Note:* The first century king, also called Woden, was probably so named in order to deify himself.

- Odin had twelve men ruling under him as high priests and judges. These are the twelve tributary kings of Troy who ruled under Priam. Twelve languages were spoken, and each king had authority over a different language group. One of these kings was Munon (Mennon or Memnon), who married Troan the daughter of Priam.
- Thor, the son of Odin, is Hector, the son of Priam. There is a generation missing because the Prose Edda identifies Thor is the grandson of Priam, through his daughter Troan. Perhaps it's near enough, or maybe daughters don't count. Thor was fully grown at the age of twelve and he was so strong he could lift twelve bear-skins. He was brought up by foster parents but he killed them and took possession of his foster-father's kingdom of Thracia, which is called Thrudheim. Hector was also the greatest man in the world, in stature and strength.
- The Fenris-Wolf[190] who killed Odin is Pyrrhus, the son of Achilles, who killed Priam.
- The Midgard-Serpent[191] is one of the heroes killed by Hector.
- Ragnarok[192] is the siege of Troy.
- Vidar, who survives Ragnarok, is Aeneas who fled from the burning city of Troy and set up his new kingdom in Italy.

Rydberg continues with a variation of the story, in which Asgard is a new city that was founded after the destruction of Troy. There were two parties that fled from Troy in different directions. One party left under the leadership of Aeneas and founded a new kingdom in Italy. The other

---

[190] The Fenris-Wolf is also a child of Loki. It was very fierce and could not be bound with chains, but was eventually bound with a thin ribbon that had magical powers. There was a prophecy that the wolf would break free at Ragnarok and would devour Odin.

[191] The Midgard-Serpent is a sea monster, a child of the trickster god Loki. The Prose Edda tells a story of how Thor went fishing with a giant called Hymir and he caught the Midgard-Serpent on his hook, using the head of an ox as bait, but Hymir was afraid and he cut the line so that the serpent got away.

[192] Ragnarok is an apocalyptic event in Teutonic mythology, normally associated with the fate of the gods or the end of the world. For further details see page 200.

party, led by Loridi the son of Thor, went to Asialand, between the Caucasus Mountains and the River Tanais which is now called the River Don. It feeds into the Sea of Azov to the north-east of the Black Sea. They founded the new city of Asgard and preserved the old customs of Troy.

Rydberg then considers the work of Saxo Grammaticus (c.1150-c.1220), a Danish historian who wrote 16 books of oral tradition and legends, called the *Historia Danica* (Danish History). The name *Grammaticus*, which means 'learned' was probably bestowed on him after his death. There is a passage from Saxo which describes how Odin used trickery and disguised himself as a female physician to have his way with a princess who had rejected him. This results in his expulsion from the company of the gods, as follows:[193]

> But the gods, whose chief seat was then at Byzantium, (Asgard), seeing that Odin had tarnished the fair name of godhead by divers injuries to its majesty, thought that he ought to be removed from their society.

Asgard, the seat of the gods, is identified as Byzantium[194] which is not far from ancient Troy. Rydberg makes the comment that Saxo was a Euhemerist who considered all the pagan gods to be deified humans, and the gods of Asgard were merely the kings of Troy.

Babylon II

The passage referenced by Rydberg, about the twelve languages and the twelve tributary kings of Troy, is from the Prose Edda.[195] There is a description of creation, the flood, the tower of Babel and the division of the world into three parts, mostly taken from the Bible, then there is a paragraph about Troy as follows:

> Near the middle of the world was built the house and inn, the most famous that has been made, which was called Troy, in the land which we call

---

[193] Elton, O., *The Nine Books of the Danish History of Saxo Grammaticus.* (The first nine of the 16 books). This passage is from Book 3, <sunsite.berkeley.edu/OMACL/DanishHistory/book3.html>, Oct. 2002.
[194] Byzantium was re-named Constantinople by Constantine the Great, and then Istanbul by the Ottoman Muslims.
[195] Anderson, R.B., *The Younger Edda*, Foreword, para.4, <www.northvegr.org/lore/prose2/001_04.html>, Oct. 2002.

Turkey. This city was built much larger than others, with more skill in many ways, at great expense, and with such means as were at hand. There were twelve kingdoms and one overking, and many lands and nations belonged to each kingdom; there were in the city twelve chief languages. Their chiefs have surpassed all men who have been in the world in all heroic things. No scholar who has ever told of these things has ever disputed this fact, and for this reason, that all rulers of the north region trace their ancestors back thither, and place in the number of the gods all who were rulers of the city. Especially do they place Priamos himself in the stead of Odin; nor must that be called wonderful, for Priamos was sprung from Saturn, him whom the north region for a long time believed to be God himself.

This is clearly a description of a cosmopolitan city, a circumstance that is not surprising considering the geography of the region. As the people were scattered from Babylon, speaking their different languages, those who travelled across Turkey towards Greece would reach a narrow land bridge where they would have to assemble at either of two strategic points:

- Byzantium, on the Bosphorus.
- Troy, on the Hellespont.

At each of these points, a narrow stretch of water had to be crossed, and it would have been necessary to set up a ferry service.

Those who arrived at the Hellespont might have had sufficient common culture to enable them to live together, regardless of their languages, so they decided to go no further and built the city of Troy. The city grew and prospered until it was eventually destroyed by the Greeks with their wooden horse. It went up in flames and those who survived were scattered.

Comparing Troy with Babylon, we can see how the city was doomed. It was not possible for people of different language groups to live together at Babylon, and neither was it possible at Troy, at least not for ever. They were destroyed, not by the might of the Greeks, but by cunning and trickery, which must have been that much easier among a population that spoke multiple languages.

Troy can be considered a second Babylon, a place where people stayed and built a great city when they should have travelled further into empty lands.

We have already seen how some of the Italians and then the Britons came from Troy, and now we see that the Saxon and Scandinavian kings came from there also. Annius of Viterbo, who we have considered in Chapter 3, would have us believe that other nations of Europe also came from Troy, and he might have been right, although it was not necessary for him to create forgeries to try and convince us about it. He should have just presented the evidence available to him. It may well be that most of the nations of Europe originated from Troy, or at least some of them, although the detailed knowledge of the events has fallen to the shipwreck of history.

Descendants of Woden

The Saxon genealogy that we have considered so far ends with Woden (the later one, in the second century AD, not the Saxon version of Priam). He had at least ten sons who became kings, or their descendants became kings, in England, Denmark, Norway and Sweden.

The sons whose descendants ruled the English provinces were:

- Wecta (Witta) - Kent. The famous Hengist and Horsa, who arrived in Britain and made way for the other Saxons, were grandsons of Wecta.
- Baeldaeg - Wessex
- Casere - East Anglia
- Seaxnet - Essex
- Waegdaeg - Northumbria
- Wihtlaeg - Mercia
- Winta - Lindsey (Lincolnshire)

Three other sons became Nordic kings:

- Skjöldr - Denmark
- Saemingr - Norway
- Yngvi - Sweden.

The succession of Saxon kings, in the English provinces, is given by Cooper.[196]

---

[196] Cooper, Bill, *After the Flood*, pp.85-86.

Chapter 6 - History of Ireland and Scotland

This chapter is not intended to provide a comprehensive review of the history of Ireland and Scotland. Instead, it focuses on the story of an Egyptian princess called 'Scota' who married a Scythian prince called Gaythelos. They left Egypt shortly after the exodus of Moses and the Israelites, because the land had been devastated by the plagues and they believed that it was cursed. They arrived in Spain and settled there, until Gaythelos died. Their two sons, Hiber and Hymec went to Ireland, but Hymec later returned to Spain. They were called the *'sons of Miletus'* because Gaythelos was surnamed Miletus. Scota also went to Ireland, and some of her company later went to Scotland, naming it after themselves, but Scota herself died and was buried in Ireland.

The name 'Scota' is clearly not an Egyptian name. Instead, it appears to have been given to her by Gaythelos, to identify her with Scythia, or perhaps Greece.

Evidence of an Egyptian presence in the Britain and Ireland is given by Lorraine Evans:[197]

- The skeleton of an adolescent male, believed to be an Egyptian Prince, was found at an ancient hill-fort near the hill of Tara, south of Trim which is not far from Dublin. He was wearing a necklace that came from Egypt, and he was called the Tara Prince and the necklace was called the Tara Necklace. The skeleton was carbon-dated to about 1350 BC.

- An almost identical necklace, believed to be from Egypt, was found on a skeleton at North Molton in Devon.

- Some boats, of Egyptian design, were found buried in the mud on the banks of the Humber at North Ferriby.

- The burial place of Scota is at Glenscota, about five miles south of Tralee in south-west Ireland. It is identified by Donald Watt in his

---

[197] Evans, L., *Kingdom of the Ark.*

1993 edition of Walter Bower's *Scotichronicon*.[198] He says that her grave is *Fert Scota*, and it is called *Glenscoheen, Scotina's Glen* or *Scota's Glen*.

However, before we look at this in detail, we need to look at some of the earlier history of Ireland.

Early History of Ireland

This section of Irish history is taken from *Holinshed's Chronicle*[199] and the *Annals of Clonmacnoise*.[200]

> Ireland long time after the flood lay waste until about the Year after the Creation of the World 1969 and after the flood 313 years in the 21st year of the age of the Patriarch Abraham and also in the first year of the Reign of Semiramis then monarchs of the world in Assyria.
>
> *Annals of Clonmacnoise, pp.12-13.*

After this time, a number of successive colonies arrived in Ireland. They are sometimes thought to be Scythian, descended from Magog, and sometimes thought to be Greek. The Scythians and Greeks lived in close proximity to each other, and there appears to have been some intermarriage. Herodotus[201] mentions a people called the Callippidae, who were 'Scythian Greeks', although it is not possible to say if these are the people who came to Ireland.

The first colony to arrive in Ireland was led by Bartolenus from Morea, and his three sons Languina, Salamis and Ruthurgus. At that time the country was entirely covered in forest, and they cut down trees to make plains. Bartolenus divided the country into four parts, one for each of his sons and one for himself. Their descendants continued after them, so that they ruled the country for about 300 years. However, a colony of giants arrived, of the race of Ham, and began to oppress the people and

---

[198] Watt, D.E.R., *Walter Bower: Scotichronicon*. The burial place of Scota is identified in Vol. 1, editor's note 11, p.112, but it originally comes from Joyce, *Irish Names of Places*, i, 159.
[199] Holinshed's *Chronicle*, Vol. 6 (Ireland), pp.73-76.
[200] Murphy, D., *Annals of Clonmacnoise*.
[201] Godley, A.D., *Herodotus: The Histories*, 4.17.1.

usurp the kingdom. There was a battle between the people of Bartolenus and the giants. The entire population of the giants was slaughtered, but they were never buried. Instead they were left to rot on the ground, causing an infection that killed about 9000 of the people of Bartolenus, almost the entire population, and those that remained left the island by sea.

The next colony to arrive from Scythia (or Greece) was Nemodus[202] and his four sons, Starius, Garbaneles (the prophet), Anuinus and Fergus. Fergus had a son called Brittan the Balde, from whom it is said that the Welsh are descended, in contradiction to their descent from Brutus the Trojan, but we will return to this matter later. The people of Nemodus inhabited Ireland for 216 years, but they were at war against the giants, like their predecessors, and were eventually driven out and went to Syria. These giants, also of the race of Ham, were pirates and they were called Fomores.

The giants took possession of the land, but they were unable to form any kind of government because they were at war against each other. When this became known in Greece, another colony of Scythians, known as the Firbolges, set out to re-possess the land. They were led by five brothers, the sons of Dela, descended from Nemodus, who were called Slanius, Gandius, Sagandus, Gemandius, and Rutheranius. They defeated the giants and drove them out, and according to Holinshed the date was 1252 BC.[203]

They divided the country into five parts, one for each brother, and set up a mere-stone in the middle of the country, to divide it equally, but the brothers were at variance against each other. Slanius, the eldest brother who had the province of Leinster, took some land from the other four,

---

[202] In the *Annals of Clonmacnoise* (Murphy p.14) he is called *Neuie McAgamemnon*.

[203] Holinshed's *Chronicles*, Vol. 6 (Ireland), p.75. The date is given as 2714 AM (Anno Mundi = year of the world from creation). This is converted to 1252 BC by comparison with Vol. 1 (England), p. 443 where the date of the arrival of Brutus in Britain is given as 2850 AM and 1116 BC. Holinshed's date of the flood, although not relevant to this calculation, is given in Vol. 6, p.76. The date of the departure of Gaythelos from his home country is 2436 AM and 780 years after the flood. Therefore the date of the flood is 1656 AM which corresponds to most other Biblical calculations.

encroaching a few miles around the mere-stone. This continued for 30 years, but then Slanius died and was buried in the mountain of Meath. The princes who were subject to him began to fight among each other for his part of the land.

While they were squabbling, another band of Scythians arrived, of the same stock as themselves, descended from Nemodus. They were the Tuatha de Danann, also called Firbolges. They claimed title to the land, and they caused havoc on all sides, with fire and sword, adding to the troubles that were already there.

The Sons of Miletus

The next company of migrants to arrive in Ireland were the sons of Miletus, but first we have to tell the story of Galatheus and Scota. At this point, our main sources of reference are John of Fordun's *Chronicle of the Scottish Nation* and Holinshed's *Chronicle*.

Gaythelos, surnamed Miletus, was a Scythian prince, the son of Neolus, although some say he was Greek. He was probably from a nation of Scythians who passed through Greece, although Keating[204] says they were not Greek, but learned some Greek customs from the Tuatha de Danann and the earlier Firbolges who were in Ireland.

Gaythelos was given no authority in the kingdom, so he raised up a band of youths and rebelled against his father, but he made the people angry and was driven out of the country. He sailed to Egypt where he became distinguished for his courage and daring, and became an ally of Pharaoh. There are different accounts of his exploits. One chronicle says that he fought against the Ethiopians who were ravaging Egypt, while another said he helped Pharaoh to keep Moses and the Israelites under control.

For his valour, and to seal the alliance, Pharaoh gave him his daughter Scota in marriage, so that he became a potential successor to the kingdom.

The dynasty into which he married is described by John of Fordun[205] as follows:

---

[204] Keating, G., *The History of Ireland*, Vol. I, p.237.
[205] Skene, W.F., *John of Fordun: Chronicle of the Scottish Nation*, p.8.

In the seventeenth dynasty, then, reigned the Pharaohs, one of whom, by Commestor called Nephres, promoted Joseph. This Pharaoh, Nephres, died in the thirteenth year of the administration of Joseph. He was succeeded by -
The Pharaoh Amosis, who reigned twenty-five years.
The Pharaoh Chebron, thirteen years.
The Pharaoh Amenophis, twenty-one years.
The Pharaoh Mephres, twenty-two years, in whose ninth year died Joseph.
The Pharaoh Mishpharmotsis, twenty-six years.
The Pharaoh Authomosis, nine years.
Ammenophis, thirty-one years, whose daughter Theremuch, in the twenty-sixth year of his reign, took the infant Moses out of the water, and adopted him as her son; after which this Ammenophis reigned five years.
The Pharaoh Horus, thirty-eight years.
The Pharaoh Accentris, twelve years.
The Pharaoh Athorisis, seven years.
The Pharaoh Chencres, eighteen years. He was swallowed up in the Red Sea, while pursuing the children of Israel. His daughter was Scota, wife of Gaythelos before mentioned.

This list corresponds to the eighteenth dynasty, but not all the kings are included. The 'seventeenth dynasty', mentioned at the beginning, is the one that precedes it.

Lorraine Evans,[206] using the same list from Bower's Scotichronicon,[207] points out that Chencres (Achencres) is the Greek rendering of Akhenaten[208] who reigned for 17 years in the mid-14th century BC - around 1350 BC, and this date corresponds to the Ferriby boats and the necklaces that came from Egypt.

Akhenaten and his queen Nefertiti had six daughters but no sons. All six daughters are accounted for, except Meritaten, the eldest, who mysteriously disappeared. The third daughter, Ankhesenpaaten, married Tutankhamun, an honour that should have been reserved for Meritaten because she was the eldest. The other four daughters died. Evans suggests

---

[206] Evans, L., *Kingdom of the Ark*, pp.27-32.
[207] Watt, D.E.R., *Walter Bower: Scotichronicon*, Vol.1, p.31.
[208] Akhenaten (glory of the Aten) used to be called Amenhotep IV (Amun is content). He built a temple dedicated to Aten, in the first year of his reign. Then in the sixth year of his reign, he changed his name to Akhenaten and abolished the other deities, particularly Amun. For details see *Akhenaten - The Glory of the Aten* <kate.stange.com/egypt/akhenaten.htm>.

that Meritaten must be the missing princess, called Scota, who married Gaythelos.

However, there could be problems with the Egyptian king lists. David Down[209] suggests that the dates have been miscalculated and the Exodus occurred, not in the 18th dynasty, but at the end of the 12th dynasty which more accurately represents a period of slavery followed by plagues. He also suggests that the reign of king Solomon of Israel was during the 18th dynasty of Egypt. Now, it just happens that there is an alternative Gaythelos and Scota story, from the *Annals of Clonmacnoise*,[210] which says that they were in Egypt at the time of King Solomon, not at the time of the Exodus. So it might all work out right in the end, but I will put this matter aside until something more can be known about it, and continue with the rest of the story.

When the Israelites went out of Egypt, Pharaoh was drowned in the Red Sea, together with his army, but Gaythelos stayed behind, refusing to go in pursuit of the innocent Israelites. He should have succeeded Pharaoh as king, but the people rose up against him because they were afraid that they might become subject to foreign tyranny. They gathered their forces, and sent word to Gaythelos, that he should quickly depart from the kingdom.

Gaythelos decided that, although he had a large army, he could not fight against the whole Egyptian people and he had to comply with their demand. He could not go back to his homeland, because of the mischief he had caused there, so he decided to go in search of another kingdom that he could occupy, either by warfare or else by finding an empty land.

Gaythelos and his wife Scota and their company, known as the Miletans, prepared their ships and set off, stopping in many places. They stayed for a while in Numidia, which corresponds approximately to modern Algeria, but they were resisted by the inhabitants. They set off again and sailed through the Pillars of Hercules (Straits of Gibraltar) and arrived at the islands of Gades (Cadiz). According to Holinshed,[211] they went to Lusitania (Portugal). They were resisted by the Spaniards, but Gaythelos had the victory and they were able to make peace. They settled

---

[209] Down, D., *Searching for Moses*, Answers in Genesis, Creation TJ, 15 (1), 2001.

[210] Murphy, D., *Annals of Clonmacnoise*, p.22.

[211] Holinshed's *Chronicle*, Vol. 5 (Scotland), p.34; Vol. 6 (Ireland), p.76-77.

on the River Mondego which runs through Portugal, along the valley to the north of Mount Estrela.

As their numbers increased, they were again at variance with the Spaniards, who were ready to go to war against them. Gaythelos prepared to defend, but the two sides negotiated peace, and the Miletans agreed to move to another region. They went to Galicia, on the north-west coast of Spain, where they built a city called Brigantia, which is now called Coruna. In the process of time, their numbers increased further so that they occupied the whole northern coast of Spain, and they founded the city of Bayonne in Gascony.

An alternative version of the story, from St. Brandan,[212] says that Gaythelos left Egypt, sailed to Spain, and built a tower called Brigancia on the River Hyber. This is thought to be the River Ebro, which emerges into the Mediterranean Sea on the east coast of Spain at Amposta, south of Tarragona. Possibly the Miletans might have gone there, but this is not where he founded Brigantia. The river Ebro is very long, starting at a lake in the Cantabrian Mountains in northern Spain, and running across almost the whole of north-east Spain to the Mediterranean, so it is possible that the Miletans could have been identified with it in some way. However, there is much more certainty about Brigantia in Galicia, so we have to stick with it.

Gaythelos was given the title of a king, and began to reign in Brigantia, and gave laws to the people. He used to sit on a marble stone, shaped like a chair, which he had brought with him from Egypt. It is called the 'Stone of Destiny' and there is a tradition that wherever it is found, the Scots shall reign supreme. It was taken to Ireland, then to Scotland, then to England, and then back to Scotland, and kings were crowned while sitting on it. However, there are some who say that the stone never came from Egypt, and instead it was dragged out of the sea by a prince of the Scots of Spain, called Simon Brech.

As the people multiplied still further, Gaythelos was concerned about further wars with the Spanish, so he sent out explorers in ships. They sailed north and discovered an island, so they explored it, then they returned to Brigantia and brought back the news to Gaythelos. Then he sent out some warlike youths, who rowed around the island and attacked

---

[212] Skene, W.F., *John of Fordun: Chronicle of the Scottish Nation*, p.12.

and killed all that they found, and returned to Brigantia. By this time Gaythelos was in bad health and about to die, and he exhorted his sons, Hiber and Hymec, to go and take possession of the island, so that they could live as free men and not as slaves which would be their inevitable fate if they stayed in Spain.

Hiber and Hymec went to the island, with a fleet, and took possession of it. Some say the island was uninhabited, while others say there were a few people, and others say there were giants. They called it Scotia, after their mother Scota who was there with them, but later it became known as Hibernia, after Hiber, and it gradually changed to Iberland and then Ireland.

When things were set in order, Hiber went back to Brigantia, leaving his brother Hymec in charge of the island. He found his father Gaythelos dead and succeeded him to his kingdom in Spain. The next in line was his son Nonael, and there was a succession of kings for about 240 years, but the nation was molested by the Spaniards who only gave them a small amount of land in the hill country, so they could hardly sustain themselves. Eventually, there was a king called Mycelius, who enabled them to live in peace and freedom, although the land was too small.

In Ireland, Hymec ruled the Scots and the former inhabitants, but failed to unite them as one people, so that there were civil wars. Eventually some of the Scots sent a request to Mycelius, to come and help them. Mycelius welcomed the opportunity to send some of his people, to live among their kinsmen in a spacious land, so he prepared a fleet and sent his three sons, Hermonius, Bartholomus and Hibertus. They easily took possession of the land, restoring order by force or by consent of the inhabitants. Hermonius returned to Spain to join his father, while his two brothers remained in Ireland.

Hermonius succeeded to the kingdom in Spain, and after that there were 19 generations of successors, up to King Fonduf. During that period there was prosperity in Ireland, but it led to contentions which could not be resolved because they were divided into factions and never had a king of all the Scots. They needed a king who was not involved in any of their factions, so they sent a request to King Fonduf, that he should send his son Simon Brech to be king of Ireland, because his valour and fame was known to them. Simon Brech was not the eldest son, nor the heir, but his father loved him more than the others, so he sent him to Ireland with an army, and he also gave him the Stone of Destiny.

Simon Brech subdued the warring factions and was crowned King of Ireland, on the marble chair in 697 BC. He placed the chair in Tara, and many successive kings were crowned upon it. This must have been an important place in the kingdom, for many years earlier, because the remains of the Tara Prince, dated 1350 BC were found there (see page 133).

The successors of Simon Brech were Fandufus, Ethion, Glaucus, Noitafilus, and Rothesay. This Rothesay, before he became king, perceived that the people were becoming too numerous so he transported some of them to the islands that were in ancient times called Ebonides, and then Hebrides. The first island that he possessed was called Rothesay, after himself, but later it was called Bute because St. Brandan had built a booth there, i.e. a shrine. Rothesay returned to Ireland when his father died and became king.

After that, more of the Scots went to the Hebrides, because it was good for breeding cattle, and some of them went to the mainland, to the northern part of Britain, which was called Albion. They settled on the west coast of Albion, which was previously uninhabited, and the date was about 584 BC. They called the place Argathelia, after Gaythelos, but now it is called Argyll.

At this time another Scythian tribe arrived, called Picts, and they wanted to live among the Scots. According to some accounts, the Picts arrived on the north coast of Ireland, and according to others, they arrived in Albion where the Scots had settled. In either case, the outcome was the same. The Scots would not allow the Picts to live among them, but advised them to go to empty lands that were not yet inhabited on the coast of Albion. The Picts complained that they had no women among them, so the Scots agreed to give them their daughters in marriage, on the condition that if there is any doubt about their royal succession, they should choose a king from the female line rather than the male. The Picts agreed, and observed this custom from that time onwards. The intermarriage of Picts and Scots was to be a perpetual alliance between them, so that if necessary they could join together and fight their common enemy, the Britons.

The Picts went off, together with the daughters of the Scots, and settled in whatever empty lands they could find in Albion. Also a larger number of Scots, both men and women, went out from Ireland because of their affection for their daughters, and lived among the Picts. This caused some friction among the Picts and Scots, so that the Picts defined their own boundaries and forbade strangers to come among them. The situation was exacerbated by the Britons who feared that the Picts and Scots together would become too powerful, so they made an alliance with the Picts which turned them against the Scots. Neither the Picts nor Scots could venture on each other's territory, not even to walk along the path, without being killed or taken hostage.

At that time there was a king of the Scots in Ireland, called Ferguhardus, who responded to the situation of his kinsmen in Albion. He sent his son Fergus with an army to help them, and also gave him the Stone of Destiny. Fergus set up his parliament in Argyll, and was crowned upon the Stone of Destiny as the first king of the Scots in Albion, in 327 BC.

He prepared for battle against the Picts and Britons, and when the two armies faced each other, ready for battle, the Picts became aware that their supposed allies, the Britons, intended to hold back and watch the Picts and Scots fight each other, and when both were weakened they would fall upon them and kill them all. The same report was given to Fergus, by someone who fled from the enemy camp and came over to his side. The Picts and Scots held back for a few days, knowing that they were both in danger from the Britons if they should fight each other, and then they had a meeting and renewed the peace that they had made in former times. Then they went to war against the Britons and defeated them, slaughtering most of their army, including their king Coill, and those that remained sent a delegation to make peace. The Picts and Scots consented, and then they held a parliament, and sent out surveyors to divide up the country among them, taking into account the fertility of the soil that would either enlarge or diminish their boundaries.

After that there is a long history where the Picts and Scots were at war against the Britons, Romans or Saxons, and sometimes they were at war against each other. The Pictish nation finally came to an end during the reign of Kenneth, King of the Scots, in AD 839. There was war between the Picts and Scots, and the Picts were almost entirely wiped out. Those that remained fled to England, Norway or Denmark. Kenneth ordered that the Stone of Destiny should be brought from Argyll and he placed it on a raised plot of ground at Scone. From that time onward it was called the 'Stone of Scone'.

In 1296, King Edward I of England took the stone to London and placed it in Westminster Abbey. It remained there until 15th November 1996, when Prime Minister John Major, with the approval of Queen Elizabeth II, sent it back to Scotland where it was placed in Edinburgh Castle.

British and Irish Histories

Earlier in this discussion, on page 135, we saw that the Welsh are supposed to have descended from Brittan the Balde, the son of Nemodus. However, as we have already seen from the British histories, the Britons are supposed to have come with Brutus the Trojan, and were named after him. The Irish histories say one thing, and the British histories say another, so which one do we believe?

It may be that there was an early migration from Ireland, before Brutus arrived, but the question remains, which one of these gave his name to the Britons? To try and answer this question, we have to look at the claims and counter-claims that the Irish and Welsh have made against each other, as each of them tries to write histories that make themselves look good.

We will begin by looking at a fairly typical summary of what the Welsh believe about themselves. Jonathan Davis begins his *History of the Welsh Baptists*[213] with the following lines:

> The Welsh, properly called Cumry, the inhabitants of the Principality of Wales, are generally believed to be the descendants of Gomer, the eldest son of Japheth, who was the eldest son of Noah. The general opinion is, that they landed on the Isle of Britain from France, about three hundred years after the flood.
>
> About eleven hundred years before the Christian era, Brutus and his men emigrated from Troy in Asia, and were cordially received by the Welsh. They soon became one people and spake the same language, which was the Gomeraeg, or Welsh; hence the Welsh people are sometimes called the Ancient Britons.

---

[213] Davis, J., *The History of the Welsh Baptists, from the Year Sixty-Three to the Year One Thousand Seven Hundred and Seventy*, p.5.
Note: The term 'Baptist' in this book is taken to mean all those who practised believer's baptism, from the time of the early church onwards, and is not limited to the post-Reformation Baptists.

About four hundred years before Christ, other emigrants came from Spain, and were permitted by Gwrgan, the Welsh king, to settle in Ireland, among the Ancient Britons, who were in that country already. They also, soon became one people, but have not retained either the Welsh or the Spanish language; for the Irish language, to this day, is a mixture of both.

This history begins with a very early settlement in Britain, not from Ireland, but from France, although it roughly coincides with the arrival of Bartolenus in Ireland, 313 years after the flood (see page 134). It seems likely, therefore, that two groups of people migrated westward at the same time, after the dispersion from Babylon. One group went to Britain and the other to Ireland.

The Welsh are Celtic Gauls, and the Irish are Scythians, and they are descended from Gomer and Magog, the first and second sons of Japheth, but the Scythians are a mixed race. Gomer was the ancestor of the Gauls, while Magog was the ancestor of the Scythians, but Ashchenaz, the eldest son of Gomer, was also the ancestor of a race called Scythians. The two groups of Scythians became assimilated with each other, so that the Scythians are descended partly from Gomer and partly from Magog.[214] In that case, the Scythians and Gauls are related tribes, and this becomes apparent as they never seemed to be far from each other as they migrated across Europe.[215]

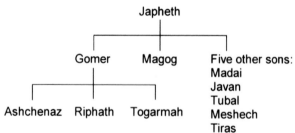

Figure 16 - Family Tree of Gomer, Magog and Ashchenaz

---

[214] Cooper, Bill, *After the Flood*, Appendix 3.
[215] Gaythelos and his company were Scythian, but they lived in Galicia, named after the Gauls. There is another place called Galicia in Poland, not far from Germany which is called 'Ashchenaz' in Hebrew.

Returning to the Irish story of Brittan the Balde, he did not arrive in Wales until at least 300 years after the early Celtic and Scythian migrations, so he cannot be the ancestor of all the Welsh, although his arrival can still be accepted.

The second paragraph from Davis is about Brutus, who we know about, and the third paragraph is a rather demeaning account of the Irish, suggesting that they settled in Ireland only with the consent of the Britons.

We have already seen, on page 98, the story of Gwrgant returning from Denmark and giving permission to a group of migrants from Spain to go to Ireland. This version of the story suggests that Ireland was uninhabited at the time, which is impossible because Gwrgant reigned during the 4th century BC, long after Simon Brech became king of Ireland in 697 BC. Needless to say, the Irish deny the story that they needed permission from the Britons to settle in Ireland.[216]

Davis conveniently side-steps the issue by giving an alternative version of the Gwrgant story. He does not claim that Ireland was uninhabited, instead he says it was inhabited by Britons. It may be possible that some Britons went to Ireland in very early times, but the Irish history says nothing about it.

What is Truth?

In cases where the nations disagree about their histories, it is sometimes almost impossible to know who is telling the truth. All we have is a series of claims and counter-claims, and some historians complain that it is so muddled, it becomes difficult even to understand the concept of truth and error (a problem that Pontius Pilate encountered).[217] They find themselves studying the history of claims and counter-claims, rather than the history itself which is just a vague shadow in the background. However, this should not cause us to become discouraged. We have already seen that behind the Greek Mythology we have the vague shadow of Noah and his family. It would have been very nice if the Greeks had told us the plain facts, without all the embellishments, but we have to accept what they

---

[216] Skene, *John of Fordun: Chronicle of the Scottish Nation*, Vol. 1, pp. 19-20.
[217] John 18:38. Pilate did not deny that Jesus was telling the truth, he had simply lost interest in it.

have given us. All ancient history is like that. You just have to study it, in all its fantastic detail, and you gradually get a 'feel' for what actually happened.

Common Ground

It always helps to look at the things on which histories are agreed, rather than on the things in which they differ, and in this regard there are two important points:

- The British and Irish histories, together with many other histories of the world, are agreed that there was a flood. Many historians date the events of antiquity from the flood onwards, or even from the creation of the world, together with their BC dates. I have not yet found a single example of flood-denial among the ancient historians. Flood-denial began only in relatively recent times, after Lyell's long-age geology and Darwin's theory of evolution, and it is perpetuated by people who think they know better than all our ancient ancestors.

- As the nations spread around the world, their main concern was overpopulation rather than extinction (except for the initial period when the family of Noah came out of the ark). The Miletans went from Portugal to northern Spain, and then migrated to Ireland because their numbers were continually increasing. This is just one example, but the same motivation existed throughout the ancient world. If they migrated because of population growth, then there must have been a time when the population of the world must have been very small. Of course our ancient ancestors would be astonished if they knew about the population we have now, which is sustained by intensive farming and technology.

Chapter 7 - Early Christianity in the British Isles

Christianity is known to have existed in Britain at a very early date, with all probability during the first century AD, and claims a most important Christian heritage with regard to the following events:

- Britain was able to build an 'above-ground' church at Glastonbury while everywhere else in Europe the Christians were meeting in secret because of persecution.
- Britain was the first country in the world to have a Christian king. All the accounts agree that during the second century, King Lucius and all his household became Christians. Many pagan temples were consecrated as places of Christian worship, and Christianity became the official religion of Britain.
- Britain supplied Rome with the Emperor, Constantine the Great, who ordered that Christianity should be the official religion of the entire Empire during the fourth century. Constantine came from York and was British on his mother's side.

The early arrival of Christianity in Britain can be attributed to a number of people, and the facts regarding each of them can be related with a greater or lesser degree of certainty. Some of these stories might seem fanciful, especially to those who are not familiar with them. My purpose in writing this chapter is to relate the histories as they have been handed down to us, so that the reader can decide whether they should be considered true or false.

I have included the history of Christianity in Ireland in this chapter, because it is linked to Christianity in Britain. In particular, St. Patrick, the patron saint of Ireland, came from Britain. Ireland is geographically considered to be part of the 'British Isles', although politically separate from Britain.

To the End of the Earth

After his resurrection, Jesus told the apostles that they would be his witnesses in Jerusalem, Judea, Samaria, and "*to the end of the earth*"

(Acts 1:8, Green's Literal Translation). They were to travel widely, to the limits of the known world, as far as it was physically possible to go. The end of the earth, in the westerly direction, was the Atlantic coast including Britain.

This commandment was made directly to the apostles, not to future generations of their converts, although it obviously applies to them as well.

The history of the early church testifies that they carried out the command, travelling all over the world, and at least one of the eleven, Simon Zelotes, is believed to have come to Britain. There were about 120 people in the upper room altogether before the day of Pentecost and this must have included most, if not all, of the 70 disciples who Jesus had sent around the towns of Israel (Luke 10:1-17). Many of these people are known to have accompanied the apostles on their journeys, and some of them are thought to have reached Britain.

It should be no great surprise that the early followers of Jesus came to Britain, because it was well known to the people of the Middle East at that time, and was an important source of tin that was needed to make bronze.

The Trade Routes

There were two trade routes to Britain from the Mediterranean areas. There was the sea route, used in ancient times by the Phoenicians, and the land route across France that was used later by the Romans.

The Phoenicians used to live in the coastal regions of the Eastern Mediterranean, to the north of Mount Carmel. They were accomplished sailors, and they are known to have been involved in long-distance trade since 1000 BC and possibly much earlier. King Solomon also had a navy, at the time when the Temple was built in Jerusalem, and they worked in collaboration with the Phoenicians, bringing great riches to the land.

> For the king had at sea a navy of Tharshish with the navy of Hiram: once in three years came the navy of Tharshish, bringing gold, and silver, ivory, and apes, and peacocks.
>
> *1 Kings 10:22*

This cargo was obviously obtained from a long distance, because ivory, apes and peacocks were not to be found in the Middle East.

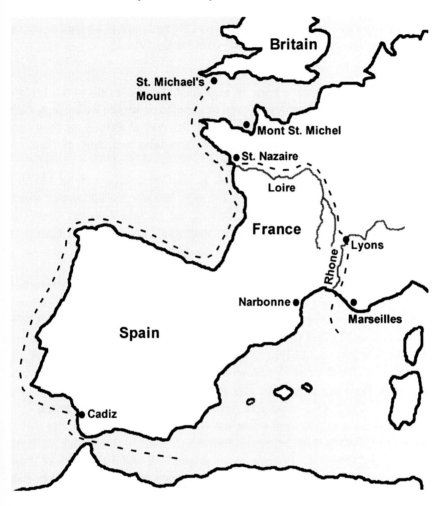

Figure 17 - Trade Routes to Britain

Tharshish (or Tarshish) can be identified with the land of Tartessus, which was the Guadalquivir river basin on the Atlantic coast of Spain just outside the Pillars of Hercules (Straits of Gibraltar). The coastal port was known as Gadir or Gades, but now it is called Cadiz, and it was used by the Phoenicians as a centre of exchange for long distance trade. In addition to the commodities already mentioned, they are known to have traded in iron, tin and lead.

> Tarshish was thy merchant by reason of the multitude of all kind of riches;
> with silver, iron, tin, and lead, they traded in thy fairs.
>
> *Ezekiel 27:12*

Britain is known to have been an important supplier of tin to the Middle East, although the Phoenicians used to guard their wealth by keeping their sources secret. They may have sailed all the way to Britain, or they may have received the goods from Celtic sailors who met them at Cadiz or some other place on the Atlantic coast.

Herodotus,[218] the Greek historian, in his *Persian Wars* about 445 BC, mentioned the "*Cassiterides (Tin Islands), whence the tin comes which we use.*" He never knew how it arrived, but he said it comes "*from the ends of the earth*". The Cassiterides were the Scilly Isles, off the tip of Cornwall, and the name represents tin ore which is called Cassiterite (SnO_2), from the Greek word for tin.

Pytheas of Massalia (Marseilles), a Greek explorer and geographer who flourished about 300 BC, wrote a book called '*On the Ocean*', describing a voyage that he made to Britain and Thule (Iceland). His work is now lost, but we know about his voyage from the Greek historian Polybius (c.200 - c.118 BC) who wrote 40 books of '*Histories*'. Book 34, which includes the description of the voyage, exists only in fragmentary citations from other authors. The relevant paragraphs about Pytheas are from Strabo (c.63BC - c.AD23), the Greek historian and geographer.[219]

Polybius was sceptical about the voyage of Pytheas, claiming that it was pure fiction and he never had the means to carry out such an expedition. Strabo shares some of his scepticism, and if the work of these two critics was all we had to go on, the journey of Pytheas would be like this:

- He walked around Britain on foot, giving it a circumference of 40,000 stadia, which works out at about 4,600 miles. This is 2.7 times

---

[218] Rawlinson, G., *Herodotus: The Persian Wars*, Book 3 - *Thalia*, para.115. <mcadams.posc.mu.edu/txt/herodotus/herodot3.htm>, Oct. 2002.

[219] Paton, W. R., *Polybius: The Histories*. For the fragments of Book 34, see <www.ukans.edu/history/index/europe/ancient_rome/E/Roman/Texts/Polybius/ 34*.html>, Oct. 2002. The sections relating to Pytheas are from Strabo (ii.4.1-3, C 104), (iv.2.1, C 190). See also Jones, H.L., *The Geography of Strabo*.

the distance of 1,700 miles that is obtained by drawing a simple triangle around Britain, and Strabo complains that it is a gross exaggeration. However, he complains about other explorers who can't get their distances right, so Pytheas is no exception. In any case, Pytheas says he walked around Britain on foot, so he might have measured the distances of the actual roads and tracks around the coast.

• He went to Thule (Iceland) where, according to Strabo, he says *"there was no longer any proper land nor sea nor air, but a sort of mixture of all three of the consistency of a jelly-fish in which one can neither walk nor sail, holding everything together, so to speak."*. Then he turned back, presumably because he could go no further. Clearly, this is a description of the fog and ice that he encountered in the region of the Arctic Circle.

• He went to the trading port of Corbilo, now known as St. Nazaire, on the Atlantic coast of France at the Loire Estuary. He asked the local people about Britain, and they gave him much information, but Strabo dismissed the journey as fiction on the grounds that other people had been there and could not learn anything. However, the mere mention of Corbilo is important, as it lies on the overland trading route that was used to transport tin and other commodities through France.

The scepticism of Polybius is understandable, considering that the Greeks knew very little about a place beyond the coast of Europe that was called the *"ends of the earth"*. To them, it was an almost mythical land of mist and darkness, barely inhabitable, and they were astonished that someone should actually go there. Strabo is more difficult to understand, because he lived at the time when Julius Caesar attempted to invade Britain. He was probably following a legacy of institutionalised scepticism that had been left behind by his predecessors.

Diodorus Siculus, the Greek historian from Sicily in the first century BC, took a more progressive approach. He wrote about Britain in his *Bibliothecha Historica*,[220] and he is widely believed to have used the work

---

[220] Diodorus Siculus, *Universal History*, Book V. Quoted from Keyser, J.D., *Joseph of Arimathea and David's Throne in Britain!*

151

of Pytheas as his source. The relevant text is as follows:

> They that inhabit the British Promontory of Belerium [old name for Cornwall], by reason of their converse with merchants, are more civilised and courteous to strangers than the rest. These are the people that make the tin, which with a great deal of care and labour they dig out of the ground; and that being rocky, the metal is mixed with some veins of earth, out of which they melt the metal and then refine it. Then they beat it into four square pieces like a die and carry it to a British isle, near at hand, called Ictis. For at low tide, all being dry between them and the island, they convey over in carts abundance of tin. But there is one thing that is peculiar to these islands which lie between Britain and Europe: for at full sea they appear to be islands, but at low water for a long way they look like so many peninsulas. Hence the merchants transport the tin they buy of the inhabitants of Gaul, and for thirty days' journey they carry it in packs upon horses' backs through Gaul to the mouth of the River Rhone.

Also from Booth's translation[221] we have:

> This tin metal is transported out of Britain into Gaul, the merchants carrying it on horseback through the heart of Celtica to Marseilles and the city called Narbo.

The following observations can be made from these two passages:

- The inhabitants of Cornwall were more hospitable to strangers than "*the rest*", which probably means the Phoenicians who wanted to prevent people from finding out about their sources of tin. In that case, the Phoenicians were not actually involved in the mining and extraction of tin. They were only involved in transporting it by sea. The local inhabitants had no reason to conceal their identity or the location of their mines, and their "*converse with merchants*" means they were always ready to do a deal with someone over the sale of tin.

- The island called "*Ictis*" is believed to be St. Michael's Mount near Penzance. It fits the description exactly because it is an island at high tide, but joins up to the mainland at low tide. The reference to "*the*

---

[221] Diodorus Siculus, translation by G. Booth in 1700, vol.1, p.311. Also from Keyser.

island" suddenly switches to the plural and becomes "*these islands which lie between Britain and Europe*", as if there is more than one of them. There is a very similar island called Mont St. Michel, near Avranches on the north coast of France, which is considered to be the counterpart of St. Michael's Mount. The relationship is ecclesiastical rather than commercial, and apart from this vague allusion from Diodorus Siculus, I have found no other evidence that Mont St. Michel was used for trade. It is better known as a place of religious pilgrimage. St. Michael's Mount in Cornwall was a centre of trade, and the ships could have sailed to any convenient port on the French coast, depending on the final destination of the goods.

• The overland route to the Mediterranean was along the Rhone Valley, although this just describes the end of the journey. The complete journey from Cornwall was first by sea to St. Nazaire on the Atlantic coast at the Loire Estuary (the ancient port of Corbilo that was mentioned by Pytheas). The journey would continue along the Loire Valley and then over a short mountain pass to Lyons, then down the Rhone Valley to the sea.

The journey of thirty days across France might seem arduous by today's standards, but it was worth it, considering the high value of tin and the profits that could be made. Their main concern was security, rather than the length of the journey. If they took the sea route along the Atlantic coast to Cadiz, they would take the risk of running into storms and getting shipwrecked. If they took the overland route they took the risk of getting robbed by bandits.

The sea route was always treacherous, but the land route was made safe by the Romans when they conquered Gaul and established a system of law and order that was essential for travel and commerce. The Romans themselves gained much benefit from the tin trade, because they needed the tin to make weapons, and this was to some extent their motivation for invading Britain.

As we come to the end of this discussion of the trade routes, which has been a digression from my main theme, we come to an important conclusion. Trade is the vehicle that enables the passage of ideas, and just as the merchants travelled from Marseilles to Cornwall, so the apostles passed along the same route, preaching about Jesus and establishing churches.

The Jews in Britain

When Jesus sent out his disciples to go and teach all nations, he meant the Gentiles, and not just the Jews who had been scattered around the world. However, it took them a few years to get used to the idea, and at first they preached only to the Jews. Even when they started preaching to the Gentiles, they would always go to the Jews first when they travelled to any new place, in accordance with the words of the Apostle Paul "*to the Jew first, and also to the Greek*". (Rom. 1:16).

In that case, would they have found any Jews, if they had come to Britain? The answer is probably yes, because there is evidence of an early Jewish community in Devon and Cornwall.

According to Bernard Susser,[222] the following evidence is available:

- A type of smelting oven, made of hard clay in the shape of an inverted cone about 3 feet across and about the same height, was called a "Jew's House". This type of oven was used from the second century BC until about AD 1350. The tin from a Jew's House was known as "Jew's House tin".
- The town immediately on the shore from St. Michael's Mount is called Marazion and it means either 'sight of Zion' or 'bitterness of Zion'. In ancient times it was called 'Market-Jew'. The main street of Penzance, leading to it, is today called 'Market-Jew Street'.
- The village of Menheniot, near Liskeard, derives its name from the Hebrew 'min oniyot' which means 'from ships'.
- The town of Mousehole, pronounced "Muzzle" might derive its name from the Hebrew word 'mazel' which means 'luck'.

There are other Jewish place names around Britain, but Susser believes that the evidence from the pre-Roman period relates mainly to Devon and Cornwall. In that case, how did the Jews arrive in Britain at such an early period? There are a number of possibilities:

- Some of them might have come with the Phoenician sailors, during

---

[222] Susser, B., *The Jews of South-West England*, Chapter 1 - *The early settlement of Jews in Devon and Cornwall*, <www.eclipse.co.uk/exeshul/susser/thesis/thesischapterone.htm>, Oct. 2002.

the time of King Solomon.

- There might have been Jewish traders who imported pottery, glass and oriental wares.
- Some Jewish soldiers may have arrived, in oriental units, with the Roman army.
- Some Jewish slaves might have been brought to Britain after the Bar Kochba uprising in AD 135.

In that case, not only do we have the trade routes that would help the apostles on their journey, but we also have the presence of Jews, which gave them a compelling reason to travel to Britain.

It is even possible that Jesus himself might have gone to Britain, before he began his ministry in Israel, although there is a lack of supporting evidence. If the story is true, it means that when he gave his disciples the command to go to the *"end of the earth"*, he was sending them to a place where he had already been himself.

Glastonbury

Before we move on to the activities of the early Christians in Britain, it is necessary to say something about Glastonbury, about four miles from Wells in Somerset. It was a major centre of Christian worship, reputed to exceed all others in antiquity, including the churches of France and Spain. In pre-Christian times it used to be a centre of Druid worship, but it was converted to Christian worship during the first century. There are various accounts of how Joseph of Arimathea came and built a simple church made of wood and wattle. After that, other churches were built and finally a great Abbey.

Outside the town there is a hill called Glastonbury Tor, which had a spiritual significance for the Druids, but now there is the tower of St. Michael's Church on the summit. On the other side of the town there is 'Wearyall Hill', otherwise known as the 'Wyrral', where Joseph first arrived after his long journey, and it is so named because he felt tired.

The town of Glastonbury is on land which is slightly higher than the surrounding countryside, although it would be an exaggeration to call it a hill. In medieval times the plain was a swamp, and it was possible for ships to sail there from the Bristol Channel at high tide, but since then earthworks have been built and the swamp has been drained.

Glastonbury, including the Tor, the Wyrral and the land where the town and Abbey now stand was known in medieval times as the 'Isle of Avalon' (Isle of Apples) and was so named because the land was good for growing apples. It became associated with King Arthur, whose career is embellished with legend, although he was a real person as we have already seen in the histories. He was buried with his Queen Guinevere at the Abbey, at first on the south side of the Lady Chapel, and then they were moved to the Great Church where their final resting place is now marked by a simple plaque.

The town is also a centre of paganism, which is currently being re-marketed under the title of 'new age', and there are many occult bookshops. There has been a revival of paganism, which is clearly an attempt to fill the spiritual void that has been left by the decline of Christianity and falling church attendances. It can be argued, that if Britain is to be regained as a Christian country, we need to understand the heritage we have lost and re-establish Glastonbury as a centre of Christian worship.

For anyone who is seriously interested in the early history of Christianity in Britain, I would highly recommend a visit to Glastonbury. The ruins of the Abbey are open to visitors, and details are available at the Glastonbury Abbey Web Site.[223]

Jesus and Joseph of Arimathea in Britain

William Blake's well-known patriotic hymn, *Jerusalem*, is otherwise known as the *Glastonbury Hymn*:

> And did those feet, in ancient time,
> Walk upon England's mountains green?
> And was the holy Lamb of God,
> On England's pleasant pastures seen?
> And did the countenance divine,
> Shine forth upon our clouded hills?
> And was Jerusalem builded here,
> Among those dark satanic mills?
> Bring me my bow of burning gold!
> Bring me my arrows of desire!
> Bring me my spear! O clouds unfold!

---

[223] <www.glastonburyabbey.com>, Oct. 2002.

Bring me my chariot of fire!
I will not cease from mental fight,
Nor shall my sword sleep in my hand,
Till we have built Jerusalem
In England's green and pleasant land.

The first verse is based on a tradition that has been perpetuated among the tin miners of Cornwall and passed on from generation to generation. They say that Jesus, when he was a young boy, came to Britain with his great uncle, Joseph of Arimathea, who was in the tin trade and used to make regular visits to the tin mines.

The reference to Jerusalem, in both the first and second verses, is about the church at Glastonbury, which was the first church to be built in Britain. It is thought by some to have been built by Jesus himself, although it is more likely to have been built by Joseph during a subsequent visit after the crucifixion. In that case, the militarism of the second verse might refer to the protection given by king Arviragus, who donated the land on which the church was built. Otherwise, the "arrows of desire" and "mental fight" could just be an expression of the determination required to build a church on a former Druid site.

It is difficult to determine whether the Cornish tradition is based on a memory of actual events, or whether it is based on conjecture derived from the following:

- Joseph must have been a close relative of Jesus, otherwise he would not have been able to go to Pontius Pilate after the crucifixion and ask for the body. Seaman[224] refers to some sources which say that Joseph of Arimathea was the younger brother of the father of Mary, the mother of Jesus. Morgan[225] says the same thing, but he is unsure of his sources and refers to them vaguely as "Eastern tradition". In that case, we have to be satisfied that Joseph of Arimathea was closely related to Jesus but the exact relationship is uncertain.

- The Gospels make no mention of Joseph, the husband of Mary, after Jesus had been to Jerusalem at the age of twelve, so it seems that he

---

[224] Seaman, *The Dawn of Christianity in the West*, p.35, referring to: Harl. MSS 38-59, f.193b, (British Museum); MS.20 (Jesus College, Cambridge).
[225] Morgan, pp.138-139, footnote.

must have died. In that case, Joseph of Arimathea might have taken responsibility for the family from that point onward, and he could have taken Jesus on business trips abroad.

- There is abundant evidence, as we shall see on page 161, that Joseph of Arimathea came to Britain after the crucifixion and resurrection of Jesus and built the church at Glastonbury. He travelled through France, along the route that was used by the tin trade, and he might have learned something about the trade, although we cannot be certain of his active involvement.

- We know that Joseph of Arimathea was wealthy (Matt. 27:57), and if he was involved in the tin trade, this would be how he gained his wealth.

- If Joseph was transporting tin from Cornwall to the Middle East, he would have sailed in ships for all or part of the journey, depending on his route. In that case, Jesus would have been very useful as a ship's carpenter.

We therefore have a story that is feasible, but is based on circumstances that do not tell us anything definite. There is a lack of supporting evidence, and we have to decide for ourselves whether or not we can believe the Cornish traditions on this matter.

Jesus at Glastonbury

Now we turn to the notion that Jesus went to Glastonbury on one of his tin mining trips, and built a church there, or at least a dwelling-place for himself that was later converted into a church. We have the following quotation from William of Malmesbury,[226] attributed to St. Augustine:

> There is on the confines of Western Britain a certain royal island, called in the ancient speech Glastonia, marked out by broad boundaries, girt round with waters rich in fish, and stagnant rivers, fitted for many uses of human indigence, but dedicated to the most sacred of deities.
>
> In it the earliest Angles, neophytes of the Catholic Rule, God guiding them, found a church, not built by art of man, they say, but prepared by God

---

[226] Lomax, *William of Malmesbury*, p.5.

himself for the salvation of mankind, which church the Heavenly Builder Himself declared - by many miracles and many mysteries of healing - he had consecrated to Himself and to Holy Mary, Mother of God. [227]

This description of a church *"prepared by God himself"* is an obvious allusion to the presence of Jesus although he is not mentioned by name. Morgan[228] gives an alternative version which uses the word *"Christ"*, and he gives his own opinion on the matter. He acknowledges widespread support for the arrival of Joseph, after the resurrection, but he denounces as superstition the notion that Jesus was ever there.

Of the general truth of the Arimathean mission there have been numerous supporters. No author, indeed, who has taken due pains to examine its evidences, rejects its main facts. "We dare not deny," writes the caustic Fuller, "the substance of the story." Bishop Godwin, in his quaint style, writes, "The testimonies of Joseph of Arimathea's coming here are so many, so clear, and so pregnant, as an indifferent man cannot but discern there is something in it."[229] Archbishop Usher defends it with his usual display of erudition, and with unusual vehemency of manner, as if the honour of ecclesiatical Britain rested on its truth. The reader will form his own judgement.

For our part, we cast aside the addenda and crescenda, the legends, poems, marvels which after ages, monk, troubadour, and historian piled high and gorgeously on the original foundation. That foundation must indeed have originally possessed no mean strength, depth, and solidity, to bear the immense superstructure which medieval superstition and literature emulated each other in erecting above the simple tomb of the Arimathean senator in the Avalon isle. This superstition was rising tide-high in the time of Augustine, AD 600. "In the western confines of Britain," he writes to the Pope, "there is a certain royal island of large extent, surrounded by water, abounding in all the beauties of nature and necessaries of life. In it the first neophytes of the catholic law, God beforehand acquainting them, found a church constructed by no human art, but by the hands of Christ Himself, for the salvation of His people. The Almighty has made it manifest by many

---

[227] The deification of Mary was obviously well established in the Roman Catholic church at the time of Augustine, although the Bible contradicts it with the statement that Mary was in need of a Saviour. (Luke 1:46-47).
[228] Morgan, pp.142-143.
[229] Godwin's *Catalogue of Bishops*, Praesul., p.11, referenced by Morgan, p.142.

miracles and mysterious visitations that He continues to watch over it as sacred to Himself, and to Mary the mother of God."[230]

William of Malmesbury, probably aware of some of the problems with this, gives a number of other accounts. During the time of King Lucius in the second century, when Phagan (Faganus) and Deruvian (Damicanus) came from Rome and went around the country preaching, they came to Glastonbury. He continues as follows:[231]

> There, God leading them, they found an old church, built, as it was said, by the hands of Christ's disciples, and prepared by God Himself for the salvation of souls, which church the Heavenly Builder Himself showed to be consecrated by many miraculous deeds and many mysteries of healing.

This gives a more feasible story, that the disciples built the church and God placed his blessing upon it by many acts of healing. Perhaps from this we can learn something of what the "church" actually consists of. It isn't a building, it's a congregation. The disciples constructed the building, and Jesus was there, although not in body, giving his blessing to the congregation.

Then he writes:[232]

> ... St. Philip the Apostle coming into France with a host of disciples, sent twelve of them into Britain to preach, and that there - taught by revelation - constructed the said chapel, which the Son of God afterwards dedicated to the honour of His Mother ...

In this version, the disciples constructed the building according to divine instructions, rather like the Israelites setting up the tabernacle in the wilderness.

Then he writes:[233]

> ... "the Church of Glastonbury was not made by hands of men, but the disciples of Christ, sent by St. Philip the Apostle, themselves built it,"...

---

[230] Epistolae ad Gregorium Papam, referenced by Morgan, p.143.
[231] Lomax, *William of Malmesbury*, p.8.
[232] Lomax, p.9.
[233] Lomax, p.11.

In this version, the disciples appear rather pompously as if they were different from ordinary men, but it probably means that they didn't hire local labour for a job they could do themselves, since it was a simple building made of wood and wattle.

So we see that there are a number of ways of interpreting Augustine's assertion that Jesus built the church at Glastonbury. The first century church that we see in the New Testament had no interest in the construction of fine buildings, and the old wattle church at Glastonbury was little more than just a shelter from the rain. By the time Augustine arrived, during the late 6th century, the word "church" had come to mean "building" and he could easily have written his account based on a misunderstanding of earlier material.

Certainly Jesus has always been at Glastonbury, but from the sources available to us we have to conclude that he was never there in the flesh.

Joseph in Britain after the Resurrection

Now that we have looked at the speculative notion of Jesus and Joseph of Arimathea coming to Britain, on a tin trade visit, we can look at the more substantive history of Joseph coming after the resurrection, together with other disciples, on an evangelistic mission.

During the early days of the church in Jerusalem, there was persecution of the believers so that they were scattered abroad throughout Judea and Samaria, and they preached the word wherever they went, but the Apostles remained behind. (Acts 8:1-4). We are then told that those who were scattered went as far as Phoenicia, Cyprus and Antioch, and there were believers in Antioch who had come from Cyprus and Cyrene, preaching to the Greeks. (Acts 11:19-20). Cyrene is in Libya, and some of these people might have been in Jerusalem on the day of Pentecost when Peter preached his first sermon (Acts 2:10).

We have a picture of a community that is mobile even in normal circumstances, travelling long distances to attend the festivals in Jerusalem, and they would not hesitate to travel during times of persecution.

Seaman[234] tells the story of how Joseph and his family and companions left Jerusalem in AD 35 and went to Caesarea where Philip

---

[234] Seaman, pp. 18-32, 42-45.

the evangelist was living. They prepared a ship and set sail for Marseilles, then they travelled across France up the Rhone Valley and crossed the channel to Britain. They arrived in AD 36 and went to Glastonbury where they set up a place of worship.

Morgan refers to a Vatican manuscript from Baronius[235] describing the events of AD 35 as follows:

> The manuscript records that in this year Lazarus, Maria Magdalene, Martha, her handmaiden Marcella, Maximin a disciple, Joseph the Decurion[236] of Arimathea, against all of whom the Jewish people had special reasons of enmity, were exposed to the sea in a vessel without sails or oars. The vessel drifted finally to Marseilles, and they were saved. From Marseilles Joseph and his company passed into Britain, and after preaching the Gospel there, died.

This account is essentially the same as the story told by Seaman, except that it does not allow time for them to prepare the boat. Instead, it says they were dumped in the boat and pushed out to sea, with the obvious expectation that either they would perish, or else they would drift to a distant place and not come back.

If they drifted all the way to Marseilles and survived the journey, it would be nothing short of a miracle. However, there is a more practical solution. They are thought to have stopped in Cyprus, just a short distance off the coast of Lebanon. They could have reached it by ripping a few timbers off the boat and using them as paddles, or by other acts of inventiveness, and once in Cyprus they could have fitted out the boat properly. It is also possible that they drifted to Caesarea, far enough away from Jerusalem to be safe for a while, and then we take up the story as it is related by Seaman.

Baronius gives us the names of the occupants of the boat, and considering the traditions that developed on their journey, there appears to have been more of them.

---

[235] Baronius, *Ecclesiastical Annals*, ad annum 35. See Morgan, pp. 139-140.

[236] A *Decurion* is a person in charge of a group of ten, or a head of ten families. It is possible that Joseph of Arimathea was the head of a family group that included the family of Jesus, or there might have been ten people in the boat altogether. Seaman (p.4) says that *Decurio* is a coveted title, given to him by the Romans.

Some of the traditions, related by Seaman, are as follows:

- Lazarus, who Jesus raised from the dead, is celebrated in Larnaca, Cyprus, where he was a priest for seven years. He is also believed to have been the first bishop of Marseilles.

- Mary Jacobé (mother of James and John), Mary Salome and Sara their black servant are celebrated in a town on the coast near Marseilles called *Les Saintes-Maries-de-la-Mer* which means *Mary's from the sea.* It is also known as *Bouches-du-Rhone.* These three women stayed in the town, and black Sara became patroness of the gypsies.

- Trophimus, who accompanied Paul on his journeys,[237] is celebrated in the cathedral at Arles where there is a statue in his honour. This is only about 20 miles inland, up the Rhone Valley, and Trophimus might have stayed there to be near his companions in the area of Marseilles.

- Martha, the practical housekeeper from Bethany, is celebrated at Tarascon, also in the same region, for getting rid of a monster, possibly a crocodile. Alternatively, the monster might represent demon possession or an illness, and Martha saved the people from it with a work of healing.

Joseph and his remaining companions continued their journey across France, then sailed across the Channel and landed at Falmouth. Then they set sail again and went up the Bristol Channel, and through the marshes to Glastonbury. King Arviragus was a pagan and showed no interest in converting to Christianity, but he recognised that Joseph and his companions had come a long way and only wished to live a modest lifestyle, so he donated twelve hides of land to them, to set up their Christian community at Glastonbury.[238] A hide of land is about 120 acres, or perhaps slightly more, so that the total area is more than two square miles and would enclose the entire modern-day town of Glastonbury.

---

[237] Acts 20:4, 21:29, 2 Tim. 4:20.
[238] Lomax, *William of Malmesbury*, pp. 3,62.

There is a clear reference to this plot of land in the Domesday Book:[239]

> The Domus Dei, in the great monastery of Glastingbury, called the Secret of the Lord. This Glastingbury church possesses, in its own villa, xii. hides of land which have never paid tax.

We have already seen that the first church in Britain was built by the disciples, and not by Jesus himself. We have also seen the account of Baronius who describes this early band of disciples as *"Joseph and his company"* as if Joseph was their leader. His status as leader of the group is affirmed by other authors, as we shall see, and he is also credited with building the church.

William of Malmesbury[240] describes the construction of the church as follows:

> ... they, quick to obey the Divine precepts, completed a certain chapel according to what had been shown them, fashioning its walls below, circular-wise, of twisted twigs...

The description goes no further, but this is sufficient to identify the building as a simple wood-framed wattle church, in the style of the wattle huts found in the area. The wattle church has long since perished, and in the 12th century it was replaced by St. Mary's Chapel which still stands among the ruins of Glastonbury Abbey.

Date of Joseph's Arrival

The very early date of AD 36, for the arrival of Joseph in Britain, is not universally accepted. There are arguments in favour of a later date of AD 63, but first we will look at further evidence of the early date, which can be deduced from the following paragraph from Gildas:[241]

> Meanwhile these islands, stiff with cold and frost, and in a distant region of the world, remote from the visible sun, received the beams of light, that is, the holy precepts of Christ, the true Sun, showing to the whole world his

---

[239] Morgan, pp. 145-146.
[240] Lomax, *William of Malmesbury*, p.4.
[241] Giles, J.A., *Six Old English Chronicles, Gildas: The Ruin of Britain*, par.8.

splendour, not only from the temporal firmament, but from the height of heaven, which surpasses every thing temporal, at the latter part, as we know, of the reign of Tiberius Caesar, by whom his religion was propagated without impediment, and death threatened to those who interfered with its professors.

Tiberius became Emperor in AD 14 and died on 16 March AD 37 according to the Roman history.[242] In that case, the most likely time of Joseph's arrival would be the summer of AD 36 when conditions were favourable for the journey across the Channel. There is a good correspondence with the account of Baronius, allowing one year for the journey since they set off in AD 35.

The date is affirmed, according to Morgan,[243] by a number of other historians, some of whom also affirm that Joseph of Arimathea was first to have preached Christ in Britain.

Morgan,[244] says that Joseph died in AD 76, and Maelgwyn of Llandaff (c.AD 450),[245] the uncle of St. David, says that he was buried at Glastonbury, together with two white silver vessels filled with the blood and sweat of Jesus.

The later date of AD 63 is supported by William of Malmesbury,[246] who says that Joseph was in France with the Apostle Philip, before he came to Britain. He mentions the persecution of the early church in Jerusalem, and the martyrdom of Stephen, and the believers being scattered around the world, but he says nothing of the journey by boat to Marseilles and along the trade route to Britain. Instead he describes the situation as follows:

Whilst, therefore, this storm of persecution was raging, the scattered believers penetrated into divers kingdoms of the earth, chosen by the Lord for Himself, to bring the word of salvation to the nations. Now St. Philip, as Frechulpus[247] testifieth in his second book, chapter iv, coming into the

---

[242] Birley, A.R., *Tacitus: Agricola and Germany*, Chronological Table, p.xlvi.
[243] Morgan, p.140.
[244] Morgan, p.144.
[245] Maelgwyn of Llandaff. See Morgan p.138.
[246] Lomax, *William of Malmesbury*, p.2.
[247] Bishop of Lisieux in the 9th century, wrote *Phillipus Gallias*. Referenced by Lomax p.2.

country of the Franks to preach, converted many to the faith, and baptized them. Therefore, working to spread Christ's Word, he chose twelve from among his disciples, and sent them into Britain to bring thither the good news of the Word of Life, and to preach the Incarnation of Jesus Christ, after he had most devoutly spread his right hand over each.

Their leader, it is said, was Philip's dearest friend, Joseph of Arimathea, who buried the Lord.

Coming therefore into Britain sixty-three years from the Incarnation of the Lord, and fifteen from the Assumption of Blessed Mary, they began faithfully to preach the faith of Christ.

This passage raises a question about the age of Joseph. If he was the great uncle of Jesus, he must have been very old when he arrived in Britain in AD 63. However, we only know that he was a close relative of Jesus, not necessarily his great uncle, so this need not concern us. The so-called "Assumption of Blessed Mary" is a Roman Catholic belief that Mary ascended into heaven, but it appears in this passage only as a date-marker, not as a part of the story.

There is a problem with the early date of AD 36 because Arviragus, who gave the twelve hides of land to Joseph, was not king at that time. The date of the Claudian campaign, when Arviragus succeeded his brother Guiderius, was AD 43 (see page 100). However, there is a possible solution. Morgan,[248] says that Arviragus was Duke of Cornwall before he became king. We already know, from page 99, that his grandfather Teneuvan was too young to succeed Lud, so his uncle Caswallon took the kingdom instead, but he gave Cornwall to Teneuvan. When Caswallon died, Teneuvan succeeded him, and this would have left the dukedom of Cornwall empty. In that case, Cornwall would have been given to each successive heir who was next in line to be king, and it would have eventually fallen into the hands of Arviragus. According to Morgan, this is exactly what happened. He says that when Guiderius became king, Arviragus was given Cornwall, which was a royal dukedom under British laws. The dukedom of Cornwall has, for a long time, included land in the West Country, far outside of Cornwall itself, and if that was the case at the time of Arviragus, he might have been able to give some land to Joseph.

---

[248] Morgan, p.95.

The Holy Thorn

There is a local legend at Glastonbury, that when Joseph and his party arrived, they climbed a hill, a short distance to the east of Glastonbury Tor. They were feeling quite tired at the end of their long journey, so they called it '*Wearyall Hill*', and it became known as the '*Wyrral*'. Joseph thrust his staff into the ground and it budded, and although this might seem like a fanciful tale, it is quite feasible that he brought a tree cutting with him from Israel and planted it in the soil.

The original tree was cut down by a Puritan fanatic during the reign of Queen Elizabeth I (1558-1603), but cuttings had been made, and descendants of the original tree are growing in Glastonbury and elsewhere. One of these is in the Abbey grounds, and another at the spot where the original tree stood on Wearyall Hill. They are collectively known as the Holy Thorn trees and they blossom twice a year in May and December.

The tradition of Joseph and the Holy Thorn is thought to be the origin of the Christmas tree, although the observance of Christmas did not begin until the fourth century and Joseph would have known nothing of it.

The Holy Grail

There is also a legend that Joseph brought with him the communion cup which Jesus used at the Last Supper, and he buried it near Glastonbury Tor, possibly by a spring called the Chalice Well. It became known as the 'Holy Grail' and is associated with the legends of King Arthur and the knights of the round table.

The British history attributed to Tysilio[249] says nothing about the Holy Grail, or even the round table, and these aspects of the Arthurian legend have to be dismissed as a later invention. It is feasible that Joseph might have brought the communion cup with him, but it would not be the jewel-studded chalice of the Arthurian legends. Instead it would be a very ordinary looking wooden cup.

---

[249] Roberts, Tysilio's *Chronicle*.

Antiquity of the British Church

Setting aside the legends, and returning to matters that can be known with greater certainty, we know that Glastonbury has for a long time been considered the mother-church of Britain, and was probably the first church in all the world, or at least in Western Europe, to be built with the approval of a king. Many famous missionaries have resided there, and according to Smithett Lewis,[250] these have included St. Patrick, St. David, St. Aidan, St. Cuthbert, St. Ninian, St. Brendan, St. Bride of Kildare, St. Dunstan and St. Columba.

The British church has a claim to antiquity that exceeds all other churches, and this is acknowledged even among those who owe their allegiance to Rome. The matter was stated by Cardinal Pole, Archbishop of Canterbury during the 16th century, in a combined assembly of the Lords and Commons at the Great Chamber in Whitehall, London.[251]

> The See Apostolic from whence I come hath a special respect to this realm above all others, and not without cause, seeing that God Himself, as it were, by providence hath given to this realm prerogative of nobility above all others, which to make it plain unto you, it is to be considered that this island first of all islands received the light of Christ's religion.

Even Polydore Vergil, who dismisses the British history as "uncertain and unknown" (see page 120), affirms that Joseph of Arimathea came to Britain.[252]

> At which time[253] that same Joseph, (as the Evangelist Matthew witnesses was born in the city Arimathea, and buried Christ's body), whether it were by chance, or of purpose, or at the appointment of God, with no small company came into Britain, whereas both he and his fellowship preaching the word of God and sincere sect of Christ, many were trained to true piety, and being endued with the right saving health were baptised. These men, surely inspired with the holy ghost, obtaining of the king a little ground to inhabit, near unto the town named Wells, or not above four miles distant, did sow the

---

[250] Lewis, Smithett, *Joseph of Arimathea at Glastonbury*, referenced by Seaman, p.47.
[251] Seaman, pp.45-46.
[252] Ellis, *Polydore Vergil*, Book 2, p.74.
[253] The time of Arviragus.

seed of our new religion, where at this day a gorgeous church, and fair monastery of religious men of the order of Saint Benet,[254] called Glastonbury. These were the first principles of Christian faith in Britain, ... For Gildas witnesses, that from the very first divulgation of the holy gospel, Britain most desirously embraced the same.

In addition to this, there were four Church councils in the 15th century[255] all affirming the antiquity of the British church:

> ... the Churches of France and Spain must yield in points of antiquity and precedence to that of Britain as the latter Church was founded by Joseph of Arimathea immediately after the passion of Christ.

Simon Zelotes in Britain

Simon Zelotes was one of the twelve disciples of Jesus (Matt. 10:4, Mark 3:18, Luke 6:15). He was called the 'Canaanite' because he came from Cana in Galilee, and he was also called 'Zelotes' in Greek because the Hebrew 'qana' means 'zealous'. He was with the disciples in the upper room, before the day of Pentecost (Acts 1:13) and after that there is no mention of him in the Bible. However, his name lives up to his reputation, because he literally obeyed the Lord's command to go "*to the end of the earth*".

Morgan[256] says that Simon Zelotes came to Britain, after Joseph of Arimathea. He gives a list of people who all came in succession, first Joseph, then Simon Zelotes, then Aristobulus, then possibly the Apostle Paul. This last name might come as a surprise, but as I said earlier, I am just relating the histories as they have been given, and the reader can decide which of them are true.

---

[254] St. Benedict (c.480-547). Obviously there were no Benedictine monks at the time of Joseph of Arimathea, but they must have taken over the Abbey some time later.
[255] The Councils of Pisa 1409, Constance 1417, Sienna 1424 and Basle 1434. See Khalaf, S., *Britain, Phoenicia's Secret Treasure*.
[256] Morgan, p.129.

Dorotheus, Bishop of Tyre during the reigns of Diocletian and Constantius, wrote the following, about AD 300:[257]

> Simon Zelotes traversed all Mauritania, and the regions of the Africans, preaching Christ. He was at last crucified, slain, and buried in Britain.

Nicephorus (c.758-829) was a Greek Orthodox theologian and historian, and patriarch of Constantinople. He wrote:[258]

> Simon born in Cana of Galilee, who for his fervent affection for his Master and great zeal that he showed by all means to the Gospel, was surnamed Zelotes, having received the Holy Ghost from above, travelled through Egypt and Africa, then through Mauritania and all Libya, preaching the Gospel. And the same doctrine he taught to the Occidental Sea[259] and the Isles called Brittania.

Baronius[260] records the martyrdom of Simon Zelotes in his 'Ecclesiastical History' for AD 44, so this must be the year of his death. In that case, he might have met up with Joseph of Arimathea in France in AD 36 and travelled with him to Britain, or he might have gone there slightly afterwards.

The Silurian Royal Family in Rome

The Silures were a powerful Celtic tribe in South Wales, and they had a chief called Caradoc (Caractacus) who fought against the Romans, within his own domain, while Arviragus was holding out against them elsewhere (see page 100). It is thought that he was a cousin of Arviragus, but it is not known for sure.

Caractacus had a number of children, including a son called Lyn (Linus) and a daughter called Gladys (Claudia). He was the son of Bran, and the grandson of Llyr who is sometimes referred to as "King Leir"

---

[257] Dorotheus, Synod de Apostol.; Synopsis ad Sim. Zelot. See Morgan p.151.
[258] Seaman, p.73.
[259] *Occidental* means 'to the west' and is associated with the setting of the sun. In this case the *Occidental Sea* probably means the Atlantic coastline of Western Europe.
[260] Seaman, p.73.

although he is not the King Leir of Shakespeare fame who lived much earlier and is dated by Cooper as 861 BC.[261]

This family is noted for the following achievements:

- Claudia married a Roman Senator, Rufus Pudens. They both became Christians and were involved in the early church in Rome.

- Linus became the second Bishop of Rome after St. Peter.[262]

- Bran is reputed to be the first British royal convert, and is known as "Bran the Blessed".

The family tree, based on a chart by Morgan,[263] is as follows:

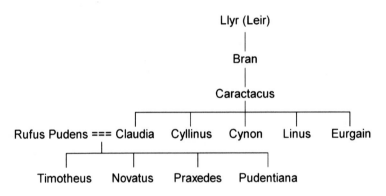

Figure 18 - Family of Claudia

Caractacus made his last stand against the Romans, in AD 50 or 51, on a hill called Caer Caradoc at Church Stretton in Shropshire. The battle was lost, and Caractacus fled to the north to take refuge with Queen Cartimandua, but she promptly betrayed him to the Romans. Some of the

---

[261] Cooper, *After the Flood*, Appendix 7.

[262] There is no reason to doubt that Peter was the first bishop of Rome, although this does not justify the so-called 'Apostolic Succession'. The word 'Apostle' means an ambassador who is specifically sent out by someone as a representative. Peter was an Apostle because he was sent out by Jesus Christ. Linus was not an apostle, he was only a Bishop.

[263] Morgan, p.192.

family of Caractacus, including his wife and his daughter Claudia, were also captured, and they were taken to Rome in chains and paraded through the city. Caractacus did not become fearful, but conducted himself with dignity and defiance. He was taken to the Senate, where he made a speech in front of the Emperor Claudius is as follows:[264]

> Had my moderation in prosperity been equal to my noble birth and fortune, I should have entered this city as your friend rather than as your captive; and you would not have disdained to receive, under a treaty of peace, a king descended from illustrious ancestors and ruling many nations. My present lot is as glorious to you as it is degrading to myself. I had men and horses, arms and wealth. What wonder if I parted with them reluctantly? If you Romans choose to lord it over the world, does it follow that the world is to accept slavery? Were I to have been at once delivered up as a prisoner, neither my fall nor your triumph would have become famous. My punishment would be followed by oblivion, whereas, if you save my life, I shall be an everlasting memorial of your clemency.

Claudius was impressed by his speech, and his bravery even when taken captive, and he pardoned Caractacus and all his family. However, it was not just the conduct of Caractacus that won the day. It is likely that their pardon had already been decided in advance. Claudius was anxious to make peace with the Britons, because he knew the fierce reputation of the Silurians who were still capable of resistance and might take up arms again if they heard that their chief had been mistreated. He also wanted to show the people of Rome that he was capable of clemency, as they were getting tired of seeing every defeated king get executed.

After their pardon, the family lived in a large residence called the "Pallatium Britannicum" (British Palace), which was either given to them, or paid for out of their tributes to Rome. However, some restrictions were placed upon them. The life of Caractacus was spared, on condition that he never takes up arms against Rome again. He was given seven years of free custody in Rome, together with his father Bran who was kept as a hostage. Caractacus and Bran both returned to Britain, but not at the same time. Caractacus is thought to have returned in AD 58, but

---

[264] Tacitus *Annals*, XII,37. See Church & Brodribb, *The Complete Works of Tacitus.*

Morgan[265] suggests that Bran might have gone back earlier. The family was at peace with the Romans, and even intermarried with them. Claudia married a Roman senator called Rufus Pudens, and they both became Christians. Her brother Linus, who is thought to have arrived in Rome later when things had quietened down, also became a Christian and was appointed by the Apostle Paul as Bishop of Rome. All three of them, Rufus Pudens, Linus and Claudia are mentioned by the Apostle Paul.

> Do thy diligence to come before winter. Eubolus greeteth thee, and Pudens, and Linus, and Claudia, and all the brethren.
>
> *2 Tim. 4:21*

To see them mentioned together in this way means they are all closely associated with each other, and Paul is obviously referring to members of the same family.

It is also very likely that the "hired house" where Paul spent two years receiving visitors (Acts 28:30) was the British Palace where Pudens and Claudia lived. This was the period of Paul's first imprisonment (Acts 28:16), but it was actually house arrest with a limited amount of freedom, and it was during the time of the Emperor Nero. It could well have been the intervention of Rufus Pudens, in his capacity as a Senator, that enabled him to live there without being imprisoned altogether.

Paul was released from his house arrest and went on another journey, but then the persecution became more severe. The whole family became martyrs, except Claudia, and the four children were canonised as saints. On the site of the British Palace, in the Via Urbana, there is now a church called St. Pudentia. There is an inscription saying that this was the house of "Sanctus Pudens" in which many martyrs were buried by Pudentiana and Praxedes.

Morgan,[266] gives the following details:

• November 26, AD 90. Martyrdom of Linus, the brother of Claudia, in Rome.

---

[265] Morgan, p.156. See also pp.118,157-158 where the 7-year periods of residence are specified for Caractacus and Bran. Clearly in the case of Bran it is just an approximate figure.

[266] Morgan, pp.196-197.

- May 17, AD 96. Martyrdom of Rufus Pudens in Rome.
- AD 97. Claudia died a natural death in the province of Samnium, in central southern Italy. Davis[267] says she went to Britain in AD 63 and was a successful evangelist, and this does not necessarily contradict Morgan, as Britain was her home country and she might have gone for a visit.
- May 17, AD 107. Martyrdom of Pudentiana in Rome, on the anniversary of the martyrdom of her father Rufus Pudens.
- June 20, AD 139. Martyrdom of Novatus in Rome.
- August 22, year unknown, but after Novatus. Martyrdom of Timotheus in Rome, aged about 90, after returning from a trip to Britain. His companion Marcus was also martyred.
- September 21, year unknown, but same year as Timotheus. Martyrdom of Praxedes in Rome.

In each case the day of a martyrdom is remembered, even if the year is forgotten, because they celebrated the anniversaries of their martyrs every year. They called it the 'natal day'[268] as if a martyrdom was like a birthday. The only person with the day missing from this list of deaths is Claudia, because she was not a martyr.

Aristobulus in Britain

When Paul was in Corinth, during his third missionary journey, he wrote to the church in Rome as follows: (Rom. 16:10)

Salute them which are of Aristobulus' household.

Aristobulus was a grandson of Herod the Great, according to the New Bible Commentary.[269] He was also the father-in-law of St. Peter, according to Morgan.[270] We know that Peter was married because the healing of his wife is described in Matt. 8:14-15.

---

[267] Davis, J., *History of the Welsh Baptists*, p.7.
[268] Morgan, p.196, says that the natal day of a martyr is the day of his martyrdom.
[269] Davidson, F., *The New Bible Commentary*, p.965, (Rom. 16:10).
[270] Morgan, p.153.

Clearly, Aristobulus himself was absent from Rome when Paul wrote his epistle, so where was he? The answer comes from Dorotheus (c.300):[271]

> Aristobulus, who is mentioned by the Apostle in his Epistle to the Romans, was made bishop in Britain.

The Greek Martyrologies[272] describe his mission in more detail, and identify him as one of the seventy disciples who had been sent out during the ministry of Jesus. (Luke 10:1-17)

> Aristobulus was one of the seventy disciples, and a follower of St. Paul the Apostle, along with whom he preached the Gospel to the whole world, and ministered to him. He was chosen by St. Paul to be the missionary bishop to the land of Britain, inhabited by a very warlike and fierce race. By them he was often scourged, and repeatedly dragged as a criminal through their towns, yet he converted many of them to Christianity. He was there martyred, after he had built churches and ordained deacons and priests for the island.

His rough treatment by the Britons, and his eventual martyrdom, was probably because he was a Roman, and therefore identified with the enemy, as much as for his Christian ministry.

Haleca, Bishop of Augusta[273] describes him as follows:

> The memory of many martyrs is celebrated by the Britons, especially that of St. Aristobulus, one of the seventy disciples.

Adonis Martyrologia (March 17)[274] says:

> Natal day of Aristobulus, Bishop of Britain, brother of St. Barnabas the Apostle, by whom he was ordained bishop. He was sent to Britain, where, after preaching the truth of Christ and forming a Church, he received martyrdom.

---

[271] Synopsis ad Aristobolum. See Morgan p.153.
[272] Greek Men., ad 15 March. See Morgan p.153.
[273] Halecae Fragmenta in Martyr. See Morgan p.153.
[274] In Diem Martii 17. See Morgan pp.153-154.

The term "brother of St. Barnabas" probably means a spiritual relationship rather than a physical one.

There are two questions arising from Haleca and Adonis Martyrologia:

- If the martyrdom of Aristobulus on March 17th is celebrated above all others, as Haleca suggests, why have we forgotten it?
- If Aristobulus was ordained as a bishop, by St. Barnabas, does it mean that St. Barnabas also came to Britain?

The British Achau, or Genealogies of the Saints of Britain, according to Morgan[275] says:

> These came with Bran the Blessed from Rome to Britain – Arwystli Hen (*Senex*), Ilid, Cyndaw, men of Israel; Maw, or Manaw, son of Arwystli Hen.

The name 'Arwystli' is identified with 'Aristobulus', and 'Hen' means 'old'. If Aristobulus was the father-in-law of St. Peter, as Morgan suggests, he would have been quite old when he went to Britain. The title *Senex* is a mark of respect for his age. Morgan continues with the suggestion that the district of Arwystli in Powys,[276] around Llanidloes, is named after Aristobulus.

We have already seen that Bran was a hostage in Rome, with his son Caractacus who was given seven years of free custody. Caractacus is not in this list of people travelling with Bran, and this is why Morgan thinks that Bran was released earlier.

In that case, Aristobulus went to Britain in AD 58 or slightly earlier, and this matches up with the date of Paul's letter to the Romans. He wrote the letter from Corinth, shortly before his journey to Jerusalem where he was taken prisoner and sent to Rome. The earliest and latest possible dates for his trip to Jerusalem are AD 56 and 59, so there is time for the departure of Aristobulus to Britain.

---

[275] Achau Saint Prydain. See Morgan p.154.
[276] At the time of Morgan, Arwystli was in Montgomeryshire, but the boundaries have changed.

The Apostle Paul in Britain

The journeys of the Apostle Paul are documented in detail in the book of Acts, and further information about his movements can be obtained from the letters he wrote to the churches.

On his third missionary journey, he was in Greece (Acts 20:2) visiting the church at Corinth. From there he wrote to the church in Rome about how he intended to go to Spain, but he would visit Rome on the way. (Rom. 15:24). However, he didn't go directly to Rome. Instead he went in the opposite direction to Jerusalem, because he wanted to be there for Pentecost. (Acts 20:16). His intention was to go from Jerusalem to Rome, but it didn't turn out the way he expected. He was arrested in Jerusalem and taken to Rome as a prisoner, where he was held under house arrest for two years, but he was able to receive visitors (Acts 28:30).

At this point the book of Acts comes to an end, but the story continues. He was released from his imprisonment and was able to travel for a few years, before he was finally taken prisoner again and beheaded. The chronology of the last few years of his life are as follows:[277]

- AD 60-62. Paul was under house arrest in Rome. He wrote some of his letters to the churches during that time, including two letters where he wrote about his expectation of imminent release. He wrote to the Philippians saying he hopes to come and see them shortly. (Phil. 2:24). He also wrote to Philemon, who was at Colosse in Asia Minor, asking him to prepare a room because he was hoping to be there soon. (Phm. 22).
- AD 62. Paul was released and went on another journey, although some of his destinations are uncertain.[278] He wrote his first letter to

---

[277] The dates are from Davidson, *The New Bible Commentary*, pp.70, 938, 1063.

[278] The places where the books of 1 & 2 Timothy and Titus were written are taken from the subscriptions at the end of the respective books, in the King James Authorised Version. These are not authoritative, and do not come from the original text, but they exist in some manuscripts. They cannot be relied upon unless confirmed from elsewhere. However, we can at least say that Laodicea and Nicopolis are feasible destinations on Paul's journey to Crete, and we can be

Timothy, possibly from Laodicea, quite close to Ephesus where Timothy was living. He also wrote his letter to Titus, possibly from Nicopolis, on the border between Macedonia and Thracia, not far from Phillipi. He must have been to Crete and was on his return journey, because he said he had left Titus in Crete. (Tit. 1:5). The first letter to Timothy, and the letter to Titus, were probably both written in AD 64.

- AD 66 approximately. Paul was taken prisoner again in Rome and brought before Nero. He wrote his second letter to Timothy, in AD 66 or 67, and mentioned his imminent martyrdom (2 Tim 4:6-8).
- He was beheaded in AD 67 or 68, and according to Morgan[279] his martyrdom was at Aquae Salviae in the Ostian Road, near Rome.

His possible itinerary, according to these letters, was Rome, Ephesus, Laodicea, Colosse, Cyprus, Nicopolis, Phillipi, and then back to Rome as a prisoner. However, since there are at least four years available for this journey, there would be plenty of time for his intended visit to Spain. He could have set off from Rome and travelled west to Spain, then travelled east towards Asia Minor and Cyprus. While in Spain, there would have been time for a visit to Britain, but is there any evidence that he actually did so?

Yes there is. Theodoret (AD 435), Bishop of Cyropolis writes:[280]

Paul, liberated from his first captivity at Rome, preached the Gospel to the Britons and others in the West. Our fishermen and publicans not only persuaded the Romans and their tributaries to acknowledge the Crucified and His laws, but the Britons also and the Cimbri (Cymry).

Also in his commentary on 2 Tim. 4:16 he writes:[281]

When Paul was sent by Festus on his appeal to Rome, he travelled, after being acquitted, into Spain, and thence extended his excursions into other countries, and to the islands surrounded by the sea.

---

more certain that 2 Timothy was written in Rome because Paul was expecting his imminent martyrdom.
[279] Morgan, p.202.
[280] Theodoret, De Civ. Graec. Off., lib ix. See Morgan, p.188.
[281] Morgan, p.188.

The journey to Spain, and possibly to Britain, and then back to the Mediterranean area might be called Paul's fourth missionary journey, but why is it not recorded in the book of Acts? Luke, who wrote the book of Acts, was in Rome at the time of Paul's imprisonment. He says that Paul was under house arrest for two years, which means he was released after that time, but he says nothing about where Paul went after his release. The obvious conclusion is that Paul left quickly on his westward journey and Luke lost track of him.

Although the journey to Britain might seem like a long way, it is actually not very far, according to the standards of Paul or any other of the apostles. We have to remember that Paul was in Corinth when he wrote to the Romans, saying that he would visit them on his way to Spain. However, he went to Jerusalem first, with the intention of going to Rome and then Spain. The total length of his intended journey, from Corinth to Jerusalem, then to Rome and to Spain, is about the same as the distance from Corinth to Iceland, as the crow flies.

Lucius, The First Christian King In All The World

We have already seen, on page 163, how Arviragus gave a plot of land to Joseph of Arimathea to build a church at Glastonbury. Lucius, the first Christian king, is descended from him as follows:

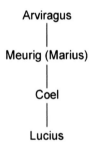

Arviragus
|
Meurig (Marius)
|
Coel
|
Lucius

Figure 19 - Arviragus to Lucius, from Tysilio's Chronicle[282]

---

[282] This genealogy comes from Tysilio's *Chronicle*, (Roberts, pp.89-90), but we have to ignore a footnote suggesting that Meurig, with the article prefixed, becomes y-Veurig and then Arviragus. There is no widespread support for Roberts in this matter. The genealogy in the main text of Tysilio is supported by

Arviragus, Meurig and Coel were all pagans, but Lucius became a Christian.[283] According to Tysilio,[284] Lucius wanted to know more about the faith, so he sent to Eleutherius, the Bishop of Rome, asking for people to come and teach him. Eleutherius sent two learned men, Fagan (Faganus) and Dyvan (Damicanus). They preached the faith to Lucius, and he was baptised, together with "all his subjects" which probably means his household and all those present at his court. Then he consecrated the pagan temples, converting them to places of Christian worship. There were thirty 'Sacerdotal Presidencies' and three superior ones in London, York and Caerleon on Uske (near Newport). This structure already existed among the pagans, and he converted the entire structure to Christianity, appointing Bishops in the smaller regions and Archbishops in the three major centres. Geoffrey of Monmouth calls them *Flamens* and *Archflamens.*[285]

Jonathan Davis[286] says that Faganus and Damicanus were Britons, but they had gone to Rome for training, and were then sent back to Britain as Christian ministers.

According to the *Liber Pontificalis*,[287] the date when Lucius sent to Rome for teachers was about AD 180. He was the first British King to become a Christian, and as far as it is possible to determine, he was the first Christian King in all the world.

Polydore Vergil (Ellis, pp.74,81-82) and Holinshed (v.1, p.199). There are some alternative genealogies: William of Malmesbury (Lomax, p.62) says that Lucius was the brother of Coel. The *Triads of the Isle of Britain*, say that Lucius was the son of Coel, the son of Cyllinus, the son of Caractacus, (see Morgan, pp.158,192).

[283] Lomax, *William of Malmesbury*, pp. 3, 62-63.
[284] Roberts, Tysilio's *Chronicle*, p.90.
[285] Thorpe, *Geoffrey of Monmouth*, p.125.
[286] Davis, *History of the Welsh Baptists*, p.7.
[287] *Liber Pontificalis*, referenced by Cooper, *Chronicle of the Early Britons*, footnote 284.

Emperor Diocletian and the Persecution of Christians

Diocletian became Roman Emperor in AD 284. He was preoccupied with the affairs of the Eastern Empire, and in 285 he appointed Maximian as his co-emperor with authority over the Western Empire based in Rome. Diocletian was the senior emperor, known as the 'Augustus', meaning 'revered one', a title that was first given to Octavius in 23 BC. His co-emperor Maximian was called 'Caesar' which means 'heir to the throne'. In the Roman Republic, the person considered most suitable was appointed Caesar, and was not necessarily the Emperor's son.

In AD 286, Dioclesian promoted Maximian to the rank of Augustus, but still maintained a veto over his decisions.

In AD 293, he established the 'Tetrarchy' or 'rule of four'. The two Augusti in the east and west each had his own Caesar who assisted by ruling part of the territory. He also doubled the number of provinces to 100, and he created 13 regional authorities, called 'dioceses' to oversee them. Each 'diocese' was governed by a 'Vicarius'.

This structure gave a lot of authority to Diocletian and Maximian, but to increase their authority still further they deified themselves. Diocletian was called 'son of Jupiter' and Maximian was called 'son of Hercules'.

In AD 303, Diocletian ordered the destruction of all churches and scriptures within the empire. All Christian clergy were expected to offer sacrifices to the Roman gods, or else they would be thrown in prison. In AD 304 it became even worse. All Christians who refused to sacrifice to the Roman gods would be executed. Maximian came to Britain, to implement the persecution, and it was during this time that Alban was beheaded, at the town of Verulamium, which later became known as St. Albans. However, Diocletian became seriously ill during the same year, and in 305 he abdicated the throne, forcing Maximian reluctantly to do the same.

Constantine, the First Christian Emperor

We have already seen, on page 102, how king Coel (not to be confused with the earlier king Coel, son of Meurig) reigned in Britain after the Diocletian persecution. His daughter Helen married a Roman Senator called Constantius Chlorus and they had a son called Constantine who conquered Rome, and subsequently conquered the Eastern Empire so that he became known as "Constantine the Great".

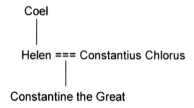

Figure 20 - Coel to Constantine the Great

Constantine was recognised by his troops as the new Augustus of the Western Empire, in AD 306 when his father Constantius Chlorus died in York. However, his position was disputed until 312 when he defeated Maxentius, the son of Maximian, at the Battle of Milvian Bridge. Constantine claimed that, during the night before the battle, he had seen the '*chi-ro*', the sign of the cross, shining above the sun. He ordered his soldiers to paint the symbol on their shields, and then they defeated the numerically superior army of Maxentius. They drove them back over the bridge and it collapsed under them.

This victory persuaded Constantine to become a Christian, because he believed that the Christian God had given him the Western Empire. He considered this to be a divine appointment, and the empire would be secure as long as he did whatever was necessary for the benefit of the church. He ordered that all persecution of Christians should cease.

Constantine appointed Bassianus as his Caesar of the Western Empire, but Bassianus rebelled against him. Constantine discovered that the rebellion had been instigated by Licinius, the Augustus of the Eastern Empire and went to war against him. After some indecisive battles and a truce, Constantine finally defeated Licinius in 324 and became the sole ruler of the Empire, so that he was called "Constantine the Great".

He declared that Christianity was the official religion of the empire, and in AD 325 he summoned the bishops of the east and west to a religious council in Nicaea, where the '*Nicene Creed*' was defined.

For some time before Constantine, each successive emperor had been given the title of 'pontifex maximus', meaning 'high priest'. It was the highest religious office of Roman paganism, and enabled the emperor to officiate at state religious occasions. When Constantine inherited the title, it became the highest religious office of Christianity.

After a while, Constantine became dissatisfied with Rome as his seat of government and sought another capital city elsewhere. After going to a number of different places, he finally settled on the ancient city of Byzantium and called it Constantinople. This turned out to be a good move, because in 476 the Western Empire collapsed, but the Eastern Empire continued for almost another thousand years and became known as the Byzantine Empire. When the Western Empire collapsed, the title of 'pontifex maximus' was transferred to the Pope and has remained there ever since.

Constantine had a distorted view of Christianity, which had more to do with the power of his empire than the salvation of the soul, and he didn't even get baptised until he was on his death bed in AD 337. While the cessation of persecution was a welcome relief for Christians, the church had become institutionalised and lost its early vitality. The succession of popes became less like priests and more like religious emperors, with power over the kings of Europe, as if they had inherited the authority of the fallen Roman Empire.

The Pelagian Heresy

At Bangor-is-y-Coed, otherwise known as Bangor-on-Dee near Wrexham, there was a monastery which was a major seat of learning. One of the monks, called Morgan, became an abbot, and about AD 380 he went to Italy and changed his name to Pelagius. He made himself famous by preaching a doctrine which became known as the "Pelagian Heresy". He maintained that salvation is not entirely the work of the grace of God within the believer, but it also depends on free choice, so that the person must work together with God, and is at perfect liberty to accept salvation or else reject it and perish forever. This doctrine is now known as "Arminianism", and the alternative doctrine which emphasises the grace of God is called "Calvinism".

Some of his followers emphasised human effort more than Pelagius himself, so that the grace of God became a matter of diminished importance. The doctrine was spread, mainly by a preacher called Agricola and his travelling companions. They taught the true faith at first, and then when they had gained people's trust they would introduce the heresy. At the same time Britain was being attacked by the Picts, Irish, French and Saxons, and many Christians were martyred by the pagans (so persecution continued even after the time of Constantine). The British church became so distressed that they sent to the French church for help, and they responded by sending two bishops called Garmon and Lupus, who opposed Agricola and restored the Christians to the true faith. The story of these events is given by Theophilus Evans.[288]

Christianity in Ireland and Scotland

As Christianity spread throughout Britain, it reached Scotland, but it is not known for certain how it first came to Ireland. There are some who say that the Apostle James, the son of Zebedee went there with some of his companions. Others say that the Queen of Ireland was converted by a Pictish woman who was her servant, and then the Queen converted her husband, and together they converted the whole of Ireland.

Paladius

According to Holinshed,[289] Pope Celestine was concerned about the spread of the Pelagian heresy in Britain, and the lack of religious instruction in Ireland. He consecrated Paladius,[290] Archdeacon of Rome, as Bishop and sent him out as a missionary. It is not certain whether Paladius went to Britain or Ireland first, but he arrived in Britain in AD 423 and was quite successful in opposing the Pelagian heresy in the southern part of the country. Then he went to Scotland, where he received some opposition from the prelates, but he was persuasive and won them over, restoring many people to the faith, and in 431 they appointed him as chief apostle of the Scots. At some stage during his ministry, he went to the northern part of Ireland, but he had to flee for his life and went to the Scottish islands.

The Annals of Clonmacnoise[291] give a different story, saying that Paladius went to Leinster and converted five parishes to Christianity,

---

[288] Roberts, G., *Theophilus Evans: A View of The Primitive Ages*, pp.175-184.
[289] Holinshed's *Chronicles*, Vol. 1, p.562, Vol. 6, p.83.
[290] The resemblance of 'Paladius' to 'Pelagian' appears to be coincidence.
[291] Murphy, *Annals of Clonmacnoise*, p.65.

although this is a small number compared with the subsequent ministry of St. Patrick.

St. Patrick

Patrick was born in Britain, probably on the border between England and Scotland, and was brought up as a Christian. At the age of 16 he was captured by a band of pirates led by 'Niall of the Nine Hostages', so called because he had taken captives from nine countries. Patrick was taken to Ireland and sold as a slave. He learned the language perfectly and always had in mind the desire to bring the gospel to Ireland, as he saw the lack of spirituality in the land.

After six years of slavery, he redeemed himself with a piece of gold that he found under a clod of earth that the swine had turned up. He went to the monastery at Auxerre in France and studied for 40 years, then at the age of 62 he went to Rome with letters from the French bishops, commending him to Pope Celestine. He told Celestine of his desire to evangelise Ireland. Celestine responded by investing him as archbishop and primate of the whole of Ireland, and sent him there with a few disciples, in the year 432.

First he went to King Laigerius, to try and persuade him to become a Christian, and during the discussion he picked up a shamrock off the ground, explaining that it had one stem but three leaves, representing the Holy Trinity. Laigerius did not become a Christian, but he permitted the gospel to be preached. According to Holinshed,[292] Patrick and his followers travelled all over the land for 30 years, preaching and founding churches and monasteries, and appointing priests and bishops, then he spent another 30 years in Armagh, in the monasteries he had founded, and he died at the age of 122. However, his great longevity is not universally accepted.

Papal Authority

Both Paladius and Patrick were sent to their respective destinations with the authority of the Pope, and were given high ecclesiatical office before they set out on their journeys. Patrick was appointed as archbishop and

---

[292] Holinshed's *Chronicles*, Vol. 6, p.85.

prelate of all Ireland, even though he had only been there as a slave, and he had been away from the country for 40 years. When he arrived in Ireland, he had to introduce himself to the king, as if he was unknown.

This is in marked contrast to the evangelisation of Britain, where Claudia and possibly many other Britons had learned the gospel from the early church in Rome, and came to Britain preaching and teaching, apparently without any ecclesiastic appointment. It is not known how King Lucius first learned about the faith during the second century, but we can be certain that there were Christians in Britain at that time. Lucius sent to the Pope for teachers, because he wanted to learn the faith more perfectly and he knew that Rome was a centre of Christian learning. The Pope responded by sending Faganus and Damicanus, and they came humbly as teachers, not as Papal authority figures.

The evangelisation of Ireland occurred later than in Britain, when the church of Rome had become more institutionalised, and has always regarded the Pope and his appointed clergy as authority figures. However, this does not mean that the Roman Catholic Church was preaching salvation by works or submission to the church. The primary purpose of sending out Paladius was to oppose the Pelagian heresy, so the Roman Catholic Church was obviously preaching salvation by faith at that time.

St. Columba

St. Columba was born in Ireland in 521, of royal descent, and according to Bowden[293] he was the great-grandson of Niall who had taken St. Patrick captive. He studied at Moville and then Leinster and was ordained, and then he spent 15 years preaching and setting up places of worship and learning at Derry, Durrow and Kells. However, he was involved in a family feud and was excommunicated for his part in a battle where 3000 people were killed. He left Ireland at about 563 with twelve of his disciples and went to Iona, a small remote island off the coast of Scotland. They set up a monastery there, which served as a base for preaching Christianity to the Picts, and hence to Scotland.

St. Columba is credited with bringing Christianity to Scotland, although as we have already seen, Paladius had already been there, and

---

[293] Bowden, M., *True Science Agrees With The Bible*, p.143, referring to d'Aubigney, *The Reformation in England*, p.27.

before Paladius there was a corrupted form of Christianity that had been infected with the Pelagian heresy. It can be said with greater certainty that Christianity became much more widespread in Scotland through the ministry of St. Columba.

St. Augustine

We have already seen, on page 109, how Augustine came to England in AD 596, sent by Pope Gregory. At that time the Britons, Scots, Picts and Irish had all been evangelised, but the Britons had been driven into Wales by the invading Saxons, who were pagan, leaving the whole of England unevangelised. Augustine came to preach Christianity to the Saxons, but he had a disagreement with the Britons which ended with the slaughter of 1200 monks. We will follow the story, as it is told by Theophilus Evans.[294]

Augustine's Christianity was not the pure faith that the Britons had learned from the beginning. Instead it was corrupted with the following superstitions and practices.

- Praying to the saints.

- The invention of a place called Purgatory, where people would wait before they go to either Heaven or Hell.

- Priests were forbidden to marry, although the practice had not become universal.

- The Bishop of Rome, otherwise known as the Pope, claimed authority over all other bishops in Christendom, although he had not attained his full power at the time but had taken the first step towards his exaltation.

- They mixed salt with the water in baptism.

- Images were introduced into the churches, although they had not yet fully observed the practice of bowing down to them.

- They taught that every piece of wood or stone in the shape of a cross had power to perform miracles.

---

[294] Roberts, G., *Theophilus Evans: A View of the Primitive Ages*, pp.197-207.

Augustine successfully converted the Saxons to his version of Christianity, and as a reward, the Pope appointed him as archbishop of Britain. However, the Britons would not submit to him, because of his superstitions, and also because he had an arrogant and pompous demeanour.

He invited the British bishops to a meeting and asked them to recognise the Pope as the head of the church world-wide, and himself as the archbishop of all Britain. Dynawt, the abbot of Bangor-is-y-Coed replied as follows:

> "Be it known to you, that we consider it our duty to obey and submit to the church of God, to the pope of Rome, and to every good Christian - to love them in every situation and in all circumstances, and to assist all both by word and deed, in becoming children of the Lord. We know of no other obedience to him you call pope, or father; and this we are prepared to render to him and to every Christian for ever. Beyond this, we are subject to the archbishop of Caerleon, who is a guide and an overseer, under God, to direct and keep us in the spiritual path."

Augustine challenged them to demonstrate their principles by performing some miracles. He summoned an old Englishman, who had lost his eyesight, and asked the Britons if they could restore his sight, but they confessed that they could not. Then Augustine prayed for the man, and immediately his sight was restored.

Evans suggests that this was not a real miracle, and instead it was stage managed. Augustine could not speak a word of English, and all his preaching and conversation was done through an interpreter. The interpreter was English, and he knew what he was supposed to say, but if he had been Welsh he might have said something different. The supposed 'miracle' was in accordance with Mark 13:22.

> For false Christs and false prophets shall rise, and shall shew signs and wonders, to seduce, if it were possible, even the elect.

A second meeting was convened, to discuss the matter further, and according to Holinshed,[295] the reason was because the Britons were impressed by Augustine's 'miracle', but they were unable to abandon their customs without wider consultation.

---

[295] Holinshed's *Chronicles*, Vol. 1, p.596.

The second meeting was held at a place called Augustine's Oak, on the boundary between Worcester and Hereford. A large number of people arrived, including seven bishops and many learned scholars, but before they arrived, some of them met an old man on the way who asked them where they were going, and the dialogue (according to Theophilus Evans) continued as follows:

> "We are going," said they, "to meet Augustine, who was sent by one he calls the Pope of Rome to preach to the Saxons. He asks us to obey him, and also to receive the same ceremonies and articles of religion as are received and held by the church of Rome. Pray, what is your opinion on this subject? Shall we obey him, or will we not?" The elder answered, "If God has sent him, obey him." "But how can we know whether he is sent by God or not?" said they. "By this shall ye know," said the elder: "consider what our Saviour says - 'Take my yoke upon you, and learn of me, for I am meek and lowly in heart;' (Matt. 11:29,) and if Augustine is a meek and humble man, and poor in spirit, hear him; if otherwise, have nothing to do with him. "But how shall we know," they rejoined, "whether he is proud or humble?" "Easily enough," said the elder: "proceed, slowly, in order that Augustine may be at the place appointed before you, [and he sits in his chair].[296] Now he is only one, and I am told there are seven bishops on our side, besides many other respectable men, therefore, if Augustine will not rise from his chair and salute you, you may then judge at once that he is a proud man: do not obey him."

The advice of this old man was universally accepted as a warning from God. They continued on their journey, and when they came into the presence of Augustine, he offered them no greeting, he did not rise from his chair, and he sat there for a long time looking at them with an air of cold indifference. Then he said that he would bear with them for a while on other matters, provided that they immediately agreed to the following demands:

* They would observe Easter according to the custom of the church of Rome.

---

[296] The text says '*and sit in his chair*' which must be an error. It obviously means '*and he sits in his chair*'.

- They would perform baptism according to the custom of the church of Rome.

- They would assist in preaching the gospel to the Saxons.

The Britons agreed to none of these, and while the demand to preach to the Saxons might sound reasonable, the Britons found it odious because they believed that a condition of true repentance was the restoration of all the land that the Saxons had taken from them. However, they did not discuss any of these matters, and instead they followed the advice of the old man they had met on the way. The dialogue continued as follows:

> The bishops of Wales replied, that they would neither coincide with the church of Rome in these particulars, nor acknowledge him as their archbishop; "for," said they to each other, "if he was too proud to rise from his seat to salute us now, how much more would he despise us if we were to submit to his authority?" "Is that your answer?" said Augustine angrily, (and his blood boiled within him as he spoke,) "Is that your story? Perhaps you will repent this hereafter. If you do not think proper to join us in preaching the gospel to the Saxons, rely upon it, the time will come, and that speedily, when you will receive death at their hands."

The events that followed have already been related (see page 109). The Saxons fell upon the monks at Bangor-is-y-Coed and slaughtered 1200 of them. Some people say that Augustine personally instigated the massacre, even though it is generally thought to have happened after his death. Others say that he never attempted to influence the Saxons, but he prophesied that it would occur as a future event.

Evans claims that the massacre occurred in 601, during the lifetime of Augustine, and he was actually present at the time giving his consent to it. Augustine is believed to have died in 604 or 605, so the validation of this depends on the date of the massacre, rather than the date of Augustine's death.

Whatever may be the case, we can be certain that Augustine was no friend of the Britons. He is credited with bringing Christianity to England (meaning the Anglo-Saxons) although it was a corrupted form of Christianity and it did not require the Saxons to make any reparations to the Britons who they had displaced.

St. Aidan

St. Aidan was an Irish monk who was appointed bishop of Clogher, but he resigned and went to the monastery of St. Columba at Iona in AD 630. Then he was appointed bishop of Lindisfarne, in AD 650, otherwise known as 'Holy Island' off the north-east coast of England near Berwick-on-Tweed. He had an effective ministry in Northumbria, with the assistance of King Oswald who helped him to learn English, and he became known as the "Apostle of Northumbria". His style of Christianity followed the Irish Celtic tradition rather than the Roman tradition that had been established elsewhere in England.

The Council of Whitby

There was a controversy between the two types of Christianity in northern and southern England, regarding various religious practices, and especially the observance of Easter. For example, when King Oswy of Northumbria (brother of King Oswald) was observing Easter, his queen who had been brought up in the south was still fasting.

A conference was held at Whitby in AD 664 where the two traditions were represented as follows:

- King Oswy, together with the bishops Colman and Chad represented the Celtic tradition.
- Alchfrid, the son of Oswy, together with the bishops Wilfred and Agilbert represented the Roman tradition.

Colman appealed to the practice of St. John, while Wilfred appealed to the practice to St. Peter and the council of Nicaea. The matter was eventually decided when King Oswy gave way to the opposition, on the grounds that St. Peter held the keys to the kingdom of heaven, and he could not offend him in case he might be refused admission.

Although it seems a small thing to give way on this matter, King Oswy was in fact accepting the growing power of the Roman Catholic Church, and Catholicism continued to spread all over England.

The Reformation

Henry VII became king of England in 1485 as a consequence of the feud between the houses of Lancaster and York. Henry was a Lancastrian, on his mother's side, being the great grandson of John of Gaunt, and he took the throne when he defeated Richard III in battle at Market Bosworth. Henry was a posthumous child, born in 1487 at Pembroke Castle. Before he was born, his father, Edmund Tudor, the Earl of Richmond, had died at Carmarthen Castle, having been taken prisoner by the Yorkists. Pembroke Castle also fell to the Yorkists when Henry was four years old, but he was still able to stay there under the guardianship of the new owner, William Herbert.

Henry was born and raised in Wales, and brought his Welsh heritage to the English throne, including the long-held aspiration to free the country from the power of Rome. He never achieved it, or even seriously attempted it during his lifetime, but his son and successor, Henry VIII, broke with Rome in 1534, declaring himself to be "Supreme Head of the Church of England".

The Reformation in Britain can therefore be seen as a consequence of the much earlier history. The Welsh had learned the true faith from the early church, before it became institutionalised. They resisted the demands of Augustine, and then they reinstated the faith in England after more than 900 years of Roman domination.

192

Chapter 8 - The End Of The World

We have now traced a continuous history, from Creation to the Flood, and then to the early inhabitants of Britain and Ireland, primarily from non-Biblical sources. We have also looked at some of the history of the church.

Since there was a beginning of all things, we should also expect that there should be an end. The question is, which part of history are we in now, and how close are we to the end? Christians have always argued that we are near the end-time, and have been able to produce evidence in terms of Bible prophecies that were being fulfilled in some way or other. For example, there have always been *"wars and rumours of wars"* (Matt. 24:6). It might seem presumptuous to suppose that we are now approaching an end-time apocalypse, as if we know better than our ancestors, but we have to take note of one important fact, that the Jews have been restored to the nation of Israel since 1948, and Jerusalem was recovered in 1967, bringing to an end the so-called *"times of the Gentiles"* mentioned in Luke 21:24.

Since then there has been a multitude of books published on Bible prophecy, and I will not dwell on any of them here, except to say that they are available in any Christian bookshop. Instead, I am going to say a few things about the pagan expectations of the end of the world, and how some of them match up with the Bible.

The Babylonian Apocalypse

Berosus identified a finite period for the existence of the world, in a passage that we saw on page 26, and the relevant part of the text is as follows:

> After the death of Ardates, his son, Xisuthrus, succeeded, and reigned eighteen sari. In his time happened the great Deluge; the history of which is given in this manner. The Deity, Kronus, appeared to him in a vision, and gave him notice, that upon the fifteenth day of the month Daesia there would be a flood, by which mankind would be destroyed. He therefore enjoined him to commit to writing a history of the beginning, progress, and final conclusion of all things, down to the present term; and to bury these accounts securely in the city of the Sun at Sippara;...

It is not clear exactly what is meant by the '*final conclusion of all things, down to the present term*'. It could mean down to the time of the flood, when the old world was concluded and a new world began, although the term '*final conclusion*' implies the end of everything. Whatever may be the case, we know that Noah had a knowledge of the future, because he knew that the flood was going to happen, and according to this passage he knew the exact date.

The following fragment from Seneca[297] tells us more definitely how the world is supposed to end.

> Berosus, who thus interprets the Babylonian tradition, says that these events take place according to the course of the stars; and he affirms it so positively as to fix the time for the (general) conflagration of the world, and the Deluge. He maintains that all terrestrial things will be consumed when the planets, which now are traversing their different courses, shall all coincide in the sign of Cancer, and be so placed, that a straight line could pass directly through all their orbs. But the Flood will take place (he says) when the same conjunction of the planets shall take place in the constellation Capricorn. The summer is in the former constellation, the winter in the latter.

Before I begin to interpret this, I will make a slight digression into the way that astronomy was understood by the ancient world. There are no surviving records to explain the Babylonian model of the solar system (not that I know of anyway). However, it is known that they were skilled astronomers, able to predict the motion of the sun, moon, and planets against the background of stars, and they could predict eclipses.

The earliest known model of the solar system is from the Greek philosopher Aristotle (384-322 BC) who believed that the earth was the centre of the universe, and the sun, moon and stars all revolved around it. This model was widely accepted for a long time, in spite of the elaborate conjectures that had to be made to explain the 'retrograde motion' of planets, as they occasionally turned backwards and went in the reverse direction against the background of stars, then went forward again. It was eventually replaced by the heliocentric (sun-centred) model of the Polish astronomer Copernicus (1473-1543). This model states that the earth and all the other planets move around the sun, while the stars remain in fixed positions but they appear to move across the sky because of the rotation

---

[297] Hodges, p.70.

of the earth on its axis. It easily explains the retrograde motion of the planets, in terms of the motion of the earth as it overtakes a planet in it's orbit around the sun. However, it was not universally accepted until it was verified by Kepler, Galileo, and Newton in the 17th century. Altogether, the earth-centred model of Aristotle had prevailed for about two thousand years before it had to be abandoned.

However, there is reason to believe that the heliocentric model of the solar system that we use today was understood by the Babylonians, before the time of Aristotle. They obviously had a model that worked, because they could plot the motion of heavenly bodies with accuracy.

There was a Greek astronomer called Aristarchus (c.310-230 BC) who lived at Samos, an island in the Aegean, off the west coast of Turkey. About 200 BC, he proposed a heliocentric model, the same as that of Copernicus, but the Greeks rejected it. They stuck to the earth-centred model of Aristotle and objected to the new ideas of Aristarchus with the following arguments:

- If the earth rotated on its axis, everything would fly off.

- If the earth moved around the sun, the birds would get left behind.

- If the earth was in orbit around the sun, we would see a parallax effect, as the nearby stars change their position in relation to the distant stars.

All of these objections can be answered easily today, in terms of gravity, the laws of motion, and the very great distances to the stars, but they couldn't be answered at the time of Aristarchus, so the earth-centred model of Aristotle prevailed.

The question is, where did Aristarchus get his ideas from? The island of Samos, where he lived, was quite close to the island of Cos where Berosus had an observatory and opened a school of astronomy about 100 years earlier. It is very probable, therefore, that Aristarchus was influenced by Berosus, from the school that he had founded.

Aristarchus is considered to be the '*Copernicus of Antiquity*', but if he got his ideas from Berosus, it is likely that they had always been known from the beginning of the world.

There is just one other point that we should know about ancient astronomy. The term 'planet' means 'wanderer' and applies to a point of light that moves across the background of stars. According to this definition, the sun and moon are both planets, but the earth is not a planet because it's down here, and not up in the sky. The distant planets, Uranus, Neptune and Pluto are invisible to the naked eye and were probably unknown in ancient times (or at least unknown to the Greeks). This leaves the so-called "seven planets of the ancient world", which are the Sun, Moon, Mercury, Venus, Mars, Jupiter and Saturn.

We have entered into this digression because any discussion of an ancient text on astronomy should be done on the basis of the models used. However, in this particular passage from Seneca (page 194), it makes no difference whether the Babylonians used the earth-centred or sun-centred model, because a straight line is the same on both of them. And now we return to the text itself.

The last sentence about summer and winter describes the position of the sun in relation to the constellations. The sun is in Cancer during the summer and Capricorn in the winter. The dates used by astrologers are June 22 to July 22 for Cancer, and December 21 to January 19 for Capricorn. Of course the concept of summer and winter applies to the northern hemisphere which includes Babylon, not the southern hemisphere where the seasons are reversed.

According to Berosus, the flood occurred in the month of Daesia, the Macedonian month which corresponds to May or June. This coincides roughly with the Biblical date which occurs sometime in May,[298] but only if the religious calendar, defined at the Exodus[299] was used by Moses to write about the flood. There are two different Jewish calendars, the agricultural and religious calendars. If the agricultural calendar was used, the Biblical date of the flood is six months out of phase and occurs in November. There is no certainty about which calendar was used, and there is no point making conjectures about the seasons of the year that would be favourable for entry or exit from the ark, because the pre-flood

---

[298] The seventeenth day of the second month, according to Gen. 7:11.
[299] The agricultural year begins at Rosh Hashana in the Autumn, and the religious year begins at Passover in the Spring. The agricultural year was used until the Exodus, and then they changed to the religious year, according to Exodus 12:2.
In the Bible, the religious year is always used, although there is some uncertainty about the flood because it is the only pre-Exodus event that uses a calendar.
Modern Judaism uses the agricultural calendar beginning at Rosh Hashana.

climate was different from what we have now, and the early post-flood climate is difficult to imagine.

If the flood was in the summer, the constellation of Cancer would be obscured by the sun. The outer planets (those in higher orbits than the earth) would be visible in Capricorn in the night sky. If the flood was in winter, the planets would not be seen because they would be obscured by the sun which is also in Capricorn.

According to Berosus, the world ends when the planets are lined up in Cancer. We have the same rules about visibility of the planets, but it's the other way round. If the world ends in winter, you can see the outer planets at night while the sun is in Capricorn. If it happens in summer you don't see the planets in Cancer because the sun is also in Cancer.

If any of the above occurred in a perfect straight line, there would be an eclipse of either the sun or moon (on the basis that the "seven planets of the ancient world" include the sun and moon).

Of course astronomers do not need to see the planets to know where they are. They just observe them at night, and they can calculate exactly where they will be at any time because they travel on precise orbits.

Planet-Gazing at Babylon

Clearly, if the predictions of Berosus are to be taken seriously, there would be great value in observing the planets, to predict the precise date of the end of the world, and perhaps we could use our ingenuity to do something about it. Indeed, there are powerful telescopes today, looking out for asteroids that might be on a collision course with the earth, and we might be able to launch a nuclear missile at the right time, to blow it up or knock it off course.

The tower of Babel is thought to have been an astronomic observatory, and they might have used it for this very purpose, to predict the end of the world. If they were aware of a planetary alignment at the time of the flood, they might have thought that another great disaster would occur at the next planetary alignment. Of course this completely ignores the reason why the flood occurred. The Bible says that God sent it to destroy humanity because of their sin and rebellion. They should have sought to avoid the next great disaster by repentance and faith, not by their own power and ingenuity, but they chose to do it their own way.

Was there really a planetary alignment at the time of the flood? I leave this question to the astronomers, except to say that planetary alignments are fairly commonplace. On May 5th 2000, the Sun, Moon, and the planets Mercury, Venus, Mars, Jupiter and Saturn were all aligned with the Earth, but the world did not end. Perhaps we were let off the hook because the planets were not lined up precisely enough, or because it happened when the sun was in Taurus and not in Cancer.

Planetary alignments have always been considered portents of doom, and sometimes they have been self-fulfilling, for example some Chinese dynasties have come to an end and been replaced because people believed that the "Mandate of Heaven" for the current dynasty had expired.[300]

Is There A Message In The Stars?

The ancient practice of astrology is now as popular as it ever was, as people daily study their horoscopes to find out how the stars might affect their personal health, wealth, fortune, and love lives. Of course there is no scientific basis for any of this, but people continue to follow it, in the belief that there is some kind of supernatural power in the stars.

Although the Bible denounces the use of supernatural methods to predict the future,[301] (and this must include the planetary alignments we have already discussed), the question still arises, that if God created the whole universe, is it possible that he could have written a message in the stars? There are reasons to believe that the answer is yes, they tell the story of the Messiah, as a sort of proto-gospel for the ancient world, before the final revelation was written down. In that case, the practice of astrology is just a perversion of the real message. We are not supposed to use the stars to make predictions for our own personal gain. Instead we are supposed to understand what they tell us about the Messiah.

There are ancient traditions associated with the Hebrew, Arabic and Aramaic names of the stars, so that the signs of the Zodiac and the stars within them represent different aspects of the life of the Messiah and the plan of redemption. They also represent the twelve tribes of Israel. The matter is discussed in detail by Chuck Missler and various others,[302] and it

---

[300] Milan, W., *Planetary Alignments: Harbingers of Doom?*
[301] Deut. 18:10-12
[302] Missler, C., *Signs in the Heavens*, audio briefing pack. See also Dolphin, Bowden, Setterfield & Fryman, *Signs in the Stars?*

has been criticised and debated,[303] but a brief summary is as follows.

Table 2 - Signs of the Zodiac

Constellation	Tribe	Interpretation
Virgo	Zebulon	The Virgin and her Promised Seed. Jesus was brought up in Nazareth, in the land allocated to the tribe of Zebulon.
Libra	Levi	The Balances, representing the price that is deficient and the price that covers.
Scorpio	Dan	The Scorpion, wounding him who comes.
Sagittarius	Asher	The Archer who goes out conquering. This probably represents the first of the four horsemen of the Apocalypse, carrying a bow. (Rev. 6:2)
Capricorn	Naphtali	The Goat-Fish, representing the sacrifice and the ones for whom it is made (the Christians use the fish as a symbol). Sometimes known as the Sea-Goat or just the Goat.
Aquarius	Reuben	The Water-Bearer, who gives water to those who are thirsty. Also the one who returns.
Pisces	Simeon	The Fishes, representing the multitudes of those who will follow. One of the decans (sub-constellations) represents a band that unites two fish.
Aries	Gad	The Ram, but originally the Lamb, who was slain for those who believe. It was changed to a ram by the Romans
Taurus	Joseph	The Bull or Ox. Once sacrificed, but now the judge who rules with strength.
Gemini	Benjamin	The Twins, representing unity. The dual nature of the Messiah, both human and divine.

---

[303] Faulkner, D.R., *Is There a Gospel in the Stars?*

Constellation	Tribe	Interpretation
Cancer	Issachar	The Crab, or the place of holding. The decans include Ursa Major, the Great Bear, and Ursa Minor, the Little Bear, which can both be interpreted as Sheepfolds.
Leo	Judah	The Lion. The judge who comes to rule and reign, and destroys the serpent.

The Zodiac begins with Virgo, the virgin who conceives and bears a son, and it ends with Leo, the lion of the tribe of Judah who appears in Rev. 5:5, opening the seals and pronouncing judgements on the world.

The Book of Revelation goes on to tell us about the thousand-year reign of Messiah, including the final judgement of the righteous and the wicked, followed by the end of the world and the creation of a new heaven and a new earth.

Ragnarok

In Norse mythology, there is an apocalyptic event called Ragnarok, which means the *'Fate of the Gods'*. We have already come across it in the section called *'Asgard - The Saxon Troy'* (page 128) together with the Fenris-Wolf and Midgard-Serpent.

The story of Ragnarok is given in the Prose Edda.[304] There are three continuous winters with no intervening summer (nuclear winter?) and there is war all over the world. Then the Fenris-Wolf, who has been bound up, breaks loose and devours the sun. Another wolf devours the moon, and the stars fall from heaven. The earth shakes and the mountains fall down. The Midgard-Serpent, the sea monster who encircles the earth, writhes in rage and attempts to gain the land, so that the sea rushes over the earth.

A ship called Naglfar, made of dead men's nails, breaks loose. The Fenris-Wolf advances with its jaws open, stretching between heaven and

---

[304] Anderson, R.B., *The Younger Edda*, Chapter 16, *Ragnarok*, <www.northvegr.org/lore/prose2/016.html>, Oct. 2002; Brodeur, A.G., *The Prose Edda by Snorri Sturluson*, Chapter LI, <www.northvegr.org/lore/prose/077080.html>, Oct. 2002.

earth, spewing out fire from his eyes and nostrils. The Midgard-Serpent advances alongside him, spewing out venom. During the commotion, the heavens are torn in two and the sons of Muspel come riding through the opening. Surt comes out first, with flames in front and behind him, carrying his sword that is brighter than the sun, and they engage in battle with the Fenris-Wolf and Midgard-Serpent.

Heimdal blows his horn to summon the other gods to battle. Thor slays the Midgard-Serpent but then he falls down dead, poisoned by its venom. Odin is swallowed by the Fenris-Wolf, but Vidar kills the wolf by tearing apart his jaws. Loki, the father of the two great monsters, fights against Heimdal and they kill each other. Finally, Surt throws fire on the earth and burns it up.

The story of Ragnarok, in the Prose Edda, uses material from Vala's Prophecy, which comes from the Poetic or Elder Edda, including the following passage:[305]

The sun turns black, earth sinks in the sea,
The hot stars down from heaven are whirled;
Fierce grows the steam and the life-feeding flame,
Till fire leaps high about heaven itself.

Clearly there is a resemblance between Ragnarok and the following passages of the Bible:

And I will shew wonders in the heavens and in the earth, blood, and fire, and pillars of smoke. The sun shall be turned into darkness, and the moon into blood, before the great and the terrible day of the Lord come.

Joel 2:30-31 (c.f. Acts 2:19-20)

For then shall be great tribulation, such as was not since the beginning of the world to this time, no, nor ever shall be… Immediately after the tribulation of those days shall the sun be darkened, and the moon shall not give her light, and the stars shall fall from heaven, and the powers of the heavens shall be shaken: and then shall appear the sign of the Son of man in heaven: and then shall all the tribes of the earth mourn, and they shall see the Son of man coming in the clouds of heaven with power and great glory.

Matt. 24:21-30.

---

[305] Bellows, H.A., *The Poetic Edda*, Voluspo, 57,
<www.northvegr.org/lore/poetic/001_01.html>, Oct. 2002.

And there shall be signs in the sun, and in the moon, and in the stars; and upon the earth distress of nations, with perplexity; the sea and the waves roaring; men's hearts failing them for fear, and for looking after those things which are coming on the earth: for the powers of heaven shall be shaken. And then shall they see the Son of man coming in a cloud with power and great glory.

Luke 21:25-27

And I beheld when he had opened the sixth seal, and, lo, there was a great earthquake; and the sun became black as sackcloth of hair, and the moon became as blood; and the stars of heaven fell unto the earth, even as a fig tree casteth her untimely figs, when she is shaken of a mighty wind. And the heaven departed as a scroll when it is rolled together; and every mountain and island were moved out of their places. And the kings of the earth, and the great men, and the rich men, and the chief captains, and the mighty men, and every bondman, and every free man, hid themselves in the dens and in the rocks of the mountains; and said to the mountains and rocks, Fall on us, and hide us from the face of him that sitteth on the throne, and from the wrath of the Lamb: for the great day of his wrath is come; and who shall be able to stand?

Rev. 6:12-17

And I stood upon the sand of the sea, and saw a beast rise up out of the sea, having seven heads and ten horns, and upon his horns ten crowns, and upon his heads the name of blasphemy... And I beheld another beast coming up out of the earth; and he had two horns like a lamb, and he spake as a dragon.

Rev. 13:1-11.

The Fenris-Wolf and Midgard-Serpent appear to be the Nordic counterparts of the two beasts, rising up out of the earth and the sea. The heavens are torn apart and Surt rides out through the gap, like a Messiah-figure, as if he is the counterpart of the '*Son of man*' coming in the clouds.

Why should the Biblical end-time prophecy have so much in common with the Norse mythology? It's unlikely that any of the Biblical authors went to Northern Europe, but if the Norse mythology came from Troy, as it is supposed, it would be known in the Mediterranean area. It seems that Christians and Pagans are using the same imagery from a very ancient source, and the two beasts of Revelation are probably derived from the book of Job where we have Behemoth, the land monster and Leviathan, the sea monster.[306]

The European Union

If there is one event that indicates we are in the end-times, apart from the restoration of Israel, it must be the European Union. First it was called the Common Market, and then the European Economic Community, as if it was just a collection of nations that wanted common trading agreements. Now it has its own currency called the Euro and is turning into a full-blown political union. It continues to expand, bringing in more countries from Eastern Europe, and then Russia, and there are even moves toward a World Government and a single world currency.

Those who follow Bible prophecy are increasingly convinced that the European Union is the empire from which the Antichrist will arise, and not without reason, because the symbols of the European Union are associated with apocalyptic events. These are:

- The twelve stars of the European Union flag, derived from the stars of the Madonna.
- The woman riding the beast, representing Europa.
- The tower of Babel.

The continuing development of the European Union, and the use of these symbols, is described in detail by Alan Franklin.[307]

Twelve Stars of the Madonna

The flag of the European Union is a circle of twelve stars, borrowed from the Roman Catholic Madonna who is often featured with either a crown or a halo of stars.

---

[306] Job 40:15 - 41:34. Behemoth and Leviathan are thought to be dinosaurs. Leviathan is a sea monster so it would have survived the flood. Behemoth is land based, but Noah could have taken a pair of young ones into the ark.
[307] Franklin, A., *End-Times News, EU: Final World Empire.*

Figure 21. Twelve stars of the European Union flag.

Figure 22. Madonna with a halo of stars.

There are a number of variations of this type of Madonna.[308] Sometimes she has a halo of stars, and sometimes a crown of stars, and the number of

---

[308] Immaculate Heart of Mary <www.immaculateheart.com/thumbnails.htm>, Oct. 2002.

stars is not always the same. Sometimes she has the moon under her feet, and in this case she also has the earth under her feet, so she is known as 'Queen of the World'.

These variants of the Madonna are based on the following passage:

> And there appeared a great wonder in heaven; a woman clothed with the sun, and the moon under her feet, and upon her head a crown of twelve stars: and she being with child cried, travailing in birth, and pained to be delivered. And there appeared another wonder in heaven; and behold a great red dragon, having seven heads and ten horns, and seven crowns upon his heads. And his tail drew the third part of the stars of heaven, and did cast them to the earth: and the dragon stood before the woman which was ready to be delivered, for to devour her child as soon as it was born. And she brought forth a man child, who was to rule all nations with a rod of iron: and her child was caught up unto God, and to his throne. And the woman fled into the wilderness, where she hath a place prepared of God, that they should feed her there a thousand two hundred and threescore days.

Rev. 12:1-6.

If the Roman Catholic Church followed this passage more literally, the number of stars around the Madonna's head would always be twelve, and on this point the European Union seems to be doing better than the Catholics. The number of stars in the European Union flag is always twelve and has nothing to do with the number of member states (unlike the flag of the USA which has one star for each state).

The passage describes both the Virgin Mary and the church, as they have a number of things in common. The Virgin Mary became pregnant and gave birth to a child, through the Holy Spirit, while she was betrothed to her intended husband Joseph, and eventually she married him. The church is also pregnant, continually giving birth to new believers, through the Holy Spirit. She is described as the "bride of Christ" and will eventually marry him (Rev. 19:7-9).

The sun is Christ, the light of the world and the clothing of the church. The moon is the Levitical system of sacrifices, which is only a shadow of things to come. The twelve stars represent the twelve apostles, upon whose teaching the church is founded. The great red dragon is the devil, and the seven heads represent Rome, the city built on seven hills (by comparison with Rev. 17:9 which we will discuss later). Here we see the reason for the use of so much imagery. If John had denounced Rome directly, he would have brought persecution on the church. The ten horns are ten kings, and we will also discuss them later. The stars of heaven are the believers who have been martyred. The dragon also attempts to kill the child as soon he is born, and this represents Herod killing the children at Bethlehem in an attempt to kill Jesus. The flight into the wilderness represents Mary, Joseph and Jesus going to Egypt and then returning when it is safe. It also represents a remnant of the church who fled to the forest during the Middle Ages and preserved the Bible when it was banned from public use. They were called the Waldenses. Jesus was caught up to God, and to his throne, and this means the resurrection and ascension. When he returns he will rule with a rod of iron.

No doubt there could be other interpretations of the passage, but we will not dwell on all of them here. The issue at hand is the use of the twelve stars by the European Union. Both Catholics and Protestants are concerned about this, for the following reasons:

- Catholics are concerned that their Madonna is being used for political purposes. For them it is a religious symbol and has nothing to do with politics.
- Protestants are not interested in icons and images. They are only interested in the written word. The passage from Revelation is for everybody, but the image of the Madonna is Roman Catholic. The use of the twelve stars in the EU flag represents the expectation that Catholicism will be the official religion of the Union, and as the Union expands, it will be at the forefront of the one world ecumenical interfaith super-church. Protestants will be expected to conform to the wishes of the super-church, contrary to their beliefs.

A Woman Rides the Beast

This is the title of a book by Dave Hunt,[309] affirming the view of the Protestant Reformers that the woman of Revelation 17, riding on a beast, is the Roman Catholic Church. Alan Franklin[310] has pointed out that the European Union is promoting this image, identifying the woman as Europa.

---

[309] Hunt, D., *A Woman Rides the Beast*.
[310] Franklin, A., *End-Times News, EU: Final World Empire*, pp. 16, 48-49.

The image appears in various places in EU buildings, and also on the Greek Euro coin. According to Greek mythology, Europa is a Phoenician princess who is abducted and taken to Crete, riding on the back of a bull, and her Phoenician family never found her. Some say that Zeus had turned himself into a bull and abducted her. Others say that it was the Cretan bull that Heracles fought against in one of his labours.

Figure 23 - Greek Euro Coin.

Figure 24 - Sculpture of Europa riding the Beast, outside the Council of Ministers building in Brussels.[311]

---

[311] Copyright: David Hathaway, Prophetic Vision magazine, 41 Healds Road, Dewsbury, WF13 4HU, UK, <www.propheticvision.org.uk>, Oct. 2002.

The relevant Bible passage is as follows:

> ...I saw a woman sit upon a scarlet coloured beast, full of names of blasphemy, having seven heads and ten horns. And the woman was arrayed in purple and scarlet colour, and decked with gold and precious stones and pearls, having a golden cup in her hand full of abominations and filthiness of her fornication: and upon her forehead was a name written, MYSTERY, BABYLON THE GREAT, THE MOTHER OF HARLOTS AND ABOMINATIONS OF THE EARTH. And I saw the woman drunken with the blood of the saints, and with the blood of the martyrs of Jesus: and when I saw her, I wondered with great admiration. And the angel said unto me, Wherefore didst thou marvel? I will tell thee the mystery of the woman, and of the beast that carrieth her, which hath the seven heads and ten horns. The beast that thou sawest was, and is not; and shall ascend out of the bottomless pit, and go into perdition: and they that dwell on the earth shall wonder, whose names were not written in the book of life from the foundation of the world, when they behold the beast that was, and is not, and yet is. And here is the mind which hath wisdom. The seven heads are seven mountains, on which the woman sitteth. And there are seven kings: five are fallen, and one is, and the other is not yet come; and when he cometh, he must continue a short space. And the beast that was, and is not, even he is the eighth, and is of the seven, and goeth into perdition. And the ten horns which thou sawest are ten kings, which have received no kingdom as yet; but receive power as kings one hour with the beast. These have one mind, and shall give their power and strength unto the beast.

Rev. 17:3-13

This is a picture of the woman, who is supposed to be the pure bride of Christ, but she has turned into a harlot, making compromises with paganism and persecuting those who were deemed to be heretics, as it was for centuries during the Middle Ages. The beast that she rides upon has seven heads and ten horns, and it is now made clear that the seven heads are seven mountains, so it must be Rome. The ten horns are ten kings who work together, giving authority to the beast, so they are rulers of nations within a united empire.

At one time, people used to think that there would be ten nations in the European Union, but now there are more than ten, and the number is likely to increase as enlargement continues. But now there is talk about a

'*World Parliament*', according to the '*Constitution for the Federation of Earth*' which contains the following provision:[312]

FOR ELECTIONS AND ADMINISTRATION, Earth is divided into 1000 Districts, 20 Regions, 10 Magna-Regions, at least 5 Continental Divisions.

Possibly the ten Magna-Regions could be the ten kings. It remains to be seen how this will all work out, but generally we can see that the prophecy is coming true, that the nations are coming together in political union.

The European Union was founded on the Treaty of Rome, so it has its origins in the very city that was identified by the Apostle John. The Roman Catholic Church, based in the same city, is likely to become the religious arm of the European Union. Church and State will rule together for a while, and will persecute the true believers:

These shall make war with the Lamb, and the Lamb shall overcome them: for he is Lord of lords, and King of kings: and they that are with him are called, and chosen, and faithful.

Rev. 17:14

Then the State will get tired of the Church, and under pressure from public opinion, will dump her:

And he saith unto me, The waters which thou sawest, where the whore sitteth, are peoples, and multitudes, and nations, and tongues. And the ten horns which thou sawest upon the beast, these shall hate the whore, and shall make her desolate and naked, and shall eat her flesh, and burn her with fire. For God hath put in their hearts to fulfil his will, and to agree, and give their kingdom unto the beast, until the words of God shall be fulfilled. And the woman which thou sawest is that great city, which reigneth over the kings of the earth.

Rev. 17:15-18

The passage finally identifies the woman herself, and not just the beast upon which she sits, as the city of Rome. This makes sense because the

---

[312] *World Parliament: How World Government Works,* <www.worldparliamentgov.net/how_works.html>, Oct. 2002.

Roman Catholic Church has always been based in that city, and the Vatican is even recognised as an independent mini-state.

The Tower of Babel

In addition to the twelve stars of the Madonna, and the woman riding the beast, we also have the tower of Babel as a symbol of the European Union.

Figure 25 - EU poster of the Tower of Babel.

This poster, published by the Council of Europe but later withdrawn, is an adaptation of a painting by the 16th Century Flemish artist Pieter Brueghel. The twelve stars above the tower are inverted to resemble upside-down pentagrams, a well known occult symbol. Further details of the poster are given by Christopher Story.[313] The poster was withdrawn, probably because its religious and political statement was too direct, but the connection with Babylon is no secret. The European Parliament building, opened in December 2000, is clearly modelled on the same image, having the appearance of an unfinished Tower of Babel.

Figure 26 - European Parliament building in Strasbourg.[314]

The European Union has a fascination for apocalyptic images, and has studied them very carefully, leaving us in little doubt that they intend to bring about the one-world government that is predicted in Revelation 17. Whatever our interpretation of prophecy might be, we can be sure that the European Union will play a major role in the end-time events that are fast approaching.

---

[313] Story, C., *The European Union Collective: Enemy of its Member States.*
[314] Photo: European Parliament, <www.europarl.eu.int/dg3/audiov/en/farch.htm>, Oct. 2002.

Escaping the Apocalypse

We have covered a lot of material in this book, drawing information from many sources to show that there is plenty of pagan and secular literature that corresponds to the Bible to some degree or other, and there is a continuous history from the beginning of the world. In particular, the study of history should show us where we are now, and where we are heading. All the ancient sources, whether they are Biblical, Babylonian or Saxon, tell us that the world exists for only a finite period and we are heading for an end time apocalyptic event. The question is, when will it happen?

The Babylonians attempted to predict the end of the world from planetary alignments, but their expectations and methods of enquiry were at variance with the teaching of Jesus. His disciples asked him:

> ... what shall be the sign of thy coming, and of the end of the world?
>
> *Matt. 24:3*

In response he tells them about the condition of the world at the end time, but he does not tell them when it will happen. Instead he says:

> But of that day and hour knoweth no man, no, not the angels of heaven, but my Father only.
>
> *Matt. 24:36*

> Watch therefore, for ye know neither the day nor the hour wherein the Son of man cometh.
>
> *Matt. 25:13*

Christian and pagan sources agree that the end will come, but there is a fundamental difference of values. The Bible teaches that there is one God, to whom we have to be obedient, and the apocalypse is the ultimate outcome of our disobedience. Pagans, on the other hand, have multiple gods with different expectations, who are sometimes at war against each other. Humans have no control over the affairs of the gods, and the apocalypse is just a matter of fate. The Greeks and Romans used to believe that if they fought valiantly and died in battle, they would go to Elysium, so they had to create their own mini-apocalypse on the battlefield to escape the big apocalypse. Otherwise, they had to pursue other values, mostly emphasising their own self-worth.

For Christians, the apocalypse is also a certainty, but the way of escape is different. Personal virtue and self-worth were lost at the fall, shortly after creation, and the escape route is through someone else who is worthy:

> And they sung a new song, saying, Thou art worthy to take the book, and to open the seals thereof: for thou wast slain, and hast redeemed us to God by thy blood out of every kindred, and tongue, and people, and nation; and hast made us unto our God kings and priests: and we shall reign on the earth.

> *Rev. 5:9-10*

Bibliography

Anderson, Rasmus B., (translator), *The Younger Edda. Also called Snorre's Edda, or the Prose Edda,* Chicago Scott, Foresman, 1901, <www.northvegr.org/lore/prose2/>, Oct. 2002.

Anderson, Rasmus B., (translator), *Viktor Rydberg: Teutonic Mythology: Gods and Goddesses of the Northland*, three volumes, London, Norroena Society, 1907. First published in Swedish, 1887, <www.hi.is/~eybjorn/ugm/ugm0.html>, Oct. 2002.

Anstey, Martin, *The Romance of Bible Chronology*, Marshall Bros, 1913, <www.preteristarchive.com/Books/anstey_chrono_index.html>, Oct. 2002.

Asher, R.E., *National Myths in Renaissance France; Francus, Samothes and the Druids*, Edinburgh University Press, 22 George Square, Edinburgh, 1993.

Bede, (b.673 - d.735), monk at Jarrow, Northumberland - see Hurst, William.

Bell, Alexander, (editor), *Geffrei Gaimar: L'Estoire des Engleis*, Oxford, Blackwell, for Anglo-Norman Text Society, 1960.

Bell, Gertrude, *Amurath to Amurath*, McMillan, London, 1924. For details of the author and her travels, see <www.noahsarksearch.com/BellGertrude/BellGertrude.htm>, Oct. 2002.

Bellows, Henry Adams, (translator), *The Poetic Edda,* The American-Scandinavian Foundation; Oxford University Press, 1923; Princeton University Press, 1936; Lewiston, Edwin Mellen Press, 1991, <www.northvegr.org/lore/poetic/>, Oct. 2002.

Birley, Anthony R., *Tacitus: Agricola and Germany*, Oxford University Press, 1999.

Bowden, Malcolm, *True Science Agrees With The Bible*, Sovereign Publications, 1998.

Bower, Walter, Abbot of Inchcolm Abbey, (d.1449) - see Watt, D.E.R.

Bibliography

Brodeur, Arthur Gilchrist, (translator), *The Prose Edda by Snorri Sturluson*, New York, American-Scandinavian Foundation; London, Humphrey Milford; Oxford University Press; 1916,1923, <www.northvegr.org/lore/prose/>, Oct. 2002.

Bryant, Jacob, *New System, or, An Analysis of Ancient Mythology*, 3 volumes, 1774-76, London, Printed for T. Payne.

Caradoc of Llancerfan, *Historie of Cambria*, originally written in Welsh containing the history up to 1270. Translated into English by Humphrey Lloyd, adding the events that occurred after that date. Augmented by David Powell and published in 1584. Reprinted for John Harding, London, 1811.

Cavazzi, Franco, *Illustrated History of the Roman Empire*, <www.roman-empire.net>, Oct. 2002.

Celebi, Emel, *Midyat - City of Stone*, Turkish Airlines Skylife Magazine, Sept. 2001, <www.bethsuryoyo.com/currentevents/skylifesept2001/ EnglishText.html>, Oct. 2002.

Christian Classics Ethereal Library, <www.ccel.org>, Oct. 2002.

Church, A.J., Brodribb W.J., (translators), *The Complete Works of Tacitus*, New York, The Modern Library, 1942. *Annals* and *History* available at <mcadams.posc.mu.edu/txt/tacitus/>, Oct. 2002.

Clothier, Stephen, *The Possible Significance of Gen. 11:2 - Does it provide us with a clue as to where the Ark landed?*, <www.noahsarksearch.com/from-the-east.htm>, Oct. 2002.

Cooper, Bill, *After the Flood*, New Wine Press, 1995.

Cooper, Bill, *Chronicle of the Early Britons*, annotated translation from the Welsh copy (Jesus College MS LXI), 2002, <www.write-on.co.uk/history/chronicle_of_the_early_britons.htm>, Oct. 2002. See also Roberts, Peter.

Cory, Isaac Preston, *The Ancient Fragments; containing what remains of the writings of Sanchoniatho, Berossus, Abydenus, Megasthenes, and Manetho*, London, William Pickering, 1828. Facsimile reprints from Ballantrae, Ontario, Canada. See also the 1876 version by Hodges.

Crouse, Bill, *The Landing Place*, Answers in Genesis, Creation TJ, 15 (3), 2001. This is an updated version of an earlier article, *Noah's Ark: Its Final Berth*, Archaeology And Biblical Research, Vol. 5, No. 3, 1992, <www.christianinformation.org/noah.html>, Oct. 2002.

d'Aubigney, M., *The Reformation in England*, Banner of Truth, 1962.

Dawood, N.J., (translator), *The Koran*, Penguin Classics, 1997.

Davidson, F., *The New Bible Commentary*, London, Inter-Varsity Fellowship, 1954.

Davis, Jonathan, *The History of the Welsh Baptists, from the Year Sixty-Three to the Year One Thousand Seven Hundred and Seventy*, Pittsburgh, D.M. Hogan, 1835, 204p. Re-published in 1976 by The Baptist, Rt. 1, Aberdeen, Miss. 39730. Re-published again in 1982 by Church History Research & Archives, 220 Graystone Drive, Gallatin, Tennessee 37066.

Dolphin, Bowden, Setterfield & Fryman, *Signs in the Stars?*, <www.ldolphin.org/zodiac/index.html>, Oct. 2002.

Down, David, *Searching for Moses*, Answers in Genesis, Creation TJ, 15 (1), 2001.

Ellis, Sir Henry, *Polydore Vergil's English History*, First 8 books published as Vol. 1 for the Camden Society, 1846. Facsimile reprint from Llanerch Press, Lampeter, Ceredigion. The original work consists of 25 books, published in several editions from 1534 to 1651, but only the first 8 books are easily available.

Elton, Oliver, (translator), *The Nine Books of the Danish History of Saxo Grammaticus*, New York, Norroena Society, 1905. Saxo wrote 16 books altogether, but only the first nine were translated by Elton. For the complete text of Elton, and references to the Latin text and other translations, see the Online Medieval & Classic Library, <sunsite.berkeley.edu/OMACL/DanishHistory/>, Oct. 2002.

Evans, Lorraine, *Kingdom of the Ark*, Pocket Books, 2001.

Evans, Theophilus - see Roberts, George.

Bibliography

Evelyn-White, Hugh G., (translator), *Hesiod: The Homeric Hymns and Homerica*, Cambridge, MA., Harvard University Press; London, William Heinemann, 1914. <sunsite.berkeley.edu/OMACL/Hesiod/>, Oct. 2002.

Faulkner, Danny R., *Is There a Gospel in the Stars?*, Answers in Genesis, Creation TJ, 12 (2), 1998. See also <www.ldolphin.org/zodiac/faulkner.html>, Oct. 2002.

Fleming, John, *Fallen Angels And The Heroes Of Mythology*, Hodges, Foster and Figgis, Dublin University, 1879, <www.mcbryan.co.uk/docs.htm>, Oct. 2002.

Flinders Petrie, W.M., *Neglected British History*, Proceedings of the British Academy, Volume VIII, pp. 251-278. Paper presented to the Academy on November 7, 1917.

Fordun, John, (c.1320 - c.1385) - see Skene, William F.

Franklin, Alan, *End-Times News, EU: Final World Empire*, Oklahoma City, Hearthstone Publishing, 2002.

Gaimar, Geffrei, (12th century), *L'Estoire des Engleis.*, c.1140 - see Bell, Alexander.

Geoffrey of Monmouth, (12th century) - see Thorpe, Lewis.

Gildas, (6th century): *The Ruin of Britain* (c.540) - see Winterbottom, Michael and Giles, John Allen.

Giles, John Allen, (translator), 1808-1884, *Six Old English Chronicles*, including *Gildas: Works*, London, G. Bell & sons, 1891. *The Ruin of Britain*, <www.fordham.edu/halsall/basis/gildas-full.html>, Oct. 2002. See also Winterbottom, Michael.

Godley, A.D., *Herodotus: The Histories*, Harvard University Press, 1920, <www.perseus.tufts.edu/cgi-bin/ptext?lookup=Hdt.+toc>, Oct. 2002.

Hales, Roy. L., various articles in Creation Social Science and Humanities Quarterly Journal: *The Original World Monotheism*, Vol. VII, No. 2, 1984, pp. 18-21; *Mythology, The Bible and the Postflood Origins of Greek History*, Vol. VII, No. 4, 1985, pp. 20-23; <www.creationism.org/csshs/index.htm>, Oct. 2002.

Herodotus, (5th century BC),
   The Histories - see Godley, A.D.
   The Persian Wars - see Rawlinson, George.

Hesiod, (flourished c.700 BC) - see Evelyn-White, Hugh G.

Hislop, Alexander, *The Two Babylons*, London, Partridge, 4th edition,
   1929, reprinted 1989.

Hodges, E.R., *Cory's Ancient Fragments*, A New and Enlarged Edition,
   London, Reeves & Turner, 1876. Facsimile reprints from Ballantrae,
   Ontario, Canada. See also the original 1828 version by Cory.

Holinshed, Raphael and others, *Holinshed's Chronicles of England,
   Scotland and Ireland*, 6 volumes. First published 1587. Reprinted
   1807 for J. Johnson and others, London. Facsimile reprint 1965 by
   AMS Press Inc., New York, NY 10003.

Homer, (8th century BC) - see Rieu, E.V.

Hull, Edward, *Deacon's Synchronological Chart of Universal History*,
   London, C.W. Deacon & Co., c.1890. Re-published as *Wall Chart of
   World History*, London, Studio Editions, 1988.

Hunt, Dave, *A Woman Rides the Beast*, Oregon, Harvest House
   Publishers, 1994.

Hurst, William, (translator), 1814, *St. Bede The Venerable: The History
   of the Primitive Church of England*. Otherwise known as *Bede's
   Ecclesiastical History*.
   <www.ocf.org/OrthodoxPage/reading/St.Pachomius/bede.html>,
   Oct. 2002.

Jackson Knight, W.F., (translator), *Virgil: The Aeneid*, Penguin Classics,
   1958.

John of Fordun, (c.1320 - c.1385) - see Skene, William F.

Jones, H.L., *The Geography of Strabo*, Cambridge, Mass., Harvard
   University Press; London, William Heinemann; 1924.
   <www.perseus.tufts.edu/cgi-bin/ptext?lookup=Strab.+toc>,
   Oct. 2002.

Josephus, Flavius, (1st century) - see Whiston, William.

Bibliography

Jowett, Benjamin, Plato's Dialogues: *Timaeus* and *Critias*, <www.activemind.com/Mysterious/Topics/Atlantis/ timaeus_and_critias.html>. For other *Dialogues* see <plato-dialogues.org/links.htm>, Oct. 2002.

Keating, G., *The History of Ireland*, Vol. 1, Containing the Introduction and First Book of History. Edited with translation and notes by David Comyn, London, Irish Texts Society, 1902.

Keyser, John D., *Joseph of Arimathea and David's Throne in Britain!*, <hope-of-israel.org/i000111a.htm>, Oct. 2002.

Khalaf, Salim, *Britain, Phoenicia's Secret Treasure*, <www.phoenicia.org/britmines.html>, Oct. 2002.

Koran, (7th century) - see Dawood, N.J.

Laing, Samuel, (translator), *Snorri Sturluson: Heimskringla: A History of the Norse Kings*, London, Norroena Society, 1907. Revised edition: Simpson, J., Everyman, 1964. <www.northvegr.org/lore/heim/>, Oct. 2002.

Lewis, Smithett, *Joseph of Arimathea at Glastonbury*, James Clarke PB, 1982.

Lomax, Frank, (translator), *The Antiquities of Glastonbury by William of Malmesbury*, c.1135, London, Talbot, 1908. Facsimile reprint by JMF Books, Llanerch, Felinfach, 1992.

Lynche, Richard, *An Historical Treatise of the Travels of Noah into Europe: Containing the first inhabitation and peopling thereof*, London, Adam Islip, 1601.

McKisack, May, *Medieval History in the Tudor Age*, Oxford University Press, 1971.

Midrash Rabbah - see Soncino Classics Collection.

Milan, Wil, *Planetary Alignments: Harbingers of Doom?*, <www.space.com/scienceastronomy/solarsystem/ planet_conjunction_000504.html>, Oct. 2002.

Missler, Chuck, *Signs in the Heavens*, audio briefing pack, Koinonia House, 1991, <www.khouse.org>, Oct. 2002.

Morgan, R.W., *St. Paul in Britain*, Oxford and London, James Parker & Co., 1880. Reprints available from Friends of the Cambrian Church, <www.grailchurch.org/booklist.htm>, Oct. 2002.

Morris, John, (editor and translator), *Nennius: British History and the Welsh Annals*, 9th century. Arthurian Period Sources, Vol. 8, Phillimore, 1980.

Murphy, Denis (editor), *Annals of Clonmacnoise*, from the earliest period to 1408, translated by Conell Mageoghagan, 1627. First published in Dublin, 1896. Facsimile reprint by Llanerch Press, Ceredigion.

Nennius, 9th century - see Morris, John.

Parada, Carlos, *Greek Mythology Link*, <homepage.mac.com/cparada/GML>, Oct. 2002.

Paton, W. R., (translator), *Polybius: The Histories*, Loeb Classical Library, 6 volumes, Greek texts and facing English translation, Harvard University Press, 1922 - 1927. <www.ukans.edu/history/index/europe/ancient_rome/E/Roman/Texts/Polybius/home.html>, Oct. 2002.

Plato, (4th century BC) - see Jowett, Benjamin.

Polybius, (c.200 - c.118 BC) - see Paton, W. R.

Porada, Edith, and others, *The Art of Ancient Iran, Pre-Islamic Cultures*, New York, Crown Publishers, Art of the World, 1962, <www.noteaccess.com/Texts/Porada/Preface.htm>, Oct. 2002.

Rawlinson, George, *Herodotus: The Persian Wars*, Modern Library Edition, 1942, <mcadams.posc.mu.edu/txt/herodotus/>, Oct. 2002.

Rieu, E.V., *Homer: The Iliad*, Penguin Classics, 1950.

Rieu, E.V., *Homer: The Odyssey*, Penguin Classics, 1948.

Roberts, George, (translator), *Theophilus Evans: A View of The Primitive Ages*. Printed and published by John Pryse. Reprinted from the American edition published at Edensburg in 1834.

Roberts, Peter, *Chronicle of the Kings of Britain*. Translated in 1811 from the Welsh copy attributed to Tysilio. Facsimile reprint by Llanerch Press, Lampeter, Ceredigion. The original 1811 edition contains some additional material from other histories that is omitted from the facsimile reprint. See also Cooper, Bill.

Rydberg, Viktor, *Teutonic Mythology*, - see Anderson, Rasmus. B.

Sandars, N.K., *The Epic of Gilgamesh*, Penguin Classics, 1972.

Seaman, Walter de M., *The Dawn of Christianity in the West*, Chrest Foundation, 1993.

Saxo Grammaticus - see Elton, Oliver.

Short, Ian, *Gaimar's Epilogue and Geoffrey of Monmouth's Liber vetustissimus*, Speculum, 69 (1994), 323-43. See also <www.write-on.co.uk/history/gaimar.htm>, Oct. 2002.

Skene, William F., (translator and editor), *John of Fordun: Chronicle of the Scottish Nation*. First published in Edinburgh, 1872, as volume IV of *The Historians of Scotland*. Facsimile reprint in two volumes by Llanerch Press, Lampeter, Ceredigion.

Soncino Classics Collection, *Talmud, Midrash Rabbah, Zohar, Bible*, Judaic Classics Library CD-ROM, Davka Corporation, 1996.

Stange, Kate, *Akhet-Aten Home Page*, <kate.stange.com/egypt/>, Oct. 2002.

Strabo, (c.63BC - c.AD23) - see Jones, H.L.

Story, Christopher, *The European Union Collective: Enemy of its Member States*, Edward Harle, 2002.

Sturluson, Snorri, (c.1179 - 1241),
Prose Edda - see Anderson, Rasmus B.; Brodeur, Arthur Gilchrist; Young & Nordal.
Heimskringla - see Laing, Samuel.

Susser, Rabbi Dr. Bernard, *The Jews of South-West England*, Exeter University Press, 1993, <www.eclipse.co.uk/exeshul/susser/thesis/thesisacknowledgements.htm>, Oct. 2002.

Tacitus, Publius Cornelius, (1st - 2nd century AD),
Agricola and Germany - see Birley, Anthony R.
Complete Works - see Church, A.J., Brodribb, W.J.

Talmud - see Soncino Classics Collection.

Thorpe, Benjamin, (translator), *The Edda Of Sæmund The Learned: From The Old Norse Or Icelandic With A Mythological Index*, 1866, <www.northvegr.org/lore/poetic2/>, Oct. 2002.

Thorpe, Lewis, (translator), *Geoffrey of Monmouth: History of the Kings of Britain*, Penguin Classics, 1966.

Tompsett, Brian, *Directory of Royal Genealogical Data*, University of Hull, <www.dcs.hull.ac.uk/public/genealogy/royal/>, Oct. 2002.

Tysilio, (6th - 7th century) - see Roberts, Peter.

Vergil, Polydore, (16th Century) - see Ellis, Sir Henry.

Virgil, (1st century BC) - see Jackson Knight, W.F.

Watt, D.E.R., (editor), *Walter Bower: Scotichronicon*, Aberdeen University Press, 1993. There are 9 volumes altogether. The first 8 volumes contain the 16 books of Walter Bower with editor's notes, and Volume 9 contains the critical studies and general indexes. Volume 1 (Books 1 & 2) is primarily the work of John of Fordun. See Skene, W.F.

Wieland, Carl, *Decreased Lifespans: Have We Been Looking in the Right Place?*, Answers in Genesis, Creation TJ, 8 (2), 1994, pp.138-141, <www.answersingenesis.org>, Oct. 2002.

Whiston, William, *The Works of Flavius Josephus*, London, Milner & Sowerby. Includes *Antiquities of the Jews*, *Wars of the Jews* and various other works.

Wicken, Dick, *Did The Vikings Name America?*, <www.orange-street-church.org/text/viking.htm>, Oct. 2002.

William of Malmesbury - see Lomax, Frank.

Williams, David, *British Israelism - An Expose*, <www.geocities.com/Athens/Forum/5951/BI.html>, Oct. 2002.

Winterbottom, Michael, (editor and translator), *Gildas: The Ruin of Britain*, Arthurian Period Sources, General Editor: John Morris, Phillimore, 1978. See also Giles, John Allen.

Young, Jean & Nordal, Sigurdar, *Snorri Sturluson: The Prose Edda: Tales from Norse Mythology*, Cambridge, Bowes & Bowes, 1954.

Index

Index

Caer Caradoc, 171
Caerleon, 188
Caerleon on Uske, 180
Caer-Ludd, 96
Caernarvon, 112
Caesar, 181
  Augustus, 28
  Bassianus, 182
  Claudius, 100
  Julius, 2, 99, 100, 114, 151
  Maximian, 181
  Tiberius, 165
Caesarea, 161, 162
Cain, 39
Cainan, 16
Caliburn, 107
Callippidae, 134
Calvinism, 183
Camboblascon, 79
Cambria, 97, 120
Cana in Galilee, 169
Cancer, 194, 196, 198, 200
Cantabrian Mountains, 139
Cape Three Points. *See* Southern
  Horn.
Caphtorim, 85
Capricorn, 194, 196, 199
Caractacus, 100, 170, 171
Caradoc
  of Llancerfan, 111
  Silurian chief. *See* Caractacus.
Caredig, 109
Carmarthen Castle, 192
Carmel, Mount, 148
Caron, 102
Carthage, 85, 92
Carthaginians, 10
Cartimandua, 171
Casere, 132
Casluhim, 85
Cassiterides, 150
Cassiterite (Greek for tin), 150

Cassius
  in Syria, 52
  Mt. Casius in Egypt, 52
Caswallon, 99, 166
Catholicism. *See* Roman Catholic
  Church.
cattle, 39
Caucasus Mountains, 130
Ceasar, 99
Cecrops, 62
Cedar Mountain, 42
Celestine, Pope, 184, 185
Celtes, 83, 87
Celtic, 5, 69, 94
  Britons, 94
  Gauls, 144
  sailors, 150
Celtica, 82, 152
Cerambus, 63
Chad, bishop, 191
Chaldea, 4, 12, 15, 18, 20, 21, 37
Chalice Well, 167
Chaos, 7, 37
Charities (Graces), 39
Chebron (Pharaoh), 137
Chencres (Pharaoh), 137
Chester, 109
chi-ro (sign of the cross), 182
Chna. *See* Caanan.
Christendom, 187
Christian rulers. *See* Lucius and
  Constantine
Christianity, 85, 87, 109, 113, 147,
  156, 184
  Irish Celtic, 191
  order of St. John, 191
  order of St. Peter, 191
  Roman, 191
Christians, 101, 102, 155, 173. *See
  also* persecution of Christians.
Christmas tree, 167
Church Island, 113

Cyrene, 161
Cyropolis, 178
Cyrus, 62
Daesia, 26, 193, 196
Dagon, 18, 51
Damicanus, 160, 180, 186
Dan, 199
Danes, 104
Danish history, 130
Daonus, 13
Daos, 14
Dardania, 80
Dardanus, 5, 64, 67, 73, 78, 79, 90,
    91, 92, 125
    first king of Troy, 65
Darwin, 3, 8, 146
David, St., 165, 168
Decurion, 162
Deira, 101
Dela, 96
deluge, 26, 193, 194. *See also*
    flood.
Demetra, 52, 57
Demigods, 17, 47
Denmark, 98, 107, 123, 125, 132,
    142, 145
Derry, 186
Deruvian. *See* Damicanus
Desius, 14
Deucalion, 60, 62
Devon, 87, 133, 154
Dido, 92
Dilmun, 44
diluvian night, 21
diocese, 181
Diocletian, 102, 170, 181
    son of Jupiter, 181
Diodorus Siculus, 151
Dionysus, 57, 86
Dioscuri, 50
Dis. *See* Belus.
Divala River, 35

Domesday Book, 164
Doral Castle, 99
Dorotheus, 175
    Bishop of Tyre, 170
Dover, 99
dragon, red, 205
Druids, 84, 155, 157
Druiyus (Druis), 82, 83, 84
Dublin, 133
Dunstan, St., 168
Durrow, 186
Durupinar, 23, 25
Dynawt, Abbot of Bangor, 188
Dyvan. *See* Damicanus
Earth. *See* Gaia.
East Anglia, 132
Easter, 189, 191
Ebonides (Hebrides), 141
Ebro River, 139
eclipse, 197
Edbert, 111
Edda. *See* Prose Edda and Poetic
    Edda.
Edinburgh Castle, 143
Edmund Tudor, 192
Edward I, 112, 143
Edward, Prince of Wales, 112
Edwin, 110
Egypt, 2, 85, 86, 133, 136, 138,
    170, 206
Egyptian Chronicle, Old, 17
Egyptian king list, 137, 138
Egyptians, 18, 90, 133
Eidiol, 107
Elder Edda. *See* Poetic Edda
Eleanor, 112
Electra, 65, 79
Eleusis, 62
Eleutherius, Bishop of Rome, 101,
    180
Elioun, 51
Elizabeth I, 167

Irish, 108, 143, 144, 184, 187
iron, 39, 149
Isiris. *See* Osiris.
Isis, 54, 69, 75, 79. *See also* Io.
Isle of Man - Manaw, 120
Israel, 148, 155, 167, 176, 193, 203
Israelites, 55, 85, 133, 136, 137,
    138, 160
Issachar, 200
Istanbul, 71
Italy, 69, 72, 75, 76, 78, 80, 86, 91,
    98, 122, 129, 183
    named after Atlas Italus, 79
Iulus, 91, 93
Iupiter Celtes, 78
Ivor, 111
ivory, 148
Jabal, 39
James, the apostle, 184
Janus. *See* Ianus.
Japheth, 5, 21, 34, 45, 58, 64, 73,
    84, 123, 125
Jerusalem, 147, 148, 161, 165, 177,
    179, 193
    Glastonbury Hymn, 156
Jesus, 147, 153, 154
    at Glastonbury, 158
    in Britain, 155, 156
Jesus College, Oxford, 114
Jew's House, 154
Jewish
    calendars, 196
    community, 154
    place names, 154
    slaves, 155
    soldiers, 155
    traders, 155
Jews
    at Cudi Dagh, 30
    in Britain, 154
    received the Gospel first, 154
    restored to Israel, 193

Job, 203
John of Fordun, 136
John of Gaunt, 192
John, the apostle, 205
Jonah, 22
Joseph of Arimathea, 122, 155,
    156, 159, 167, 169, 179
    great uncle of Jesus, 157, 166
    Holy Thorn, 167
    in Britain, 161, 164, 168
    the Decurion, 162
Joseph, husband of Mary, 157, 205
Joseph, son of Jacob, 137, 199
Josephus, 4, 16
Jubal, 39
Judah, 200
Judea, 147, 161
Julians (Julii), 93
Julius Caesar, 2, 99, 100, 114, 151
Jupiter, 8, 181, 196. *See also* Zeus.
    priests, 53
    successor to Saturn, 47
Jupiter Belus, 78
Jutes, 123
Jutland, 123, 125
Kaerlundein, 96
Kamber, 97
Katherine of Aragon, 121
Katigern, 106
Kells, 186
Kenneth, King of Scots, 142
Kent, 99, 106, 109, 132
Kepler, 195
keys to the kingdom, 191
Kirkham, Yorkshire, 119
Kittim, 78. *See also* Cyprus.
Kolpia, 7
Kronus, 14, 26, 38, 41, 46, 47, 64,
    74, 193
    castrates Ouranos, 58
    Ilus, 51, 58
    Saturn of Egypt, 47

son of Ouranos and Hestia, 52
Kurdistan, 24, 25, 28, 30
Kytim, 78. *See also* Italy.
Lady Chapel, Glastonbury, 156.
  Also known as St. Mary's
  Chapel.
lady of the lake, 107
Laigerius, 185
lamb, 199
Lamech, 16, 39
  as Zeus, 40
Lancaster, house of, 192
Langebek, 125
Languina, 134
Laodicea, 56, 178
Laranchae, 13
Larnaca, Cyprus, 163
Latin, 114, 117, 118, 122
Latinus, 92
Lavinia, 92, 94
Lazarus, 162, 163
  Bishop of Marseilles, 163
lead, 149
Lear, 97
Lebanon, 42, 162
Lehabim, 75, 85
  Hercules Lybicus, 85
Leinster, 135, 184, 186
Leir, 170
Lemanus, 83
Leo, 200
Lestrigo, 86
Lestrigones, 76
Leto, 40
Levi, 199
Leviathan, 203
Lhewelyn ap Gruffyth, 112
Lhuyd, Humphrey, 111, 120
Libanum, 56
Libra, 199
Libya, 57, 161, 170
Licinius, 182

Lincoln, 118
Lindisfarne, 191
Lindsey (Lincolnshire), 132
Linus, 170, 173
  Bishop of Rome, 173
lion, 200
Liskeard, 154
Little Bear, 200
Little Britain, 11, 104
Llanidloes, 176
Lles. *See* Lucius
Llewelyn, 103
Llychlyn, 98
Llyr, 170
Locrinus, 97
Loegria, 97, 107
Loire Estuary, 151, 153
Loire Valley, 153
Loki, 201
Lomnimi, 86
London, 96, 99, 105, 143, 180
long knives, 106
longevity, 17, 66, 125, 127, 185
Longho, 83
Loridi, 130
Lucius, 160, 186
  first Christian King, 101, 147,
    179, 180
  Roman general, 107
  successor of Coel I, 101
Lucus, 83
Lud, 96, 99, 166
Ludgate, 96
Ludim, 85
Lugdus, 83
Lugulbanda, 42
Luke, 179
Lupus, French bishop, 184
Lusitania (Portugal), 138
Lybidicus. *See* Hercules Lybicus.
Lycaeon, 62
Lydus, 80

Simon Zelotes, 148, 169
Sippara, 14, 25, 26, 193
Sisithrus. *See* Xisuthrus.
Siton, 51. *See also* Dagon.
Siward, 97
Skjöldr, 132
Slanius, 135
slavery, 138, 155, 185
snake-woman of Scythia, 76
Snowdon, 107
Solomon, king of Brittany, 110
Solomon, king of Israel, 138, 148, 155
Solon, 60
Solway Firth, 101
Somerset, 155
sossus, 14
Southern Horn, 10
Spain, 79, 86, 98, 102, 110, 133, 139, 144, 145, 146, 149, 155, 169, 177, 178, 179
Spanish, 138, 139, 144
sport, 99
St. Albans, town, 181
St. Asaph, diocese, 116
St. George's College, Oxford, 116
St. Mary's Chapel, Glastonbury, 164. *Also known as* Lady Chapel.
St. Michael's Church, Glastonbury, 155
St. Michael's Mount, 152, 154. *See also* Ictis.
St. Nazaire, 151, 153. *See also* Corbilo.
St. Pudentia, church, 173
St. Suliac, 113
stakes, in river bed, 99
Starius, 135
Stephen, 165
Stone of Destiny, 139, 140, 142
Also called Stone of Scone, 142

stones, 87
Strabo, 150
Straits of Gibraltar, 10, 95, 138, 149
Strasbourg, 211
Strong-Castle, Earl of, 103
Sturluson, Snorri, 128
summer, 194, 196
Sun, city of, 14, 193
Supremacy, Act of, 121
Surt, 201
Sussex, 123
Sweden, 98, 132
Sydyk, 50, 56
Enoch, 51
Syncellus, 4
Syria, 52, 135
Taautus, 46. *See* Thoth.
Tacitus, Cornelius, 120
Tammuz, 22, 57
Tanais River, 130
Tara, 133, 141
necklace, 133
Prince, 133, 141
Tarascon, 163
Tarragona, 139
Tarshish, 148, 149
Tartarus, 37, 59
Tartessus. *See* Tarshish
Taurus, 198, 199
Tefnut, moisture, 54
temple
at Babylon, 37
at Jerusalem, 148
of Belus, 9
of Zeus, 52
temples, 20, 27, 147, 180
Teneuvan, 99, 100, 166
tents, 39
Tethys, 64
Tetrarchy, 181
Teucer, 65
Thabion, 55

Lightning Source UK Ltd.
Milton Keynes UK
UKOW02f1115160914

238661UK00001B/11/A